Praise for the *My New*™ series

Praise for *My New*™ iPad

"Down to earth, practical and straightforward. Wang takes you through anything you could want to know about your iPad."
—MacTips

"I found this book to be a handy reference and a straightforward guide to everything I needed to know about my new iPad."
—Mac Smarts

"Each chapter is small and comes in easily consumable chunks of information that can instantly help new users complete a certain task with easy to follow step-by-step instructions."
—Gizmos for Geeks

"A pleasure to read. If you have an iPad, you'll be well served to get this."
—Technology Tidbits

"Nifty and user-friendly. This is a very good book to give to anyone who is getting or seriously considering getting a new iPad."
—TCM Reviews

"Wang has written a book that completely removes the mystery of the iPad and holds the hand of the timid first-time iPad user, revealing features that one may have never discovered on their own."
—SvenOnTech

Praise for *My New*™ Mac

"Highly recommended for newbies and switchers."
—Macworld

"Wallace Wang has hit the nail on the head. . . . Some people just learn better and faster by doing projects rather than trying to stay awake doing tedious lessons."
—InfoWorld

"An excellent book for the novice to intermediate Mac user."
—Mac User Group for Seniors (M.U.G.S.)

My New™ iPad 2

A User's Guide

WALLACE WANG

Printed in Canada

15 14 13 12 11   1 2 3 4 5 6 7 8 9

ISBN-10: 1-59327-386-X
ISBN-13: 978-1-59327-386-6

Publisher: William Pollock
Production Editor: Serena Yang
Cover and Interior Design: Octopod Studios
Developmental Editor: Tyler Ortman
Compositor: Serena Yang
Proofreader: Riley Hoffman

For information on book distributors or translations, please contact No Starch Press, Inc. directly:

No Starch Press, Inc.
38 Ringold Street, San Francisco, CA 94103
phone: 415.863.9900; fax: 415.863.9950; info@nostarch.com; http://www.nostarch.com/

The Library of Congress has catalogued the first edition as follows:

```
Wang, Wally.
  My new iPad : a user's guide / by Wallace Wang.
      p. cm.
  Includes index.
  ISBN-13: 978-1-59327-275-3
  ISBN-10: 1-59327-275-8
1.  iPad (Computer) 2.  Tablet computers.  I. Title.
  QA76.8.I863W36 2010
  004.16--dc22
```

                                                           2010020596

Brief Contents

Contents in Detail

Acknowledgments

The most important person responsible for nurturing this book from a wild idea into an honest-to-goodness product is Bill Pollock, the founder and publisher of No Starch Press, who took a chance years ago to publish the types of books he wanted to see and to allow authors free reign to take risks and see what might happen next.

Some other people who were crucial to getting this book completed were Tyler Ortman, Kim Wimpsett, Ansel Staton, and Riley Hoffman. They looked over this manuscript and designed the pages to make sure that everything I wrote actually made sense and looks easy to read as well.

Two other people who deserve thanks include Bill Gladstone and Margot Hutchison from Waterside Productions. Without their help for so many years, I might never have gotten the chance to write so many books on a variety of computer topics over the past two decades.

I also want to acknowledge all the stand-up comedians I've met, who have made those horrible crowds at comedy clubs more bearable: Darrell Joyce (*http:// www.darrelljoyce.com/*), Leo "the Man, the Myth, the Legend" Fontaine, Chris Clobber, Bob Zany (*http://www.bobzany.com/*), Russ Rivas (*http://www.russrivas .com/*), Doug James, Don Learned, Dante, and Dobie "The Uranus King" Maxwell. Another round of thanks goes to Steve Schirripa (who appeared in HBO's hit show *The Sopranos*) for giving me my break in performing at the Riviera Hotel and Casino in Las Vegas.

Additional thanks goes to Moe Abdou (*http://www.learnfrommylife.com/*) for opening my eyes on a variety of topics all the time, Jon Fisher (*http://jonbfisher .blogspot.com/*) for showing me how an entrepreneur should work (with his book *Strategic Entrepreneurism*), Dane Henderson for getting me involved in various radio shows all the time, and Joe Polish (*http://www.joepolish.com/*) for sharing crazy ideas that prove how creativity and imagination can be far more important than any formal education.

Final thanks go to my wife (Cassandra), my son (Jordan), and my cat (Nuit) for being part of my life and always wondering how anyone can make a living by just sitting in front of a computer all day long.

Introduction

There's an old story about blind men examining an elephant. Based on what they feel, each man concludes that the elephant is something completely different—one man believes the elephant is a tree, another man a snake, the third a wall. When you first share your iPad with your family and friends, you might find them disagreeing in much the same way.

The iPad offers so many features that one person may focus on its ebook reading features, another may focus on its video and music playing capabilities, someone else might be interested in browsing the Internet, and still another might focus on the ability to type and edit text to create slide show presentations, spreadsheets, or business reports.

To help you learn the multiple features of the iPad, this book will gently guide you through the basics of using your iPad for personal and business use. With an iPad, you actually have a miniature computer for both viewing and creating content, and this book will show you how to make your iPad work best for you.

If you already use an iPhone or an iPod Touch, you already know how to use most of the iPad's features. If you use any type of smartphone that offers touch screen gestures, you'll find many of the iPad's touch screen gestures familiar as well. Even if you've never used any type of touch screen device before, you'll find that the iPad can be friendly, forgiving, and fun.

Think of the iPad as a multipurpose, portable computer that you can take wherever you go and use whenever you need it. The iPad isn't just a replacement for an existing computer, but a versatile device that offers an infinite number of possible uses, limited only by your imagination.

How This Book Is Organized

To help you get started using your iPad right away, this book is divided into short chapters that act like recipes in a cookbook. Each chapter explains how to accomplish a specific task and then lists all the steps you need to follow.

By following the book's hands-on instructions for accomplishing common tasks, you can learn how to achieve specific results using your iPad right away. Best of all, you don't have to read this book in any specific order. Just bounce around and follow the chapters that catch your interest while ignoring the chapters that you don't care about.

Although the iPad comes packed with plenty of features, don't feel you need to learn everything at once. Just learn the features that you need right now and have fun right away. By following the chapters in this book, you'll learn how to use your iPad and make it a useful and indispensable tool that you can rely on wherever you go.

PART 1

Basic Training

Turning Your iPad On and Off

Your iPad can be in one of three states: *on*, *off*, or *sleep*. If you have the 3G model that can connect to a cellular phone network, you can also put your iPad in *airplane mode*. By learning the advantages of each state, you'll know when and why to use them.

When your iPad is on, you can use it. When your iPad is in sleep mode, you'll conserve its battery power while keeping it ready to start up right away. Sleep mode is best when you are not using your iPad but plan to return to it soon.

Airplane mode turns off your iPad's ability to access email or surf the Web through a 3G cellular phone network. This essentially cuts off your iPad from the rest of the world while letting you do most other tasks, such as play music, read books, check your calendar, or browse your list of contacts. As its name suggests, airplane mode is perfect for when you're in an airplane and can't risk having your iPad interfere with the airplane's navigation systems.

If you know you won't need to use your iPad for a lengthy period of time, you might as well turn it off to keep it from running down its battery.

In this chapter you'll learn how to turn on your iPad, put it to sleep, put it in airplane mode, and shut it off completely.

What You'll Be Using

To turn an iPad on and off, you need to use the following:

▶   The Sleep/Wake button   The Settings screen

Turning On Your iPad

When your iPad is off, you can turn it on by following these steps:

1.   Hold down the **Sleep/Wake** button at the top of your iPad, as shown in Figure 1-1, until the Apple logo appears on the screen.

Sleep/Wake

FIGURE 1-1: *The Sleep/Wake button is located on the corner of the iPad.*

∗ *NOTE:* **If you see a blank screen after pressing the Sleep/Wake button, your iPad may not have enough power to start.**

2.   Wait a few seconds until the Home screen appears. This tells you that your iPad is now on.

Turning Off Your iPad

The main difference between turning your iPad off and putting it to sleep is that turning the iPad off conserves its battery power. The drawback is that if you turn the iPad off, it takes a few seconds longer to start up again when you need it.

When your iPad is on, you can turn it off by following these steps:

1. Hold down the **Sleep/Wake** button until a red "slide to power off" arrow button appears at the top of the screen.
2. Slide the red arrow button to the right (or tap **Cancel** if you don't want to turn off your iPad after all).

Putting Your iPad to Sleep

After you've turned on your iPad, you can change it from on to sleep mode to conserve battery power while still being able to quickly access your iPad the moment you need to use it again (rather than wait for it to boot up).

At a glance, you cannot tell whether an iPad is turned off or in sleep mode. If you press the Home button and your iPad turns on, then you'll know it was asleep. If you press the Home button and nothing happens, then you'll know that it's turned off. You'll have to hold down the Sleep/Wake button to start it.

To put an iPad to sleep that is already turned on, press the **Sleep/Wake** button. The screen darkens.

✳ *NOTE:* **If you have a Smart Cover, just use it to cover your iPad's screen to put the iPad to sleep.**

Putting Your iPad to Sleep Automatically

Since sleep mode is critical in conserving your iPad's battery, you may be happy to know that if you leave an iPad on, it will put itself into sleep mode after a fixed period of time. To change this fixed period of time, follow these steps:

1. From the Home screen, tap **Settings**. The Settings screen appears.
2. Tap **General**. The General settings screen appears, as shown in Figure 1-2.
3. Tap **Auto-Lock**. The Auto-Lock settings screen appears, as shown in Figure 1-3.
4. Tap one of the available options: 2 Minutes, 5 Minutes, 10 Minutes, 15 Minutes, or Never.
5. Press the **Home** button to return to the Home screen.

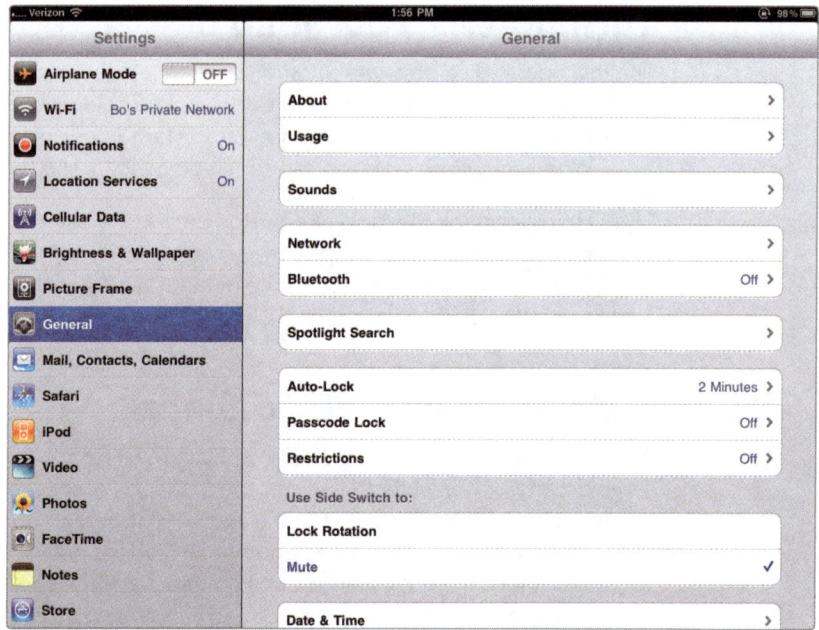

FIGURE 1-2: *The General settings screen*

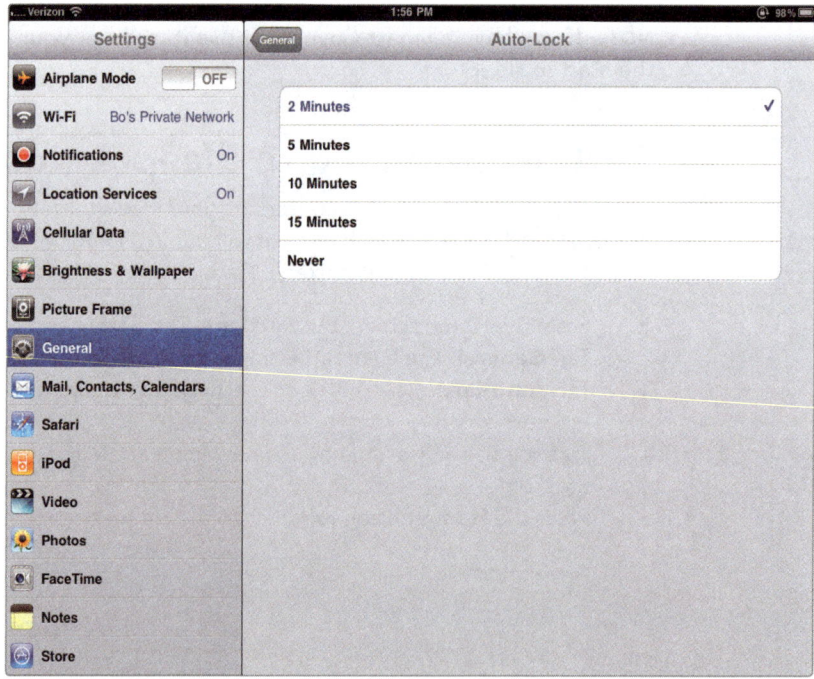

FIGURE 1-3: *The Auto-Lock settings screen lets you define a fixed amount of time before your iPad goes to sleep automatically.*

Waking Up Your iPad from Sleep Mode

When you put an iPad to sleep, you must wake it up to change its state from sleep mode to on. To wake up an iPad in sleep mode, do this:

1. Press the **Sleep/Wake** button on top of the iPad, press the **Home** button, or, if you have a Smart Cover, lift an edge away from the screen. A slider appears on the screen.
2. Drag the slider to the right. The Home screen appears.

   The slider forces you to slide your finger to unlock your iPad. That way, your iPad won't accidentally turn on if you press its Sleep/Wake button in your briefcase or purse.

* *NOTE:* **If you fail to use the slider to unlock your iPad after a few seconds, your iPad will automatically return to sleep mode.**

Turning Airplane Mode On and Off (3G iPad Models Only)

On many airlines, you are not allowed to access a cellular phone network to avoid possible interference with the plane's navigational systems. To comply with this rule but still use your iPad for other tasks, such as jotting down notes or watching videos, you can put your iPad in airplane mode by following these steps:

1. Make sure your iPad is turned on.
2. From the Home screen, tap **Settings**. The Settings screen appears.
3. Tap **Airplane Mode**. The button will show *ON*, and an airplane icon will appear in the upper-left corner of the screen, as shown in Figure 1-4.

   To turn off airplane mode, just go into Settings again and tap the Airplane Mode switch a second time. It should now read *OFF*.

Airplane icon

FIGURE 1-4: An iPad in airplane mode

Additional Ideas for Turning Your iPad On and Off

As a general rule, turn off your iPad whenever you know you won't be using it for a while. If you plan on using your iPad soon, then put it in sleep mode.

Airplane mode is most useful when you're stuck in an airplane and don't feel like interacting with any of your fellow passengers, preferring to let your iPad amuse you instead. It's also a good way to save your battery life.

Now that you understand the basics of turning your iPad on and off (and everything in between), the rest of this book will teach you how to use all the other features of your iPad so you can do something useful with it.

2 Charging and Conserving Battery Power

Your iPad should last approximately 10 hours on a single charge. Of course, playing videos will likely drain the battery faster than just reading an ebook, so your actual battery life may differ depending on what you do. There are ways you can minimize power usage, thereby extending the daily life of your battery.

Like all batteries, your iPad's battery will eventually wear out, but by then you'll probably have a newer iPad model anyway (or you can take your iPad to an Apple store and pay a minimal fee for an entirely new iPad).

In this chapter you'll learn how to maximize the charge of your battery to allow your iPad to run as long as possible.

What You'll Be Using

To maximize your iPad's battery life, you need to use the following:

▶ The iPad USB cable The Settings screen

▶ The iPad USB power adapter

Recharging an iPad

There are two ways to recharge your iPad. If you want to use your iPad while it's recharging, plug its USB cable and adapter into an electric outlet. This is also the fastest way to recharge your iPad.

You can also plug your iPad into a computer's USB outlet to recharge it. Some computers with high-powered USB outlets will let you use your iPad as it charges. But if you plug the iPad into your computer and try to use it, you may see a "Not Charging" notice near the battery indicator. This indicates that your computer's USB outlet is not high-powered, and that you cannot use the iPad as it is charging. (If you put your iPad to sleep while it's plugged in, it will slowly recharge.)

✳ **NOTE: To ensure a full battery, plug your iPad into a wall outlet overnight. That way, the iPad will be fully charged the next morning.**

✳ **WARNING: Hot weather (95°F, or 35°C) can irreversibly harm your iPad's battery, so avoid storing your iPad in direct sunlight. If your iPad feels excessively warm while it's recharging inside a carrying case, take it out of its case before recharging. Cold weather will only temporarily prevent your iPad's battery from holding a charge. Once you move your iPad to a warmer area, its battery will hold its charge normally.**

Turning Off Push Accounts

One handy feature of the iPad is the *push account.* If you have a supported email account, your email server can deliver new messages to your iPad automatically so you receive the information almost the instant someone sends it to you.

Since a push account requires that your iPad periodically contact your email account over the Internet, it uses energy. If you don't need or care to receive email messages as quickly as possible, you can turn off the push account by following these steps:

1. From the Home screen, tap **Settings**. The Settings screen appears.
2. Tap **Mail, Contacts, Calendars**. The Mail, Contacts, Calendars settings screen appears, as shown in Figure 2-1.
3. Tap **Fetch New Data**. The Fetch New Data settings screen appears, as shown in Figure 2-2.
4. Tap the **Push** on/off switch to make it read *OFF.*

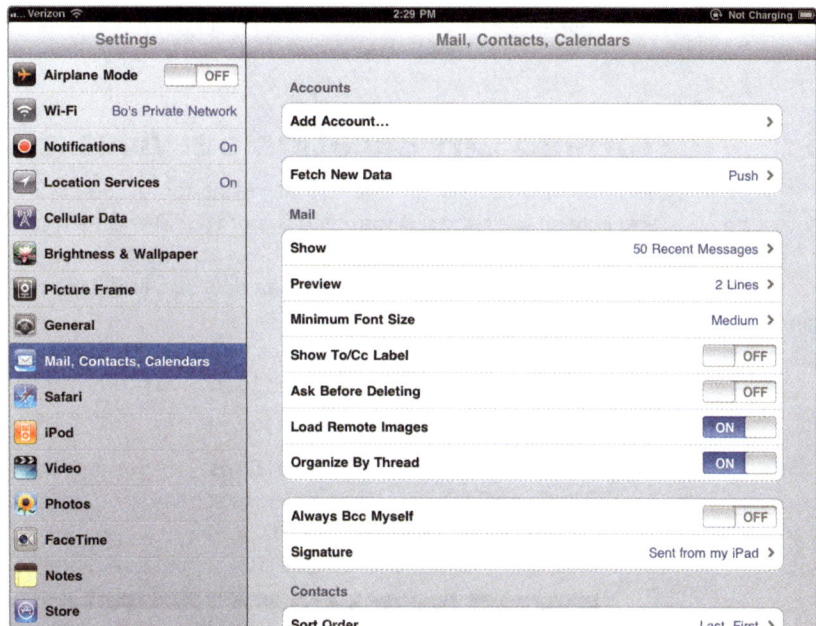

FIGURE 2-1: *The Mail, Contacts, Calendars settings screen*

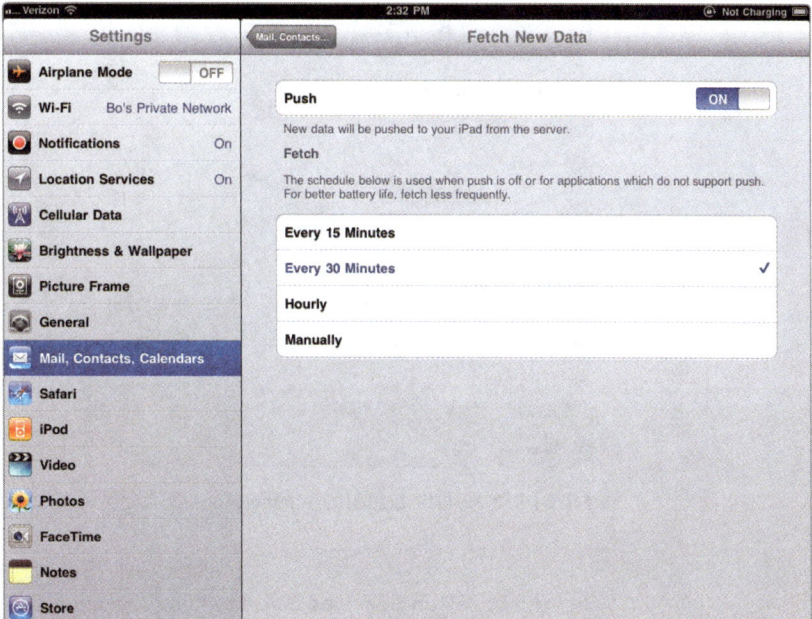

FIGURE 2-2: *The Fetch New Data settings screen*

5. Tap an option under the Fetch category, such as Every 15 Minutes or Hourly.
6. Press the **Home** button to return to the Home screen.

Turning Off Location Services

Location Services is a fancy term that means some iPad apps, such as the Maps app, rely on the Global Positioning System (GPS) and triangulation of cellular phone towers to identify the physical location of your iPad. If it knows your physical location in the world, an iPad app can then help you find the nearest restaurant or gas station, for example.

Unfortunately, Location Services burns up battery energy. If you don't need this type of service, you can turn it off to reduce power consumption by following these steps:

1. From the Home screen, tap **Settings**. The Settings screen appears.
2. Tap **General**. The General settings screen appears.
3. Tap **Location Services**. The Location Services settings screen appears on the right side of the screen, as shown in Figure 2-3.

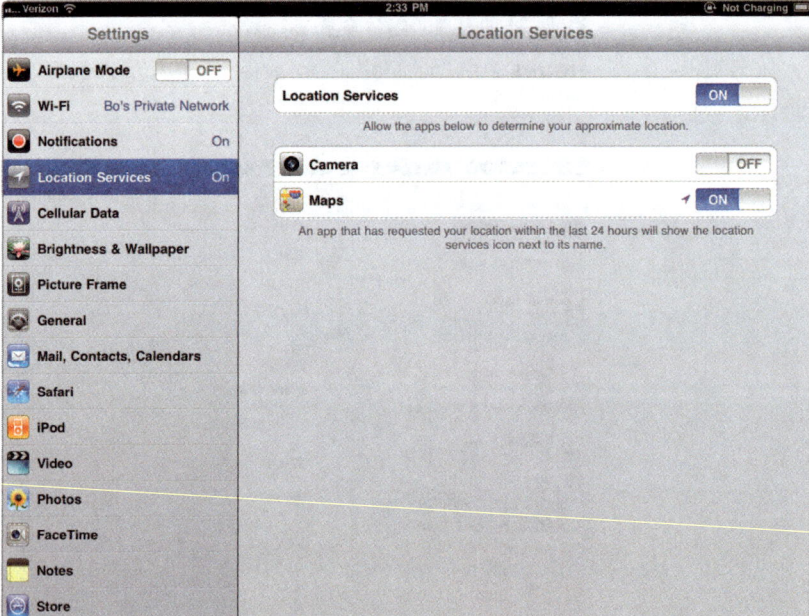

FIGURE 2-3: *The Location Services settings screen*

4. Tap the **Location Services** on/off switch so it reads *OFF*. As an alternative, you can selectively tap the on/off switch of the different apps stored on your iPad. That way you can turn off Location Services for certain apps but keep it turned on for other apps.
5. Press the **Home** button to return to the Home screen.

Monitoring Battery Life

To let you know how much battery life is left, your iPad displays a battery gauge in the upper-right corner of the screen. The more filled this battery gauge appears, the more charge your battery has remaining.

Since this small visual gauge may be hard to read, your iPad can also display the battery charge remaining as a percentage. A fully charged battery appears as 100% charged, while a weaker battery charge will have a lower percentage. When your battery life reaches 20% and 10%, warning messages alert you to recharge your iPad soon.

In case you find this battery percentage indicator annoying, you can turn it off (or on) by following these steps:

1. From the Home screen, tap **Settings**. The Settings screen appears.
2. Tap **General**. The General settings screen appears.
3. Tap **Usage**. The Usage settings screen appears, as shown in Figure 2-4.

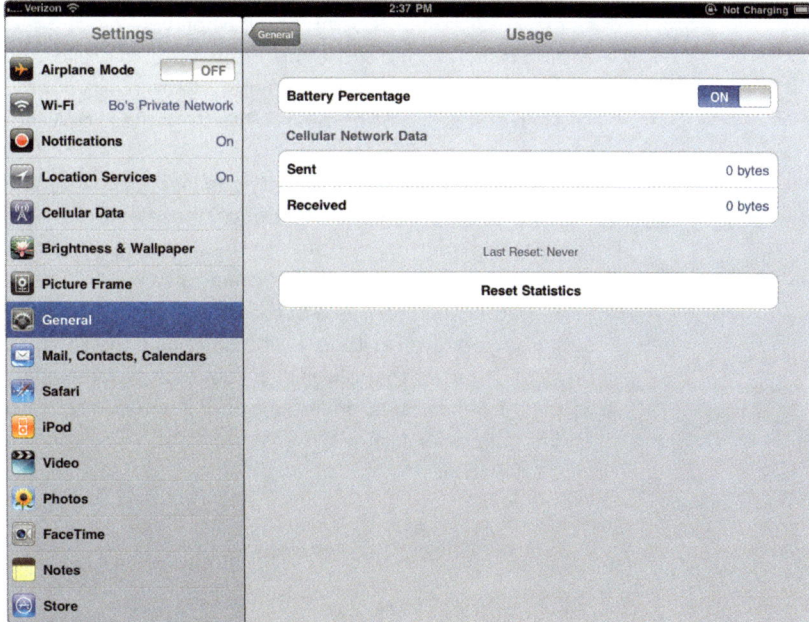

FIGURE 2-4: *The Battery Percentage on/off switch appears on the Usage settings screen.*

4. Tap the **Battery Percentage** on/off switch. When set to *ON*, the battery percentage indicator appears next to the battery gauge. When set to *OFF*, the percentage indicator does not appear.
5. Press the **Home** button to return to the Home screen.

Turning Off Bluetooth

Bluetooth is primarily used to connect an iPad wirelessly to a headset or keyboard. If you don't use Bluetooth devices such as an external keyboard, turning off Bluetooth can save power and increase your iPad's battery life. To turn off Bluetooth, follow these steps:

1. From the Home screen, tap **Settings**. The Settings screen appears.
2. Tap **General**. The General settings screen appears.
3. Tap **Bluetooth**. The Bluetooth settings screen appears.
4. Tap the **Bluetooth** on/off switch to change it to read *OFF*.
5. Press the **Home** button to return to the Home screen.

Additional Ideas for Conserving Power

The most important way to conserve battery power for your iPad is to put it to sleep (or to turn it off completely) when you're not using it. The iPad's brightness setting is the second-most important factor in preserving its battery (though there's no sense in preserving the battery but straining your eyes looking at a dim screen). You can adjust the brightness in the Brightness & Wallpaper pane of the Settings screen.

Although the iPad's battery can last approximately 10 hours, you may want to invest in a battery pack. Although these external battery packs may be cumbersome to lug around, you can use them in emergencies when you need to use your iPad but find that its power has drained away.

Rather than rely on a battery pack, you could also buy a solar panel that can recharge your iPad as long as you can place the solar panel in the sun. You can also buy a car charger that plugs into your car's cigarette lighter to provide power to your iPad while you're driving around. If you combine conservation techniques with additional power sources, there's no reason why you should ever run out of power for your iPad.

3

Using Your iPad's Physical and Virtual Controls

The iPad represents a minimalist design, so you won't see ugly ports or extra buttons protruding from every side like a typical laptop or netbook. Instead, the iPad offers only four physical buttons: Sleep/Wake, Silent/Screen Rotation Lock, Volume Up/Down, and the Home button. By learning how to use these buttons, you can control how your iPad behaves.

Besides these physical controls, the iPad also provides virtual controls for locking the screen orientation or adjusting the sound. By learning to use the iPad's physical and virtual controls, you can control the major features of your iPad.

What You'll Be Using

To learn how to control your iPad via its physical buttons, you need to use the following:

▶ The Home button

▶ The Volume Up/Down buttons

▶ The Silent/Screen Rotation Lock switch

Viewing the Home Screen

The Home button appears at the bottom of the iPad on the front, as shown in Figure 3-1. No matter what app you may be using at the time, pressing the Home button immediately displays the Home screen, which displays icons that represent all the apps you can run on your iPad. (Try it now!)

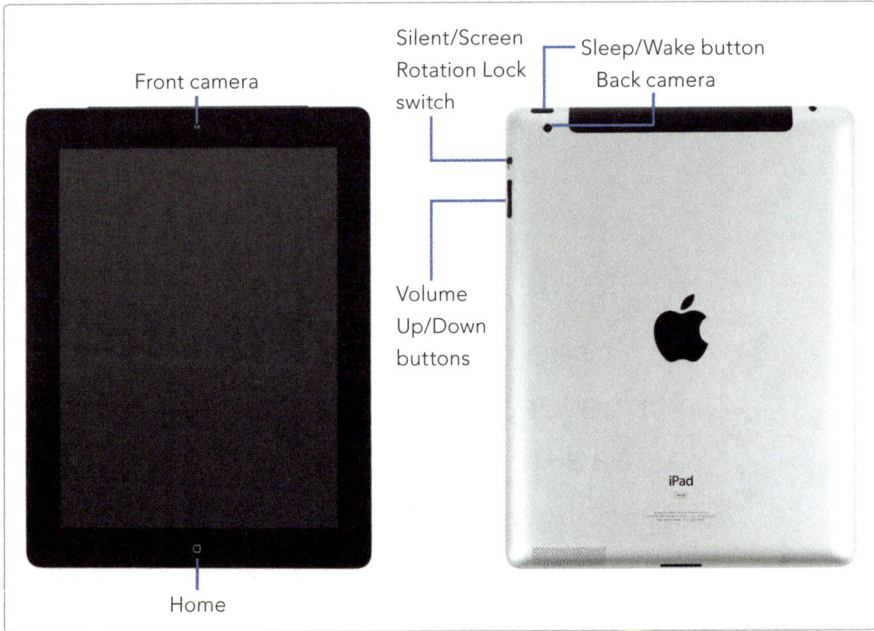

FIGURE 3-1: *The physical controls on the iPad*

Adjusting the Volume

To make it easy for you to increase or decrease the volume, the iPad includes Volume Up and Volume Down buttons on its right side (shown earlier in Figure 3-1).

You can adjust the volume by pressing one of the volume buttons or by holding it down. When you adjust the volume, the iPad displays a ringer icon with a horizontal bar underneath that visually displays the current volume level, as shown in Figure 3-2.

FIGURE 3-2: *A volume icon shows how loud (or soft) your volume is.*

✱ NOTE: **Many apps, such as the iPod or YouTube app, also let you adjust the volume with a volume slider that appears on the screen. By moving this volume slider left or right, you can lower or raise the volume without touching the physical Volume Up/Down buttons on the side of the iPad.**

Another way to adjust the volume is through the volume slider on the screen, which you can display and adjust by following these steps:

1. Press the **Home** button twice. A list of icons, representing different apps, appears, as shown in Figure 3-3.

FIGURE 3-3: *The bottom of the screen lists all apps you can switch to.*

2. Swipe this list of icons to the right. You may need to do this several times until you see the Volume Control slider, as shown in Figure 3-4.
3. Slide the **Volume Control** slider left or right.
4. Press the **Home** button when you're done.

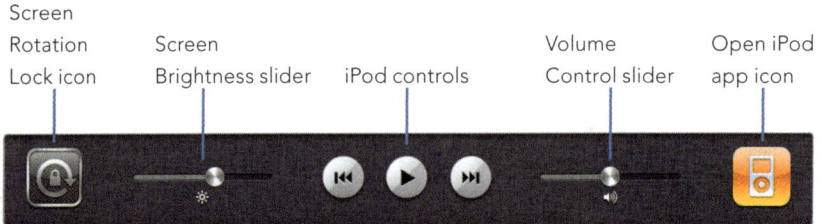

Screen Rotation Lock icon · Screen Brightness slider · iPod controls · Volume Control slider · Open iPod app icon

FIGURE 3-4: *The Volume Control slider appears after you swipe the bottom icons to the right.*

Multitasking with the Home Button

The iPad can run two or more apps simultaneously and switch between them at the touch of the Home button.

To switch between multiple apps, follow these steps:

1. Press the **Home** button twice. A list of icons, representing different apps, appears (shown earlier in Figure 3-3.)
2. Tap the icon of the app you want to switch to using.

✳ **NOTE:** **If you want to remove an app from this list, you can press and hold your fingertip over an icon until all the icons wriggle. You'll see a small red minus sign on the apps—tap it to remove an app.**

Configuring the Silent/Screen Rotation Lock Switch

The Silent/Screen Rotation Lock switch appears on the side of the iPad. If you play audio often and need to quickly mute the sound in a hurry, you'll want to configure this switch to silence the audio. If you don't want your iPad to adjust the screen rotation automatically, such as when you're holding the iPad while laying down, then you may prefer to configure this switch to lock the screen rotation instead.

To configure the Silent/Screen Rotation Lock switch, follow these steps:

1. Tap the **Settings** icon. The Settings screen appears.
2. Tap **General**. The General settings screen appear.
3. Tap either **Lock Rotation** or **Mute**, as shown in Figure 3-5.
4. Press the **Home** button once.
5. Test it out by flicking the switch. An icon appears to let you know you were successful. Your iPad is now muted or locked.

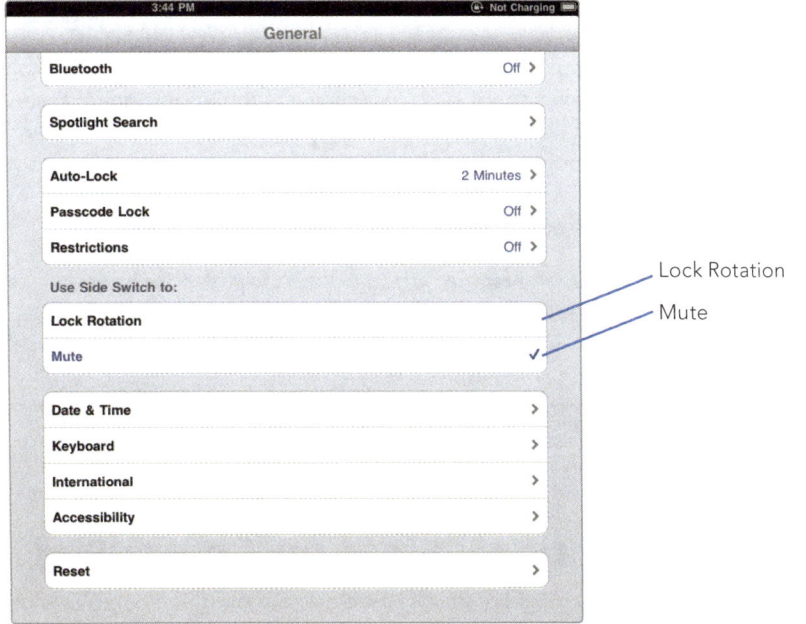

FIGURE 3-5: *Choosing between Mute or Lock Rotation*

Muting the Volume or Locking the Screen Rotation Without the Side Switch

You can also mute your iPad or lock its screen using the Home button. If you've configured your side switch to mute the iPad, you can still quickly lock the screen using these steps (and vice versa):

1. Press the **Home** button twice. A list of icons appears (see Figure 3-3).
2. Swipe this row of icons to the right until you see the Mute or Screen Rotation Lock icon, as shown in Figure 3-6.
3. Tap the **Mute** or **Screen Rotation Lock** icon to mute the volume or lock or unlock the screen rotation. The icon that appears will depend on whether you configured the side switch to Mute or Lock Rotation.

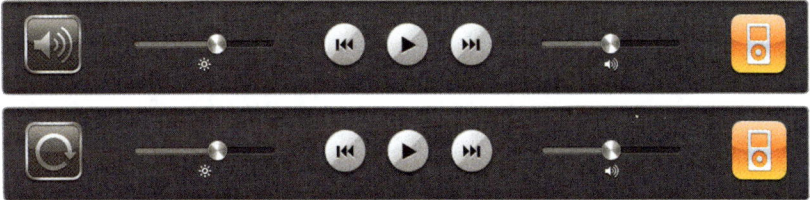

FIGURE 3-6: *The Mute or Screen Rotation Lock icon appears*

Adjusting the Screen Brightness

Since you can take your iPad anywhere you go, you'll probably use it in different lighting conditions, such as out in the bright sunlight or in a dark room while someone else is giving a boring presentation. In case you need to adjust the screen brightness, you can drag a brightness slider to make your iPad's screen easier to see.

To adjust screen brightness, follow these steps:

1. Tap the **Home** button twice. A row of icons appears at the bottom of the screen.
2. Swipe the icons at the bottom to the right until the controls appear (shown earlier in Figure 3-4).
3. Drag the **Screen Brightness** slider to the left or right.
4. Press the **Home** button once.

Additional Ideas for Controlling Your iPad

The two most commonly used buttons are the Sleep/Wake button and the Home button. Since you'll be using the Home button often, take the time to practice returning to the Home screen by pressing the Home button once. If you press the Home button twice in rapid succession, you can lock the screen rotation, adjust the volume, or switch to another app.

Locking the screen rotation can be handy if you like curling up in a chair or sofa with your iPad. Without locking your screen, the image might flip back and forth between portrait and landscape mode.

Switching between apps can be handy when you don't want to end an app but want it to retain its current state, such as letting you play a game while temporarily checking your email.

Finally, don't forget that the Volume Up/Down buttons can help you crank up your music or lower it so you don't disturb others. Physically adjusting the volume through the Volume button is easy, but you can also adjust the volume by pressing the Home button twice and then swiping your app icons to the right to view the volume control slider.

If you really need to quiet your iPad down in a hurry, just configure the side switch to Mute and then use the physical Silent/Screen Rotation Lock switch instead.

By acquainting yourself to the purpose of these physical and virtual controls, you can quickly control your iPad. Once you know how to control your iPad with these physical and virtual buttons, the next step is to start learning how to control it using the more common touch gestures on the screen.

4 Controlling the iPad User Interface

If you're already familiar with using an iPhone or iPod touch, you practically already know how to use the iPad's user interface. However, if you're new to any Apple products that use a Multi-Touch interface, you'll still find that the iPad is easy to learn.

The Multi-Touch screen is how you'll interact with your iPad. By tapping, pinching, or sliding your finger across the screen, you can select items, manipulate objects, or scroll across the screen. Nearly every app uses one or more touch gestures, so it's important to learn how to use them all.

In this chapter you'll learn how to control your iPad using touch gestures on the Multi-Touch screen.

What You'll Be Using

To learn how to control your iPad's user interface, you need to use the following:

 The Safari app   The Maps app

Using the Multi-Touch Screen

The Multi-Touch screen functions as both a display and a user interface that you can control with your fingertip. These are the three main touch commands:

- ▶ Select (tap)
- ▶ Scroll (drag)
- ▶ Zoom (pinch or double-tap)

✳ *NOTE:* **The Multi-Touch screen lets you tilt the iPad vertically (portrait mode) or horizontally (landscape mode) to make it easy to view data. No matter how you tilt your iPad, the Tap, Drag, Pinch, and Double-Tap touch commands work the same.**

Using the Select Command

The simplest command is Select, which lets you touch an item that you want to select. To use the Select command, point at an icon or button, press it lightly, and then lift your finger off the screen. When done correctly, the Select command involves nothing more than a quick tap on the screen. This Select command is called *tapping* throughout the rest of this book.

✳ *NOTE:* **The Multi-Touch screen works only when it detects your fingertip touching the screen. If you tap the screen with your fingernail or while wearing gloves, the Multi-Touch screen won't recognize this physical contact.**

To see how the Select command works, follow these steps:

1. Press the **Home** button. The Home screen appears, showing all the apps available on your iPad.
2. Tap any icon, such as the Calendar. Your chosen app appears on the screen.
3. Press the **Home** button. Notice that your iPad displays the Home screen once more.

Using the Scroll Command

Sometimes an app might need to display more information than can comfortably fit on the screen. When this happens, you can view multiple screens by choosing between two different scrolling commands: Controlled Scroll and Quick Scroll.

Controlled Scroll lets you scroll horizontally or vertically by sliding or dragging your finger across the screen. To practice the Controlled Scroll and Quick Scroll commands, try the following to acquaint you with the App Store, where you can buy and download new apps for your iPad:

1. From the Home screen, tap **App Store**.
2. Tap the **Featured** icon at the bottom of the screen. The App Store appears, as shown in Figure 4-1.

FIGURE 4-1: *The App Store*

3. Near the bottom of the screen, slide your finger up and down the screen. Notice that the screen scrolls up and down as your finger slides up and down the screen. As soon as you lift your finger off the screen, it stops scrolling. This is a *Controlled Scroll*.
4. Near the bottom (or top) of the screen, slide your finger up or down quickly, and lift your finger off the screen in a quick flicking motion. Even after you lift your finger off the screen, the screen should continue scrolling in the direction you flicked your finger. This is a *Quick Scroll*.

5. Repeat the previous step, except before the screen can stop scrolling, tap your finger on the screen. This immediately stops the scrolling and is known as a *Quick Scroll Stop.*

6. Press the **Home** button. The Home screen appears.

Since the iPad's screen can't display multiple, overlapping windows like an ordinary computer screen, apps often display multiple windows as individual, side-by-side *panes.* One pane is always visible, but other panes are tucked out of sight to the left or right of the screen.

To let you know that a screen consists of multiple panes, two or more dots are displayed at the bottom of the screen—each dot represents a screen (see Figure 4-2). A bright dot represents the current screen, while dimmed dots represent hidden screens. To view these additional screens, you need to slide the current screen left or right with your finger.

FIGURE 4-2: *This Home screen has three panes.*

The Home screen actually consists of multiple panes (up to a maximum of 11 panes). To practice scrolling horizontally to view other panes, follow these steps to get acquainted with the Home screen:

1. From the Home screen, slide your finger to the right across the screen. The Search screen appears, as shown in Figure 4-3.

2. Slide your finger to the left across the Search screen. The Home screen pane appears again.

✳ **NOTE:** **When you start downloading apps, they'll appear on additional Home screen panes, which you can access by pressing the Home button and then sliding your finger to the left to view each additional pane.**

Using the Zoom Command

The iPad's screen can display entire web pages. Of course, the images and text may appear too small to read comfortably, so the iPad gives you the option to zoom in and zoom out. To enlarge or shrink an image, you can use two fingers in a pinching motion. Touch the screen with your fingers spread out and bring them closer together to cause the iPad image to shrink. If you start with your fingers together and slide them apart, the iPad image enlarges. This gesture resembles a pinching motion with two fingers.

FIGURE 4-3: *Sliding your finger horizontally to the right displays the Search screen.*

To practice zooming in and out, try the following steps to get acquainted with the Maps app:

1. From the Home screen, tap **Maps**. The Maps app appears, as shown in Figure 4-4.
2. Zoom in using the pinching gesture: Place two fingers close together and slide them apart while maintaining contact with the iPad screen. Notice that the map zooms in.
3. Zoom out using the pinching gesture: Place two fingers apart and slide them together while maintaining contact with the iPad screen. Notice that the map zooms out.

✱ **NOTE:** **Some apps, like Maps, allow you to zoom in by double-tapping one finger and zoom out by single-tapping two fingers.**

4. Zoom in by tapping one finger on the screen twice in rapid succession. Notice that the map zooms in.
5. Zoom out by tapping two fingers on the screen at the same time. Notice that the map zooms out.
6. Press the **Home** button. The Home screen appears.

FIGURE 4-4: *The Maps app*

✳ *NOTE:* Not all apps allow you to zoom in and out. If you find yourself wanting to zoom in closer on the Home screen or within apps that don't allow it, you can enable the accessibility feature called Zoom. Read Chapter 27 for instructions on how to enable it.

Additional Ideas for Controlling Your iPad

Touch gestures represent the primary way to control your iPad, so be sure to practice using the tap, scroll, and pinch gestures until they become second nature. By knowing these three commands, you'll be able to get the most out of your iPad no matter which app you may be using at the time.

In a few apps, such as the Photos app, you can use a fourth touch gesture known as the rotate command, which lets you rotate an image on the screen. Just place two spread fingers on the screen, and then rotate your two fingers in either a clockwise or counterclockwise direction to rotate the image currently displayed on the screen.

Try these common touch gestures on different apps, both the built-in ones that come with your iPad and any additional ones you may have downloaded from the App Store. You'll quickly see how you can control almost any app with your fingers alone. Some applications also use the iPad's orientation as a control, and nearly all apps will change depending on how you hold your iPad: in portrait or landscape mode.

 5 Using and Customizing the Virtual Keyboard

One of the most unique features of the iPad is its virtual keyboard, which displays a keyboard on the screen and lets you type directly on the surface of the iPad. While typing on a flat piece of glass might initially feel odd, you'll soon find that you'll adjust and be able to use the virtual keyboard nearly as well (or perhaps even better) than using a physical keyboard that can get clogged with crumbs, dust, and spilled liquids.

To make the virtual keyboard easier to use, you can customize its behavior. After a little practice, you'll soon find yourself capable of typing happily away on the iPad whether you need to type a note to yourself, an email message, or a website address.

In this chapter you'll learn how to customize and use the virtual keyboard on your iPad.

What You'll Be Using

To customize the virtual keyboard, you need to use the following:

 The Notes app   The Settings screen

Displaying Different Virtual Keyboards

Because of the limited screen size available on the iPad, the virtual keyboard behaves differently than a physical keyboard. A physical keyboard displays every key, including letter and number keys in addition to cursor movement keys and function keys. Although this makes all the keys available, it also tends to clutter the keyboard with groups of keys you might rarely use, such as the function keys or the numeric keys.

The iPad's virtual keyboard works differently by displaying only the groups of keys you're most likely to use. The three main types of virtual keyboards display letters, numbers, and symbols.

To see what these three virtual keyboards look like, follow these steps:

1. From the Home screen, tap **Notes**. The Notes screen appears.
2. Tap anywhere on the right side of the screen that looks like a yellow notepad. The virtual keyboard displaying letters appears, as shown in Figure 5-1.

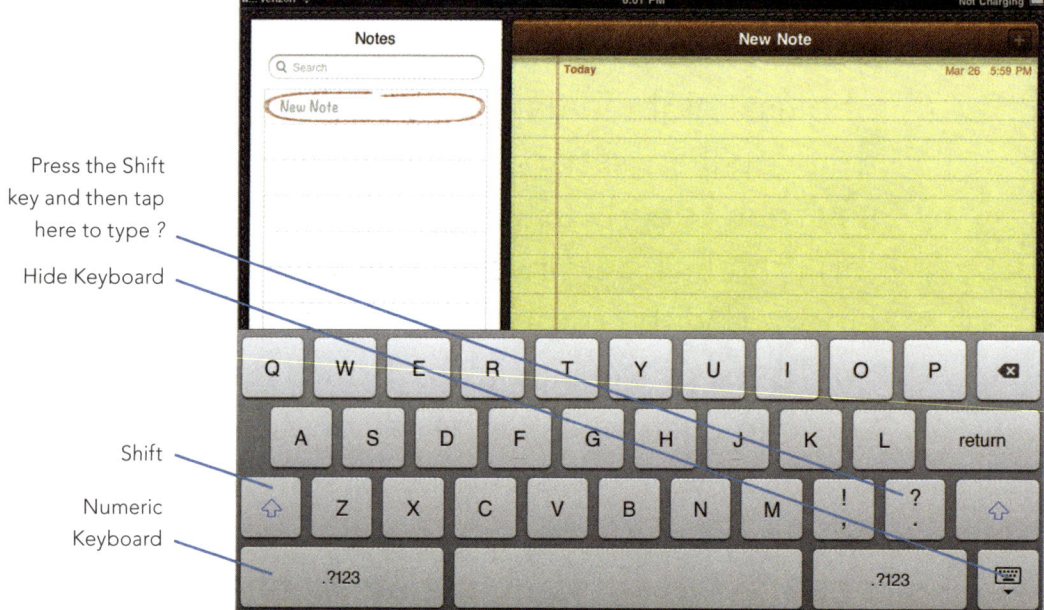

FIGURE 5-1: *The main virtual keyboard displays letters.*

3. Tap either of the **.?123** keys. The virtual keyboard changes to display numbers and additional symbols, as shown in Figure 5-2.

FIGURE 5-2: *The virtual keyboard can display numbers.*

✳ **NOTE:** To save yourself a few extra taps when typing a single piece of punctuation, you can just press and hold the .?123 key and then release it once you've found the right character. Your keyboard will automatically swap back to the ABC keyboard.

4. Tap either of the **#+=** keys. The virtual keyboard changes to display symbols, as shown in Figure 5-3.

FIGURE 5-3: *The virtual keyboard can display symbols not found on the letter or number virtual keyboards.*

5. Tap either of the **123** keys. The numeric virtual keyboard reappears (shown earlier in Figure 5-2).
6. Tap either of the **ABC** keys. The main virtual keyboard with letters reappears (shown earlier in Figure 5-1).
7. Tap the **Hide Keyboard** key in the bottom-right corner of the screen. The virtual keyboard disappears completely.
8. Tap anywhere on the right side of the screen on the yellow notepad image. The virtual keyboard appears.

Typing on a Virtual Keyboard

Typing on the virtual keyboard is nearly identical to typing on a physical keyboard. The main difference is that the virtual keyboard does not offer any arrow keys. (You have to touch the screen to move the cursor.) In addition, if you type part of a word, the virtual keyboard may display the correct and complete spelling of that word, which you can choose by pressing the spacebar.

Typing Text

To create text, you can type it yourself or let the virtual keyboard suggest and automatically type any words that you've partially typed. To see how typing on the virtual keyboard works, follow these steps:

1. From the Home screen, tap **Notes**. The Notes screen appears.
2. Tap anywhere on the right side of the screen that looks like a yellow notepad. The virtual keyboard displaying letters appears (shown earlier in Figure 5-1).
3. Start typing **Appl**. Notice that when the virtual keyboard thinks it recognizes what you're typing, it displays *Apple* as a suggested word, as shown in Figure 5-4.

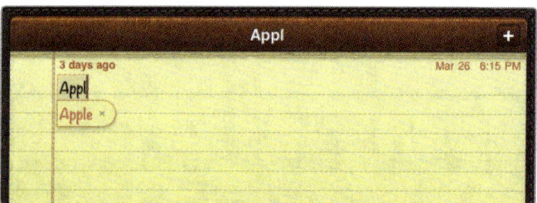

FIGURE 5-4: *The virtual keyboard tries to guess the word you want before you finish typing.*

4. Tap the spacebar to let the virtual keyboard finish typing the suggested word automatically. (If you don't want to choose the suggested word, keep typing or tap the X in a circle that appears to the right of the suggested word.)
5. Type more text. Try misspelling a word by typing **Testung**—the iPad will automatically correct your spelling to *Testing*. To make your new text appear on another line, tap the **Return** key.
6. Tap the **Shift** key, then try pressing a letter. Notice it's now uppercase. Tap the **Shift** key again, and press the button labeled **!/,**—you have inserted the ! character.

Moving the Cursor

With a physical keyboard, you can move the cursor by pressing the arrow keys or by pressing any of the other cursor movement keys such as Home or End. With the virtual keyboard, there are no cursor movement keys since you must directly place and move the cursor by touching the iPad's screen.

You can move the cursor in two ways: tapping your fingertip to move the cursor before or after a word or touching and sliding your fingertip to move the cursor within text. Holding your finger on the screen displays a magnifying glass that lets you see the exact position of the cursor so you can slide your finger to move the cursor where you want it to appear.

To see how to move the cursor, follow these steps:

1. From the Home screen, tap **Notes**. The Notes screen appears.
2. Type a few sentences of text.
3. Tap anywhere in your text. Notice that the cursor appears wherever you tap. (However, the cursor will not appear in blank areas where there is no text.)
4. Hold your finger on any part of the text that you've typed. A magnifying glass appears, letting you see the current position of the cursor, as shown in Figure 5-5.

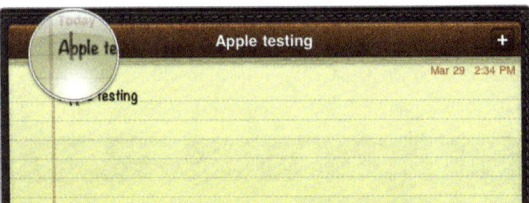

FIGURE 5-5: *A magnifying glass lets you precisely place the cursor within text.*

* *NOTE:* **If you're having trouble getting the magnifying glass to appear, make sure you do not slide your finger up or down.**

5. Slide your finger to move the cursor. Notice how this method lets you move the cursor accurately.
6. Lift your finger when you're happy with the current location of the cursor. A Select, Select All, and Paste menu appears, as shown in Figure 5-6.
7. Press the **Home** button.

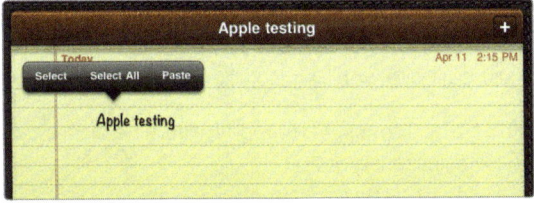

FIGURE 5-6: *After you move the cursor, a Select, Select All, and Paste menu appears.*

Selecting, Copying, and Cutting Text

Just like with a regular computer, you can select text to copy, cut, and paste it in another location. When selecting text, you have three choices: select a single word, select all of your text, or just select part of your text.

After you select text, you can delete it by tapping the Backspace key, or you can cut or copy the selected text to paste it somewhere else.

Selecting a Single Word

You can select a single word in two ways. First, you can tap a word twice to select it. Second, you can hold your finger on a word for a moment and then release. When a menu appears, tap Select. To try selecting a single word, follow these steps:

1. From the Home screen, tap **Notes**. The Notes screen appears.
2. Type a sentence of text.
3. Tap a word twice. Your chosen word appears highlighted, as shown in Figure 5-7, along with a Cut, Copy, Paste, and Replace menu. At this point, you can tap Cut or Copy to cut or copy your selected text.

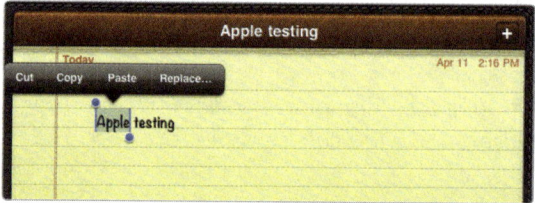

FIGURE 5-7: *Tap a word twice to select it.*

4. Press your fingertip over another word, and lift your finger off the screen. Notice that a Paste menu now appears.
5. Tap **Select**. (If you tap Select All, you'll select all the text.) Your chosen word appears selected, and a Cut, Copy, Paste, Replace menu appears. At this point, you can tap Cut or Copy to cut or copy your selected text.

Selecting Part of Your Text

Normally the virtual keyboard only selects entire words. However, you may want to select just part of a word, which you can do by following these steps:

1. From the Home screen, tap **Notes**. The Notes screen appears.
2. Type a sentence of text.
3. Tap any word twice. Your chosen word appears highlighted along with beginning and ending markers; each marker appears as a vertical line with a circle on the top or bottom of the line.
4. Hold your finger on one of the vertical lines, and slide your finger to select more or less text, as shown in Figure 5-8.
5. Lift your finger when you've selected all the text you want. At this point you can tap Cut or Copy to cut or copy your selected text.

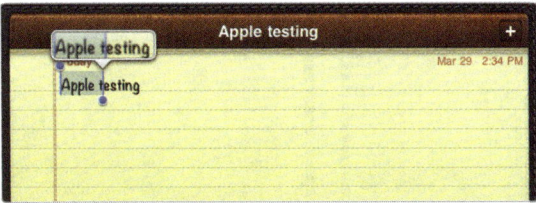

FIGURE 5-8: *Dragging the beginning or ending marker lets you select parts of a text.*

Pasting Text

After you have selected and cut or copied your selected text, you can paste it in a new location. To see how to cut, copy, and paste text, follow these steps:

1. From the Home screen, tap **Notes**. The Notes screen appears.
2. Type a sentence of text.
3. Tap any word twice to select it and display the Cut, Copy, and Replace menu.
4. Tap **Cut** or **Copy**. (If you tap Cut, your selected text disappears. If you tap Copy, your selected text remains.)
5. Hold your fingertip on a different part of your text to position the cursor. The magnifying glass appears to let you see where the cursor appears.
6. Lift your finger off the screen. A Select, Select All, and Paste menu appears.
7. Tap **Paste**. Your previously cut or copied text appears at the cursor's location. Note that you can even copy and paste to and from different applications. For example, you might copy the recipe from a web page in Safari into an email message to your aunt in Mail.

✳ *NOTE:* **You can shake your iPad to Undo a Cut, Paste, or even a bit of typing— just be careful not to drop it!**

Spellchecking

The iPad's virtual keyboard offers a limited form of spellchecking that flags possibly misspelled words with a red underline. You must first tap a possibly misspelled word, and then the virtual keyboard displays a list of possible correct spellings.

To see how to spellcheck text, follow these steps:

1. From the Home screen, tap **Notes**. The Notes screen appears.
2. Type **Greeetings**. (Make sure you deliberately misspell the word by typing three es.) The misspelled word appears with a dotted line underneath to identify it as a possible misspelling, as shown in Figure 5-9.
3. Tap the word. A menu appears, listing possible correct spellings, as shown in Figure 5-10.
4. Tap the correct spelling, and your iPad replaces your word.

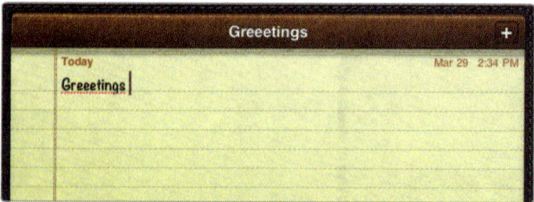

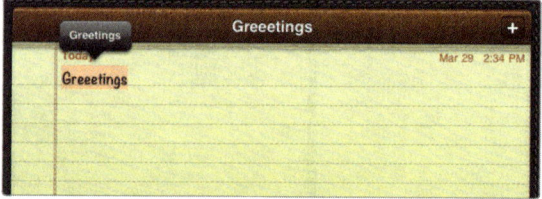

FIGURE 5-9: *Possible misspelled words appear with a dotted underline.*

FIGURE 5-10: *A menu lists possible correct spellings for your misspelled word.*

✳ **NOTE:** **If you tap a word twice to select it, a Cut, Copy, Paste, and Replace menu appears. If you tap Replace, you can select a list of alternate words to replace your currently selected word.**

Customizing the Virtual Keyboard

To make the virtual keyboard easier to use, you may want to customize its behavior. Five features you can customize include auto-correction, auto-capitalization, spell-checking, caps lock, and a neat shortcut to insert periods (".") automatically.

Auto-correction means the virtual keyboard tries to guess which word you want to type after you've typed only part of that word—the iPad will also attempt to autocorrect misspellings as you type. *Auto-capitalization* means that the first letter of every sentence automatically gets capitalized. *Spellchecking* automatically highlights potentially misspelled words. *Caps lock* lets you tap the Shift key twice to turn on caps lock so you can type capital letters without tapping the Shift key each time. The shortcut for inserting a period automatically is to simply press the spacebar twice. All of these features are on by default—if you find them annoying, just turn them off.

To customize the virtual keyboard, follow these steps:

1. From the Home screen, tap **Settings**. The Settings screen appears.
2. Tap **General**. The General settings screen appears.
3. Tap **Keyboard**. The Keyboard settings screen appears, as shown in Figure 5-11.

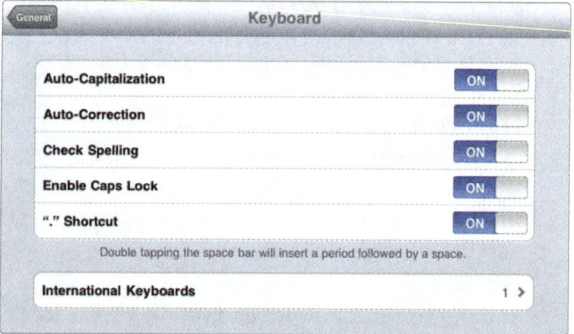

FIGURE 5-11: *The Keyboard settings screen*

4. (Optional) Tap the **Auto-Capitalization** on/off switch.
5. (Optional) Tap the **Auto-Correction** on/off switch.
6. (Optional) Tap the **Check Spelling** on/off switch.
7. (Optional) Tap the **Enable Caps Lock** on/off switch.
8. (Optional) Tap the **"." Shortcut** on/off switch.
9. Press the **Home button**.

✳ *NOTE:* Additionally, your iPad can speak any corrections it makes to your typing aloud. You can enable this feature by tapping Settings, General, Accessibility and then tapping the Speak Auto-text on/off switch.

Turning Off Audible Keyboard Clicks

Typing with the virtual keyboard doesn't give you any physical feedback when you've pressed a key. To overcome this problem, you can turn auditory feedback on or off so your iPad makes a slight clicking sound to let you know when you've pressed a key. By default, this auditory clicking is turned on, but if it annoys you, you can turn it off.

To turn on (or turn off) these auditory keyboard clicks, follow these steps:

1. From the Home screen, tap **Settings**. The Settings screen appears.
2. Tap **General**. The General settings screen appears.
3. Tap **Sounds**. The Sounds settings screen appears, as shown in Figure 5-12.

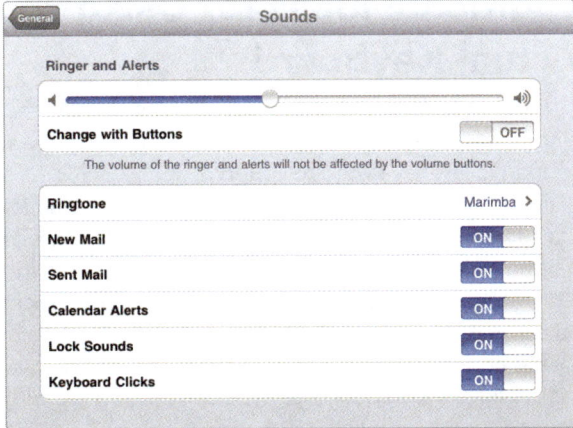

FIGURE 5-12: *The Sounds settings screen lets you turn auditory keyboard clicks on or off.*

4. Tap the **Keyboard Clicks** on/off switch.
5. Press the **Home** button.

Typing Foreign Characters

If you regularly need to type characters in foreign languages that display accent characters above or below the letter, or type the symbol for euro dollars or yen instead of American dollars, the virtual keyboard offers a unique press-and-hold feature. Just press your finger over a key and hold it there. After a few seconds, a menu of different characters appears, allowing you to slide your finger over the character you want to type.

To see how to type foreign characters, follow these steps:

1. From the Home screen, tap **Notes**. The Notes screen appears.
2. Tap on the Notes screen to make the virtual keyboard appear.
3. Press your finger over the **E** key and hold it until a menu of different characters appears.
4. Press and hold your finger over the **A**, **I**, **O**, **U** and **C** keys to see the character choices for those letters.
5. Tap the **.?123** key to switch to the numeric keyboard.
6. Press and hold your finger over the **$** and **?** keys to see the choices for those characters.

To learn more about customizing the iPad for foreign languages, read Chapter 28.

Additional Ideas for Using the Virtual Keyboard

Getting familiar with the virtual keyboard may take time, especially if you're used to using physical keyboards. If you're a hunt-and-peck typist, you may find the iPad's keyboard perfectly suited to your typing style.

The key to using the virtual keyboard is to practice in order to get over your initial unfamiliarity. To make typing more comfortable and natural, consider buying an optional case, which can prop the iPad up at an angle.

If you prefer a physical keyboard even after practicing with the virtual one, you can wirelessly connect any Bluetooth-enabled keyboard to your iPad. If you buy the optional camera connection kit, you can plug an adapter into your iPad that provides a USB port. Then you can plug an ordinary USB keyboard into this port and type on this keyboard.

PART 2

Making the Most of Your iPad

6

Customizing the Home Screen

The Home screen displays icons that represent all the apps available on your iPad. Since you'll be staring at the Home screen all the time, you may want to customize its appearance by rearranging icons on the screen, moving them off (or on) to additional panes, or just deleting certain apps altogether.

In addition, the Home screen lets you choose a background image as your wallpaper. You can choose one of the photographs that Apple provides or use any of your own pictures that you've loaded on your iPad. You can put a picture of your kids making silly faces on your iPad or use a picture of your dog or cat. The choice is yours.

In this chapter you'll learn how to customize the Home screen of your iPad.

What You'll Be Using

To customize your iPad's Home screen, you need to use the following:

▶ The Home button   The Settings screen

▶ The iPad's USB cable   iTunes on your computer

Rearranging Icons on the Home Screen

You might find yourself using the Calendar and iPod apps every day but rarely using the Contacts or Notes apps. To make it easy to access the Calendar and iPod apps, you might want to put these icons in the corner of the screen and bury seldom-used app icons in another pane that's hidden out of sight. There are two ways to rearrange your Home screen: directly on the iPad or through iTunes on your computer.

Rearranging Icons on the iPad

The fastest way to rearrange icons on your Home screen is to manipulate and move those icons directly on your iPad. To rearrange icons on the Home screen, follow these steps:

1. Press the **Home** button. The Home screen appears. (Skip this step if the Home screen is already visible.)
2. Press and hold your finger on the icon that you want to move to a new location until all the icons on the Home screen start wriggling, as shown in Figure 6-1.
3. Drag the icon to where you want to move it. When you move an icon in between two other icons, those two icons glide out of the way. You can now drag any app to a new location.

FIGURE 6-1: *Pressing and holding your finger on an icon will make all the Home screen icons wriggle.*

✳ NOTE: Remember, the Home screen actually consists of multiple panes. To move an icon off one pane and onto another one, slide your finger to the left or right of the screen until the other pane appears.

4. (Optional) Tap the close button of any app icon that you want to remove from your iPad. It's the little X in the upper left.
5. Press the **Home** button to stop all the Home screen icons from wriggling.

Rearranging Icons Through iTunes

If you have a lot of apps stored on your iPad or want to move app icons from one pane to another, it's much faster to do it through iTunes instead. Not only can you use your mouse (or laptop trackpad) to move icons across multiple panes faster than you could do this on your iPad, but you can also see thumbnail images of each Home screen pane, which makes it easier to see the arrangement of all your app icons at once. To rearrange icons on the Home screen through iTunes, follow these steps:

1. Connect your iPad to your computer through the USB cable.
2. Run iTunes on your Mac or PC.
3. Click the name of your iPad under the Devices category in the iTunes window.
4. Click the **Apps** tab and make sure a check mark appears in the **Sync Apps** check box. The right side of the screen displays your Home screen panes, as shown in Figure 6-2.
5. Drag any app icons to a new location using the mouse.

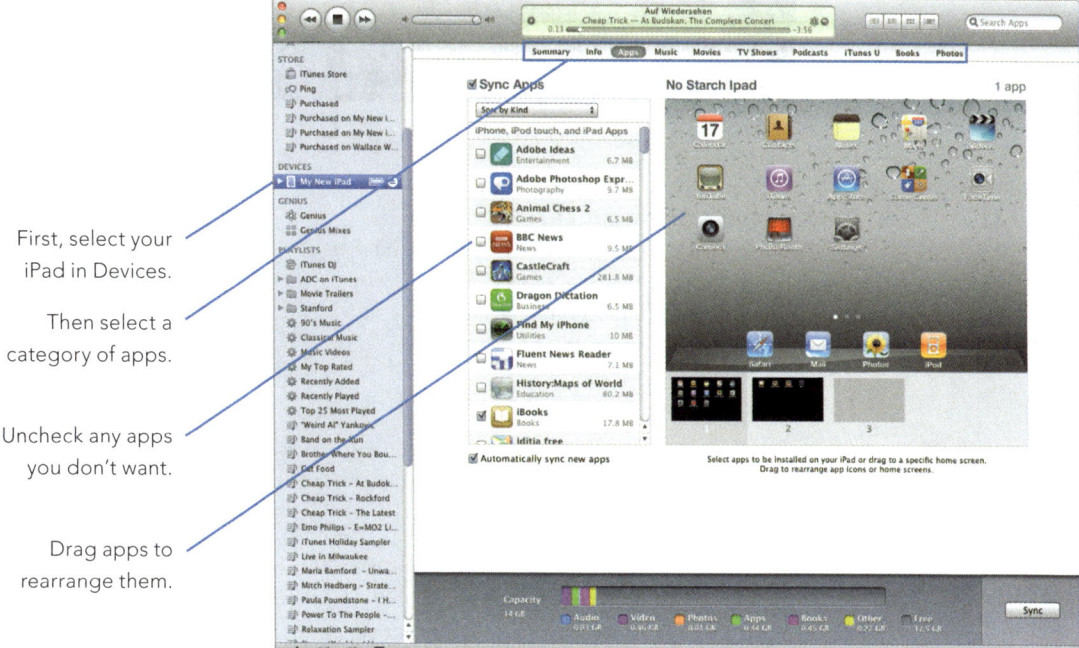

First, select your iPad in Devices.

Then select a category of apps.

Uncheck any apps you don't want.

Drag apps to rearrange them.

FIGURE 6-2: *iTunes displays your Home screen.*

6. (Optional) Using the mouse, point to any app icon that you want to delete. A close button appears in the upper-left corner of that app. Click this close button to remove the app from your iPad.
7. Click **Apply**. Wait until iTunes finishes syncing your iPad before disconnecting it from the USB cable.

Rearranging Icons into Folders

One problem with storing too many apps on your iPad is that your screen can soon look cluttered with so many app icons all over the place. To fix this problem, you can organize multiple apps into folders. To create a folder, follow these steps:

1. Press your finger over any app icon that you want to store in a folder. All the app icons start wriggling.
2. Drag the app icon toward a second app icon that you want to store in the same folder. A dark border appears around this second app icon.
3. Drag the app icon over this app icon with the dark border around it. After you lift your finger from the screen, the contents of your folder appear on the screen, allowing you to drop your currently selected icon into the folder, as shown in Figure 6-3.

FIGURE 6-3: *Dropping an icon into a folder*

4. Press the **Home** button.
5. (Optional) If you want to change the name of your folder later, just tap and hold an icon until they wiggle. Tap the folder you wish to rename, tap the title, and use the virtual keyboard to type a new folder name. Press the Home button when you're done typing.

Taking Icons out of a Folder

After you have created a folder that contains two or more app icons, you can always take an app icon out of a folder and place it back on the desktop. To remove an icon from a folder, follow these steps:

1. Tap the folder icon that you want to modify. The contents of the folder appear underneath the folder icon (see Figure 6-3).
2. Press your finger over the app icon that you want to move out of the folder. The app icons start wriggling.
3. Drag the icon out of the folder and on to the desktop.
4. Press the **Home** button to stop all your app icons from wriggling.

Putting Apps on the Dock

At the bottom of the screen, your iPad initially displays four app icons (Safari, Mail, Photos, and iPod). This area acts like the Dock in Mac OS. It displays its apps at all times, even if you switch to a different Home screen pane. If you find yourself using certain apps all the time, you may want to place those apps on this Dock area so they will always be available. You can put up to six applications on the Dock.

Adding App Icons to the Dock

To add an app icon to the Dock, follow these steps:

1. At the Home screen, touch and hold the app icon that you want to move to the Dock. All your app icons start wriggling. You can release your finger.
2. Drag the app icon to the Dock and then lift your finger off the screen. Your app now appears on the Dock.
3. Press the **Home** button to stop all your app icons from wriggling.

* NOTE: You can also put folders on the Dock.

Taking App Icons off the Dock

If you find that you don't use certain apps on the Dock very often, you can always move them off the Dock by following these steps:

1. At the Home screen, touch the app icon that you want to move off the Dock until all your app icons start wriggling.
2. Drag the app icon off the Dock, move the app icon anywhere on the screen, and then lift your finger off the screen.
3. Press the **Home** button to stop all your app icons from wriggling.

Modifying the Wallpaper

The wallpaper image appears behind all your app icons so you have something interesting to look at rather than just a blank screen. To customize the appearance of your wallpaper, you can adjust the brightness or just choose a new image altogether.

Adjusting the Wallpaper Brightness

The wallpaper on your iPad is meant to provide an interesting image to look at, but if it seems too light or too dark, you can always modify this brightness by following these steps:

1. From the Home screen, tap **Settings**. The Settings screen appears.
2. Tap **Brightness & Wallpaper**. The Brightness & Wallpaper settings screen appears, as shown in Figure 6-4.

FIGURE 6-4: *The Auto-Brightness slider lets you modify the brightness of your current wallpaper.*

3. Drag the **Auto-Brightness** slider left or right.
4. (Optional) Tap the **Auto-Brightness** on/off switch. When the Auto-Brightness switch reads *ON*, your iPad will adjust the brightness of the screen based on the surrounding lighting conditions.
5. Press the **Home** button. The Home screen appears.

Changing the Wallpaper

If you want to choose a different wallpaper image for your iPad, you can either pick one of the wallpaper images included with your iPad or use a picture that you've already transferred from your computer to your iPad. (Chapter 15 explains how to transfer pictures from your computer to your iPad.)

To change the wallpaper image, follow these steps:

1. From the Home screen, tap **Settings**. The Settings screen appears.
2. Tap **Brightness & Wallpaper**. The Brightness & Wallpaper settings screen appears (see Figure 6-4).
3. Tap anywhere inside the curved rectangle under the Wallpaper group. The screen displays a Wallpaper button along with a list of photo albums such as Camera Roll.
4. Tap **Wallpaper** (to choose from an image included on your iPad), or tap a photo album that you've transferred from your computer to your iPad. Thumbnail images of your available pictures appear, as shown in Figure 6-5.
5. Tap the image you want to use as your wallpaper. Your iPad shows what your chosen image looks like and displays three buttons (Set Lock Screen, Set Home Screen, and Set Both) in the upper-right corner, as shown in Figure 6-6.

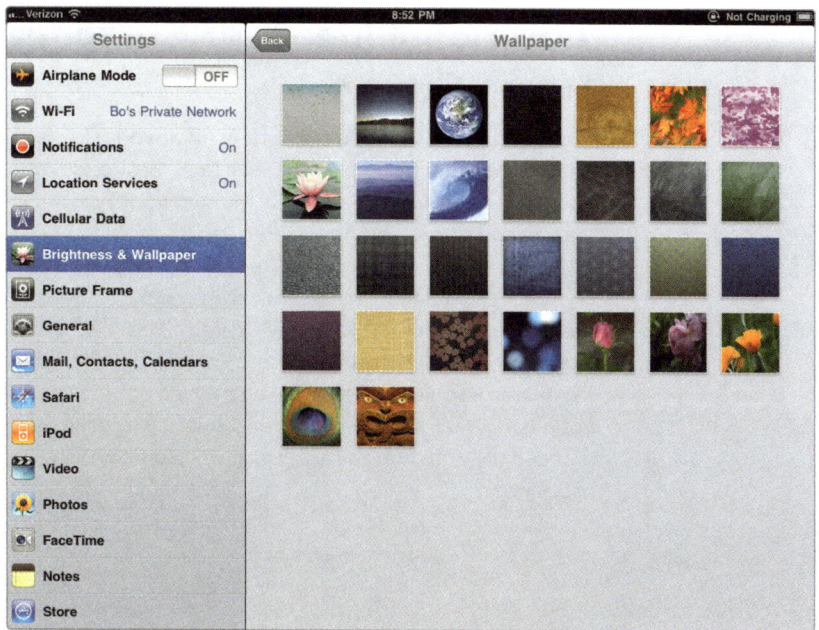

FIGURE 6-5: *Viewing a list of available wallpaper images*

FIGURE 6-6: *From the top of the preview pane, you can choose where you want the image to be used.*

✳ **NOTE:** The Lock screen is the image that appears when your iPad first turns on and requires that you drag a slider across the screen to access your iPad. The Home screen is the image that appears behind all your apps.

6. Tap **Set Lock Screen**, **Set Lock Home Screen**, or **Set Both**. (You can also tap **Cancel** if you change your mind.) Your chosen image now appears as the wallpaper on your Lock screen and/or your Home screen, depending on which option you chose.

7. Press the **Home** button. The Home screen appears.

Additional Ideas for Customizing Your Home Screen

You'll spend most of your time looking at your Home screen, so you might as well customize it so you'll enjoy looking at it. Group together your most commonly used apps on the Home screen, and set your favorite image as your wallpaper. Chapter 10 shows you how to find, buy, and install new apps. Chapter 12 explains how to add your favorite websites to your Home screen.

Since you can choose your own wallpaper images, put pictures of animals, landscapes, artwork, or people on your iPad. If you're comfortable with creating graphic images and transferring them to your iPad, turn your daily or weekly to-do list into a graphic image and then make it your wallpaper. Every time you turn on your iPad, you'll see your tasks and goals. By putting your own images on your iPad, you can truly customize its appearance so nobody will ever mistake your iPad for their own.

7 Using Parental Controls

Doesn't it seem that children gravitate toward the most expensive and valuable items we own, just so they can play with them, break them, or lose them? Although you do need to protect your iPad from excessive handling from over-eager children, you also need to protect your children from your iPad—or at least the adult-oriented content they could access on it.

Since banning your children from touching your iPad is probably not a practical solution, you can turn on parental controls to limit what a child can see on your iPad.

Making an iPad child-friendly involves restricting access to certain features, including playing videos with explicit content, browsing the Internet, watching YouTube videos, playing iTunes, and installing new iPad applications.

What You'll Be Using

To restrict access to certain iPad features, you need to use the following:

 The Settings screen

Blocking iPad Features

To restrict access to certain iPad features, you use a four-digit passcode. The only way someone (including you) can access these blocked features is by typing the correct four-digit passcode.

✳ *NOTE:* **The four-digit passcode needed to modify parental controls can (and should) be completely different from the four-digit passcode used to access your iPad, as explained in Chapter 8.**

Some of the features that you can block include:

▶ Accessing the Internet with the Safari web browser

▶ Watching YouTube videos

▶ Listening to music through iTunes

▶ Installing and deleting iPad apps

▶ Defining your iPad's location

▶ Changing email accounts

▶ Making in-app purchases

▶ Playing multiplayer games in Game Center

▶ Adding friends to Game Center

✳ *NOTE:* **Your iPad can block only those video and audio files tagged as Explicit that you bought through iTunes. If you load an R-rated movie or adult-content audio file onto your iPad that you received from another source, your iPad may not recognize the file as explicit.**

By blocking access to different parts of your iPad, you can prevent your kids (or anyone else) from peeking at adult-oriented content, goofing off when they should be doing something more productive, or running up charges by installing apps or burning up time connecting to the Internet through your iPad's cellular telephone network plan.

Finally, you may want to turn off Location Services, which can prevent your iPad from identifying its current location. Turning Location Services on can be handy for using the Maps app, but it can also pinpoint the location of your child (carrying your iPad) as well, which you may not feel comfortable allowing.

To block access to one or more of these features, follow these steps:

1. From the Home screen, tap **Settings**. The Settings screen appears.
2. Tap **General**. The General settings screen appears.
3. Tap **Restrictions**. The Restrictions settings screen appears. Notice that all the on/off buttons appear dimmed since you cannot restrict access until you first tap the Enable Restrictions button.
4. Tap **Enable Restrictions**. A Set Passcode screen appears, as shown in Figure 7-1.

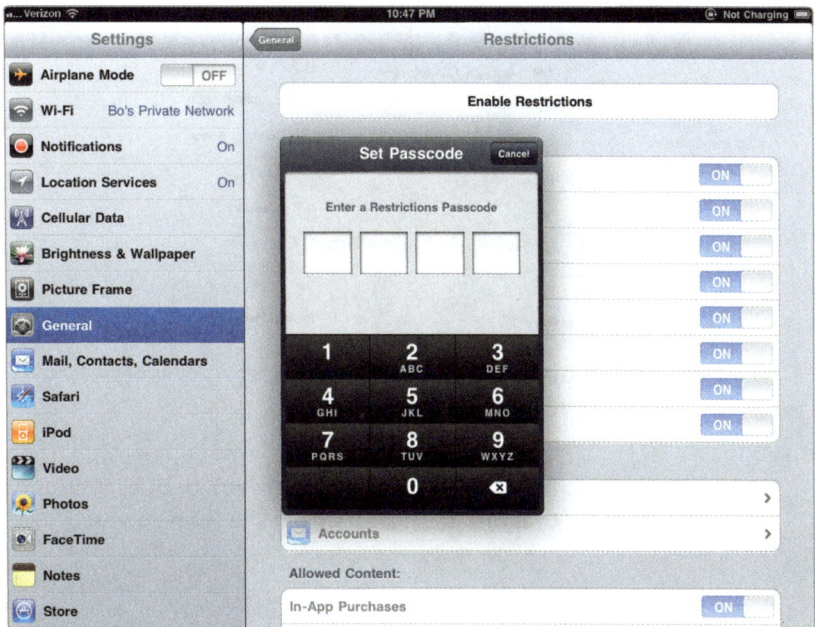

FIGURE 7-1: *The Set Passcode screen lets you selectively block access.*

5. Type a four-digit number on the numeric keypad that appears on the screen. A second Set Passcode screen appears, asking you to reenter your four-digit passcode.
6. Type your four-digit number again. The Restrictions settings screen appears again, allowing you to tap the on/off switches of different features, as shown in Figure 7-2.
7. (Optional) Tap the on/off switch for the **Safari**, **YouTube**, **Camera**, **FaceTime**, **iTunes**, **Ping**, **Installing Apps**, **Deleting Apps**, **Location**, **Accounts**, or **In-App Purchases** features. To turn a feature off, tap the switch until *OFF* appears.
8. (Optional) Scroll down until you see the Game Center category. Then tap the on/off switch for **Multiplayer Games** or **Adding Friends**.
9. Press the **Home** button.

FIGURE 7-2: *The Restrictions settings screen lets you select the on/off switches of different features.*

* **NOTE:** When you turn a feature off, such as YouTube or Safari, the icon for that feature disappears from the Home screen.

Filtering Content

Another way the parental controls feature can protect your children is by letting you choose what type of content (music, podcasts, movies, TV shows, and apps) you'll allow on your iPad. For example, you may not want your children to view any movies rated R or higher or listen to any music or podcasts rated Explicit. The following are some of the content you can filter:

▶ **In-App Purchases**   Blocks or allows installed apps to purchase additional content, such as a magazine app that charges a fee for new content.

▶ **Ratings For**   Defines which nation's ratings system to use, such as United States or Germany.

▶ **Music & Podcasts**   Blocks or allows music or podcasts labeled Explicit.

▶ **Movies**   Blocks all movies or just those above a certain rating such as R or NC-17.

▶ **TV Shows**   Blocks or allows TV shows depending on their ratings such as TV-14 or TV-MA.

▶ **Apps**   Blocks or allows apps depending on their ratings such as 9+ or 17+.

To define what's allowable on your iPad, follow these steps:

1. From the Home screen, tap **Settings**. The Settings screen appears.
2. Tap **General**. The General settings screen appears.
3. Tap **Restrictions**. An Enter Passcode screen appears.
4. Type your four-digit passcode. The Restrictions settings screen appears.
5. Under the Allowed Content category, tap a button to define what to block, such as tapping the on/off switch to block or allow in-app purchases or to define the movie ratings allowed on your iPad such as PG-13 or R.
6. Press the **Home** button.

Disabling Restrictions

By tapping the on/off buttons, you can selectively disable certain iPad features. However, if you want to remove restrictions altogether, follow these steps:

1. From the Home screen, tap **Settings**. The Settings screen appears.
2. Tap **General**. The General settings screen appears.
3. Tap **Restrictions**. A Turn Off Passcode screen appears.
4. Type your four-digit passcode on the numeric keypad that appears on the screen. A Restrictions settings screen appears.
5. Tap **Disable Restrictions**. A Turn Off Passcode screen appears.
6. Type your four-digit number on the numeric keypad that appears on the screen.
7. The Restrictions settings screen appears again.
8. Press the **Home** button.

Additional Ideas for Using Restrictions on Your iPad

The main reason to restrict access to different iPad features is to keep your kids from certain content. However, you may also want to restrict your own access to certain features to avoid the temptation to waste time.

For example, suppose you're addicted to the Internet and keep paying way too much for Internet access through your cellular network provider. Simply restrict access to Safari and/or YouTube and remove the temptation from your home screen.

To make this even more effective, have someone else type in a passcode to restrict your access to certain features. Now you won't be tempted to turn off these features since even you won't have the proper four-digit passcode. (Just make sure that you trust the person restricting your access to your own iPad, or else you may never gain access to those features without completely resetting your iPad.)

8

Protecting Your Privacy

Right now, anyone can pick up your iPad, turn it on, and see all the information stored on it, such as your email messages, appointments, or important contacts (names and phone numbers). To help keep your iPad's information private, you can turn on the passcode feature.

The passcode feature, which is different from the parental controls discussed in Chapter 7, lets you set a four-digit code that someone must enter before they can use your iPad. If someone tries guessing your passcode, you can even have your iPad automatically erase its data after 10 failed passcode attempts. By turning on this passcode feature, you can protect your data from spies and nosy relatives.

In this chapter you'll learn how to define a passcode to limit access to your iPad and keep others from identifying the location of your iPad.

What You'll Be Using

To protect your privacy, you need to use the following:

 The Settings screen

Setting (or Removing) a Passcode

Initially, your iPad does not require a passcode to start using it. Just press the Home button or the On/Off button, slide your finger across the screen to unlock the Home screen, and you (or anyone else who gets a hold of your iPad) can start peeking through your data. A passcode simply acts like a password that locks out strangers from using your iPad.

Setting a Passcode

You can define a simple or regular passcode to block access to your iPad. A simple passcode lets you define a four-digit number to block access. A regular passcode lets you define a passcode of more than four characters that can consist of letters and symbols. To set a simple or regular passcode, follow these steps:

1. From the Home screen, tap **Settings**. The Settings screen appears.
2. Tap **General**. The General settings screen appears.
3. Tap **Passcode Lock**. The Passcode Lock settings screen appears, as shown in Figure 8-1.

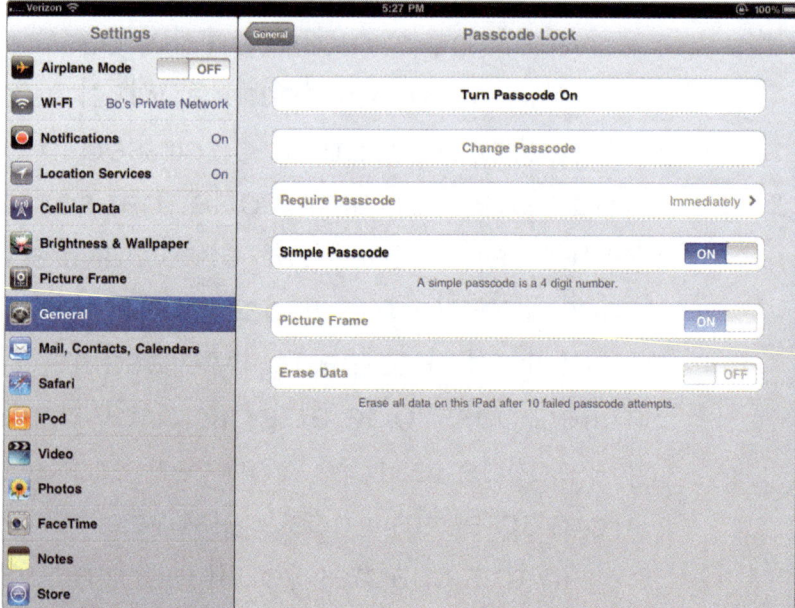

FIGURE 8-1: *The Passcode Lock settings screen lets you turn the passcode feature on or off.*

4. (Optional) Tap the **Simple Passcode** on/off switch. When set to *ON*, you can define a four-digit passcode. When set to *OFF*, you can define a passcode of letters and symbols.

5. Tap **Turn Passcode On**. A Set Passcode screen appears, as shown in Figure 8-2.

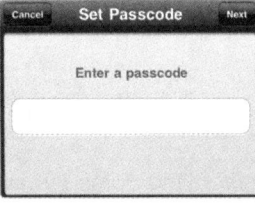

FIGURE 8-2: *The Set Passcode screen lets you type a four-digit or alphanumeric passcode.*

6. Type a code using the number pad or virtual keyboard.

7. A second Set Passcode screen appears. Type your code a second time to verify that you remember what it is.

8. Press the **Home** button.

✳ *WARNING:* **If you forget your passcode, you'll lock yourself out of your iPad, so make sure you remember it!**

Changing or Removing a Passcode

If you have already defined a passcode but want to change it to a different one or remove it entirely, you can by following these steps:

1. From the Home screen, tap **Settings**. The Settings screen appears.

2. Tap **General**. The General settings screen appears.

3. Tap **Passcode Lock**. An Enter Passcode screen appears.

4. Type your current passcode. The Passcode Lock settings screen appears.

5. (Optional) Tap **Change Passcode**. A Change Passcode screen appears.

6. (Optional) Tap **Turn Passcode Off**.

7. Type your current code.

8. Type a new code.

9. A second Set Passcode screen appears. Type your new code a second time to verify that you remember what it is.

10. Press the **Home** button.

Defining When to Ask for a Passcode

If you often turn your iPad off and on in short intervals throughout the day, you may not want to keep typing in a passcode. In that case, you can adjust the time interval before your iPad will ask for the passcode. The longer the time interval, the less chance you'll constantly need to keep typing in a passcode each time you turn on your iPad. However, the longer the time interval, the greater the chance that someone can steal or peek at your iPad and see all your data.

To define the time interval before your iPad asks for a passcode, follow these steps:

1. From the Home screen, tap **Settings**. The Settings screen appears.
2. Tap **General**. The General settings screen appears.
3. Tap **Passcode Lock**. An Enter Passcode screen appears.
4. Type your passcode. The Passcode Lock settings screen appears.
5. Tap **Require Passcode**. The Require Passcode settings screen appears, as shown in Figure 8-3.

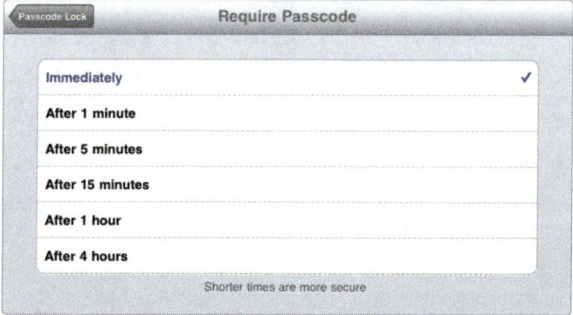

FIGURE 8-3: *The Require Passcode settings screen lets you define a time interval for the iPad to wait before asking for a passcode.*

6. Tap an option such as Immediately, After 5 minutes, or After 1 hour.
7. Press the **Home** button.

Erasing Data After 10 Incorrect Passcodes

Turning on the passcode feature can prevent a thief from peeking at your iPad's data. However, for even more security, you can make your iPad automatically erase its data if someone tries 10 incorrect passcodes in a row. To turn on this data-erasing feature after you have already defined a passcode, follow these steps:

1. From the Home screen, tap **Settings**. The Settings screen appears.
2. Tap **General**. The General settings screen appears.

3. Tap **Passcode Lock**. An Enter Passcode screen appears.
4. Type your passcode. The Passcode Lock settings screen appears.
5. Tap the **Erase Data** on/off switch. If you turn it *ON*, a message appears letting you know that your iPad will erase its data after 10 failed passcode attempts, as shown in Figure 8-4.
6. Tap **Enable** or **Cancel**.
7. Press the **Home** button.

FIGURE 8-4: You can enable a data-erasing feature for when someone types an incorrect passcode 10 times.

Additional Ideas for Protecting Your iPad

Since the iPad is so small and light (and popular), use a passcode to deny thieves access to your data if they happen to steal your iPad. For more security, read Chapter 30 to learn how to use MobileMe (*http://www.apple.com/mobileme/*) to locate your iPad whenever it's turned on and near a Wi-Fi or 3G network. You'll also learn how to encrypt your backups.

Perhaps the best way to keep strangers from peeking at your iPad is to keep your iPad out of sight whenever you're in a public area, especially when you're outdoors. If you stare at your iPad in a public place, your attention will be diverted from your surroundings, which makes it easy for a thief to grab your iPad since you'll be unaware of the thief's approach. Use your iPad indoors, or make sure you're aware of your surroundings if you use the iPad outside. By always being alert for possible thieves who might target your iPad, you can minimize the chances that you'll lose your iPad.

9

Setting Up an Internet Connection

There are two ways to connect to the Internet. First, you can connect through any Wi-Fi network. Second, if you have the 3G version of the iPad, you can connect through a cellular telephone company's network.

A Wi-Fi network is faster, but it won't always be available, especially if you're outside. 3G service is usually available almost everywhere. Since connecting to the Internet can make your iPad so much more useful, you need to learn both ways of getting on the Internet with your iPad.

In this chapter you'll learn how to set up an Internet connection for your iPad.

What You'll Be Using

To set up an Internet connection, you need to use the following:

 The Settings screen

Setting Up a Wi-Fi Connection

No matter which type of iPad you have, you can always connect to the Internet through a Wi-Fi connection. Many public places offer free Wi-Fi connections, and your home or office may have a Wi-Fi network.

To set up a Wi-Fi connection with your iPad, follow these steps:

1. From the Home screen, tap **Settings**. The Settings screen appears.
2. Tap **Wi-Fi**. The Wi-Fi Networks settings screen appears, as shown in Figure 9-1.

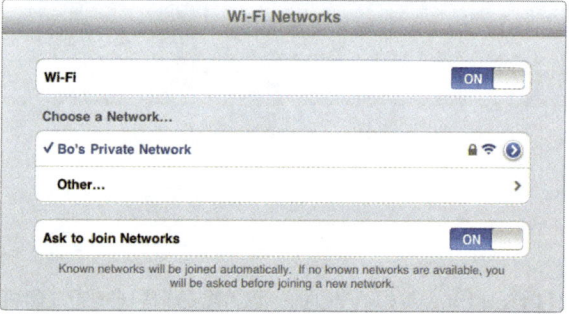

FIGURE 9-1: *The Wi-Fi Networks settings screen lets you define and choose a Wi-Fi network to use.*

3. (Optional) Tap the **Ask to Join Networks** on/off switch. When turned on, your iPad always asks for permission before accessing a Wi-Fi network. This can let you see exactly which Wi-Fi network your iPad may be accessing. It's usually a good idea to know exactly what network you're connecting to, especially when you're travelling.
4. Tap the **Wi-Fi** on/off switch so that the switch reads *ON*. Your iPad tries to recognize any Wi-Fi networks. If there are multiple Wi-Fi networks available, a window lists them all and you can tap the one you want to use. If the Wi-Fi network is password-protected, a Password screen appears. (If your iPad can't recognize a Wi-Fi network that you know exists, you'll need to tap **Other** and type in Wi-Fi settings yourself.)
5. (Optional) Type the password to access the Wi-Fi network and tap the **Join** key on the virtual keyboard. Your iPad connects to your chosen Wi-Fi network.

Forgetting a Wi-Fi Network

After you've connected to a Wi-Fi network once, your iPad will try to automatically connect to it in the future. This can be handy the next time you need to use that particular Wi-Fi network. However, if you find your iPad trying to latch on to a Wi-Fi network that you don't want to join, you can have your iPad forget that network. Forgetting a network is especially useful when a Wi-Fi connection is very slow or doesn't work at all (many Wi-Fi networks in hotels or airports allow you to connect but require payment, for example).

To forget a Wi-Fi network, follow these steps:

1. From the Home screen, tap **Settings**. The Settings screen appears.
2. Tap **Wi-Fi**. The Wi-Fi Networks settings screen appears, as shown earlier in Figure 9-1.
3. Tap the white arrow inside the blue circle that appears to the right of the network you want your iPad to forget. The network info screen appears.
4. Tap **Forget this Network** at the top of the screen.
5. Tap either **Forget** or **Cancel** when prompted.

Connecting to a 3G Cellular Network

If you have the 3G version of the iPad, you have the option of connecting to the Internet through a 3G cellular telephone network. Depending on your cellular telephone provider, you can purchase 3G access on a monthly basis for a fixed fee that gives you a fixed amount of data.

To set up a 3G account on your iPad, follow these steps:

1. From the Home screen, tap **Settings**. The Settings screen appears.
2. Tap **Cellular Data**. The Cellular Data settings screen appears, as shown in Figure 9-2.

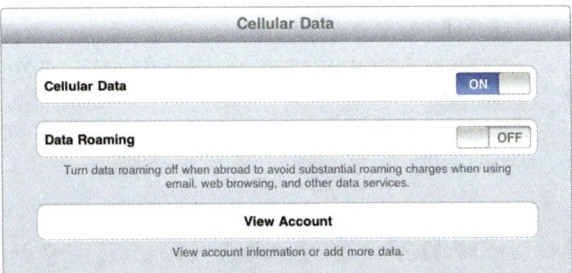

FIGURE 9-2: *The Cellular Data settings screen lets you define cellular data settings.*

3. Tap the **Cellular Data** on/off switch to make sure it reads *ON*.
4. (Optional) Tap the **Data Roaming** on/off switch to turn it *ON* or *OFF*. (Data Roaming means that your iPad constantly checks the Internet for

email messages, and, in many countries, each time it checks the Internet you could incur a fee.)

5. Tap **View Account**. The Cellular Data Account window appears, as shown in Figure 9-3.
6. Type in the required information and choose a data plan.

✻ **NOTE:** To sign up for a data plan, you must type in a credit card number. If you are in an area where you can't get 3G cellular telephone access, you will have to wait to sign up for a 3G data plan when you can access a cellular network.

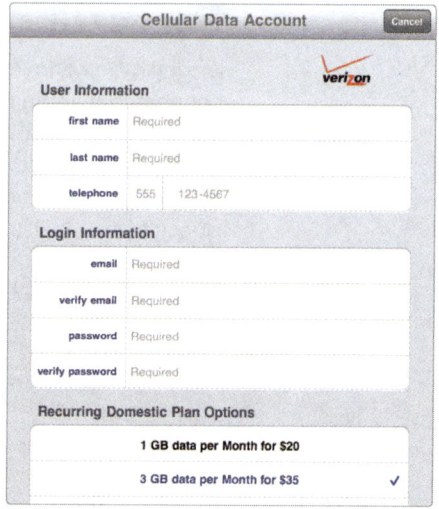

FIGURE 9-3: *The Cellular Data Account window lets you choose a data plan.*

Canceling (or Switching) a Cellular Data Plan

When you sign up for a data plan, it runs for a fixed amount of time, such as 30 days, starting with the date that you signed up for that data plan. You'll receive three alerts when your data plan limit reaches 20 percent, 10 percent, and zero. Each alert gives you the chance to sign up for your current plan or choose a different plan.

Your data plan will automatically renew every time period until you specifically turn it off. To turn off (or switch) your data plan, follow these steps:

1. From the Home screen, tap **Settings**. The Settings screen appears.
2. Tap **Cellular Data**. The Cellular Data settings screen appears (see Figure 9-2).
3. Tap **View Account**. The Cellular Data Account window appears showing your current data plan.
4. Tap **Cancel Plan** or one of the other data plan buttons to switch to that data plan.

Additional Ideas for Connecting to the Internet

Don't forget, you can also connect your iPad to the Wi-Fi broadcast from a portable hotspot device and to certain smartphones (including the latest iPhones). Piggybacking off your device's existing wireless Internet connection will let you use any provider's wireless connection—and spare you the second bill.

10 Installing (and Uninstalling) Apps

If you use a Windows or Macintosh computer, you can buy software in a store, over the Internet, or through the mail. No matter how you get a program, you can install it on your computer. The iPad is different. You can't buy iPad software from anyplace other than through Apple's App Store.

The reason for this is security. When you install programs from any source, there's always the chance of malicious software (aka malware) sneaking on to your computer and infecting it. By distributing iPad software (more commonly known as applications or just apps), Apple can inspect all apps to make sure they don't do anything sneaky like capture your password and send it to some hacker in another part of the world.

In this chapter you'll learn how to install (and uninstall) apps on your iPad.

What You'll Be Using

To install and uninstall apps on your iPad, you'll use the following:

▶ The iPad's USB cable   iTunes on your computer

 The App Store

Finding Apps on Your iPad

Before you can install apps on the iPad, you need to visit the App Store and find an app that you want. You can visit the App Store directly through your iPad or you can use iTunes on your computer.

The advantage of accessing the App Store on your iPad is that after you download an app, you can start using it right away. The drawback is that you need an Internet connection to access the App Store.

The advantage of using iTunes on your computer to access the App Store is that you can download apps much faster than you can on the iPad. The drawback is that after you download an app into iTunes, you'll need to transfer that app to your iPad before you can start using it.

To find an app for your iPad, follow these steps:

1. From the Home screen, tap **App Store**. The App Store screen appears.
2. Tap the **Featured** icon at the bottom of the screen. The Featured list of iPad apps appears at the bottom of the screen, as shown in Figure 10-1.

FIGURE 10-1: *The Featured list shows certain apps that Apple wants people to notice.*

3. Tap the Left or Right white arrows on the left or right side of the screen to view a different group of apps.

4. Tap the **New**, **What's Hot**, or **Release Date** tab at the top of the screen. The New tab lists the latest apps, the What's Hot tab lists the most popular of the new apps, and the Release Date tab lists apps chronologically by the dates they were first made available.

5. Tap the **Genius** icon at the bottom of the screen. (The first time you do this, you'll need to turn this Genius feature on.) A list of apps, similar to what you've already downloaded, appears on the screen, as shown in Figure 10-2.

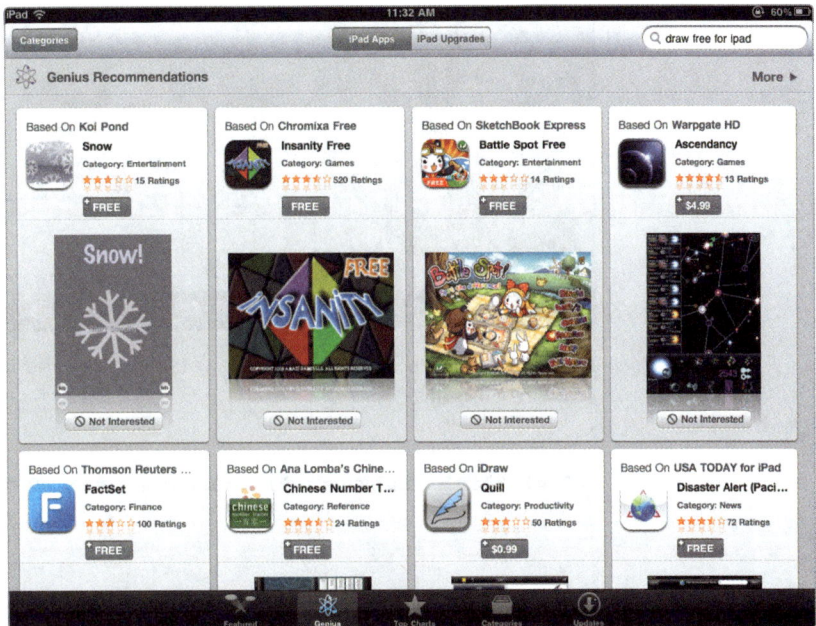

FIGURE 10-2: *The Genius feature lists apps that are similar to ones already installed on your iPad.*

6. Tap the **Top Charts** icon. A list of the most popular commercial and free apps appears, as shown in Figure 10-3.

7. Tap the **Categories** icon. A list of different app categories appears.

8. Tap the **Updates** icon at the bottom of the screen. If you have any apps that need updating, you'll see a list of them here.

9. Tap the **Featured** icon at the bottom of the screen and then tap the **Search** field in the upper-right corner of the screen. The virtual keyboard appears at the bottom of the screen.

10. Type a word or phrase that describes the type of app you want to find, such as **horoscope** or **medical**, and then tap the **Search** key on the virtual keyboard. A list of apps that matches your criteria appears. You can restrict your search results to look only for Free apps, find the newest apps, search by category, and so on, as shown in Figure 10-4.

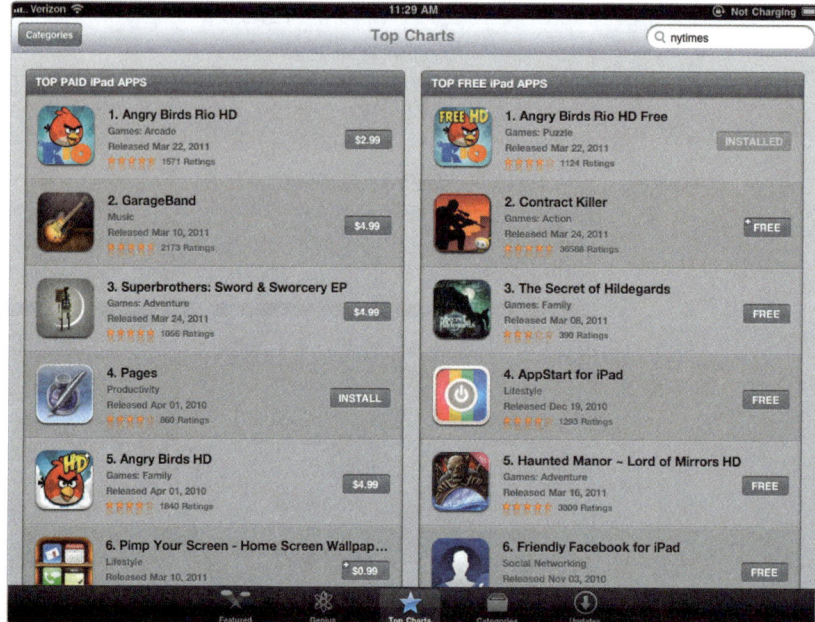

FIGURE 10-3: *The Top Charts icon lets you find the best free (and commercial) apps.*

FIGURE 10-4: *You can restrict your search for better results.*

✳ *NOTE:* The iPad can run both iPhone and iPad apps—if you already have an iPhone, all the apps you purchased or downloaded will be available to install on your iPad. However, iPhone apps may not take advantage of the iPad's ability to rotate or fill out the entire iPad screen.

Installing an App

There are so many choices that just browsing through the App Store can feel like getting lost in a shopping mall. But once you find an app that you want, you can install it by following these steps:

1. Browse through the App Store until you find an app that you want.
2. Tap the **Price** button that appears to the right of the app name. Common prices are FREE or $4.99, as shown in Figure 10-5.

FIGURE 10-5: *Tapping the Price or FREE button will display a green INSTALL (for free apps) or BUY APP (for commercial apps) button.*

✳ *NOTE:* If you tap the BUY APP button, you'll install the app and the cost of the app will be charged to your iTunes account, so make sure you really want to pay for an app before installing it.

3. Tap **BUY APP** or **INSTALL APP**. An iTunes Password dialog appears, asking you to type in your password.
4. Type your password and tap **OK**. The app icon appears on the Home screen with the message "Loading." When the app's name appears, you can tap its icon to run that app.

Finding Apps in iTunes

You can also download apps through iTunes on your computer and then transfer those apps to your iPad. To search and download apps through iTunes, follow these steps:

1. Run iTunes on your computer.
2. Click **iTunes Store** in the left pane of the iTunes window. The iTunes Store screen appears.
3. Click **App Store** at the top of the screen. The App Store screen appears.
4. Click the **iPad** tab at the top of the screen. The App Store displays only those apps designed to work on the iPad.

5. Find an app you want and click its **INSTALL APP** or **BUY APP** button. A dialog appears, asking for your iTunes account password.
6. Type your iTunes account password and click **Get**. Your chosen app downloads to your computer. The next time you connect your iPad to your computer, you'll be able to transfer the app to your iPad.

Updating Apps on the iPad

Software developers frequently update their apps, so to check if any of your apps need updating, peek at the Updates icon that appears in the App Store screen on your iPad. To use the Updates icon, follow these steps:

1. From the Home screen, tap **App Store**. The App Store screen appears.
2. Tap the **Updates** icon at the bottom of the screen. The Updates screen appears, listing any applications that you need to update. At this point, you can choose which updates you wish to update and install.

Deleting Apps from the iPad

If you've installed any apps on your iPad, you can always delete those icons and uninstall those apps. (You cannot uninstall any apps that came pre-installed on the iPad, such as Notes, Maps, or the Calendar.) You can delete apps from your iPad or using iTunes on your computer.

Deleting an App from the iPad

The simplest way to delete an app is directly from your iPad. To delete an icon and uninstall the app that the icon represents, follow these steps:

1. From the Home screen, press and hold your finger on the app icon that you want to delete. Your apps will start wriggling. An X in a circle appears in the upper-left corner of your chosen icon. (If an X in a circle does not appear, that means you cannot delete that icon and uninstall that app.)

＊ **NOTE:** Press the Home button if you suddenly decide you don't want to delete the icon after all. The X in the circle disappears from your chosen icon.

2. Tap the **X** in the circle. A Delete dialog appears, as shown in Figure 10-6.
3. Tap **Delete**. Your chosen icon disappears from the Home screen.
4. Press the **Home** button to stop your apps from wriggling.

FIGURE 10-6: The Delete dialog alerts you that you are uninstalling an app.

Deleting an App Using iTunes

To delete an app by using iTunes on your computer, you need to connect your iPad to your computer and then follow these steps:

1. Run iTunes on your computer.
2. Click the name of your iPad under the Devices category in the left pane of the Tunes window.
3. Click the **Apps** tab. The screen displays your Home screen panes with all your currently installed apps.
4. Move the mouse pointer over an app icon that you want to delete. An X in a circle appears in the app icon's upper-left corner.
5. Click this close button (the X in the circle). Your chosen app icon disappears.

✳ **NOTE: If you select the check boxes of apps displayed in the Apps tab of the iTunes window, you can re-install any downloaded apps back on to your iPad.**

Running iPhone Apps on the iPad

If you have an iPhone and have already bought iPhone apps, you can install them on your iPad too. Although you can run iPhone apps on the iPad, most iPhone apps won't use up the full screen of the iPad, as shown in Figure 10-7.

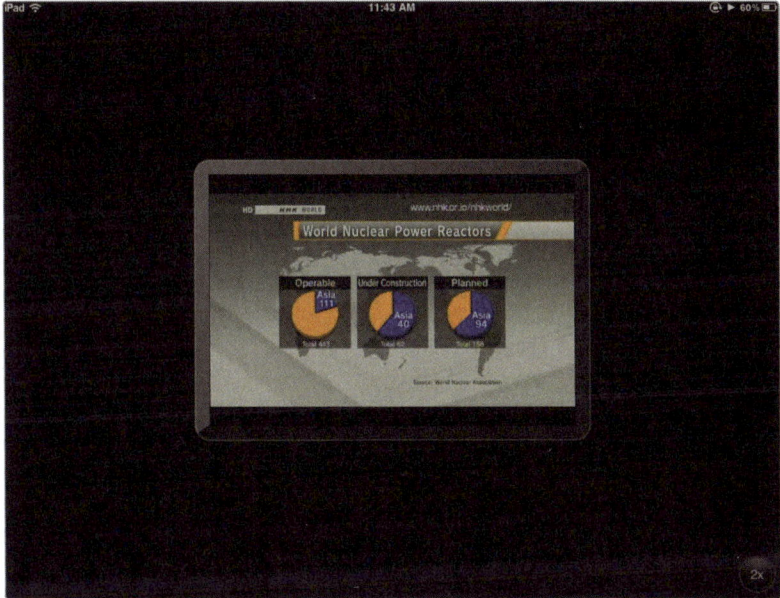

FIGURE 10-7: *Most iPhone apps won't use the entire iPad screen.*

However, you can expand an iPhone app so it fills up the entire iPad screen. Just tap the **2x** button in the bottom-right corner of the iPad screen to blow up an iPhone app, as shown in Figure 10-8.

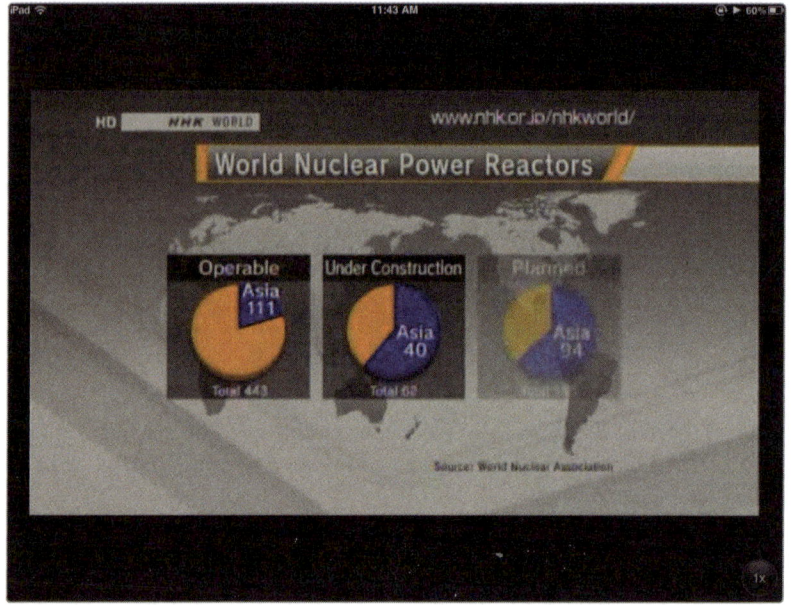

FIGURE 10-8: *You can expand an iPhone app to fill up the iPad screen.*

To shrink an expanded iPhone app screen back to its normal size, tap the **1x** button in the bottom-right corner of the screen.

Additional Ideas for Installing and Uninstalling Apps

Every day, new apps pour into the App Store, so to avoid cluttering up your iPad, resist the temptation to keep downloading the latest free and commercial apps. Since you can easily delete and re-install apps, you could always pick those apps you need right now, such as installing a bunch of children's apps so your kids can play them on your iPad during a trip, and then delete those apps after you get back home and can retrieve your iPad from your kids again.

By deleting apps you don't need and selectively installing and removing apps you may not need temporarily, you can keep your iPad lean and uncluttered so you can actually get your work done and have fun at the same time. As an alternative to deleting apps, consider combining multiple apps into a folder as explained in Chapter 6.

To turn your iPad into a productivity tool, download and install the iWork office suite for the iPad, which will allow you to transfer files between iWork on your iPad and iWork on your Macintosh, as described in Chapter 29.

PART 3

Getting on the Internet

11 Browsing with Safari

Every iPad comes with the Safari app, which lets you browse websites on the Internet. If you have used any browser on a computer before, you will find Safari on the iPad works in similar ways. While you're surfing the Web, you can rotate your iPad to portrait or landscape mode. Portrait mode lets you see more vertical content of a web page, while landscape mode makes it easier to see the entire width of a web page. No matter which way you decide to view Safari, you'll find that browsing with Safari is easy and fun.

What You'll Be Using

To browse the Internet with Safari, you need to use the following:

▶ An Internet connection (Wi-Fi or 3G) The Safari app

Navigating Safari

When using a browser on a regular computer, you can use a mouse to click links, menus, and icons. Safari on the iPad works similarly except instead of menus, it just displays icons to tap. Any link that you would normally click with the mouse, you can just tap with your finger.

To see how to navigate with Safari on the iPad, follow these steps:

1. From the Home screen, tap **Safari**. The Safari screen appears, as shown in Figure 11-1.

FIGURE 11-1: *Safari offers common web browsing features.*

2. Tap the **Address** field. The virtual keyboard appears.
3. Press the **Backspace** key, or tap the **X** that appears to the far right of the Address field to clear the contents of the Address field.
4. Type a website address such as **www.nostarch.com**. As you type, a list of previously viewed website addresses appears.

5. (Optional) Tap one of the website addresses in the displayed list.
6. Tap the **Go** key on the virtual keyboard. Your chosen website appears.
7. Tap the **Back** arrow icon. Your previous web page appears.
8. Tap the **Forward** arrow icon. The web page you viewed after the current one now appears.
9. Place two fingertips on the screen, and move them away from each other to zoom in on the currently displayed web page.
10. Place two fingertips on the screen, and move them closer together to zoom out on the currently displayed web page.
11. Double-tap on a column of text. Safari zooms to the column. Double-tap again, and Safari zooms out.
12. Tap the very top of the iPad's display, without hitting the address or search bar. You jump all the way to the top of the page you were reading.
13. Tap any link on the currently displayed web page. The new page opens.

Searching in Safari

Typing a website address can be cumbersome, so a faster way to find a website is to use a search engine. Safari displays a Search field in the upper-right corner of the screen, which lets you search using Google, Bing, or Yahoo!.

To search the Web, follow these steps:

1. From the Home screen, tap **Safari**. The Safari screen appears.
2. Tap the **Search** field that appears in the upper-right corner of the screen. The virtual keyboard appears at the bottom of the screen.
3. Tap the **Backspace** key, or tap the **X** that appears to the far right of the Search field to clear the contents of the Search field.
4. Type a word or phrase that you want to find, and tap the **Search** key on the virtual keyboard. (While you're typing, a list of possible words   phrases appears, which you can select by tapping.) Safari displays the results from your search.

Safari's default search engine is Google. You can change your search engine by tapping the Settings icon from the Home screen, tapping the Safari section, tapping the Search Engine button, and then tapping the search engine you want to use, such as Google, Yahoo!, or Bing.

Opening Multiple Web Pages

On a regular computer, you can open multiple browser windows or display web pages in separate tabs within a single window. On an iPad, Safari handles multiple open web pages differently. You can still open multiple web pages, but only one web page can appear on the screen at a time.

There are two ways to open multiple web pages in Safari. First, you can open a blank web page and then type in an address (such as *www.nostarch.com*) or use a search engine. Second, you can hold your finger on a link and choose to open the link in a new page.

Opening a Blank Web Page

If you're looking at a website (such as one related to work) and suddenly decide you want to check out another website (such as one displaying the latest sports scores or movie listings) but don't want to close the first website, open a blank web page and view another website in this other web page.

To see how to open and switch between multiple open web pages, follow these steps:

1. From the Home screen, tap **Safari**. The Safari screen appears.
2. Tap the **Address** field. The virtual keyboard appears.
3. Tap the **Backspace** key, or tap the **X** that appears to the far right of the Address field to clear the contents of the Address field.
4. Type a website address such as **www.nostarch.com**, and tap the **Go** key on the virtual keyboard. Your chosen website appears.
5. Tap the **Pages** icon (it looks like two overlapping pages). The screen shows your currently open web pages and a New Page web page icon, as shown in Figure 11-2.

FIGURE 11-2: *Safari displays open web pages as thumbnail images. The X in the upper-left corner allows you to close web pages.*

6. Tap the **New Page** icon. Safari displays a virtual keyboard at the bottom of the screen and Address and Search fields at the top of the screen.

7. Tap the **Address** field, type a website address (such as **www.apple.com**), and tap the **Go** key on the virtual keyboard. (Alternatively, tap the **Search** field, type a word or phrase to search, and tap the **Search** key.) Safari displays your chosen web page.

8. Tap the **Pages** icon. Safari displays thumbnail images of your open web pages. Now you can switch between the web pages just by tapping on the web page thumbnail image that you want to view. You can have up to nine web pages open at a time.

9. (Optional) Tap the **Close** button of a web page that you want to close. Your chosen web page disappears.

Opening a Link in Another Web Page

Normally if you tap a link on a web page, the linked web page replaces the currently displayed web page. If you don't want to lose track of a website, you might prefer having a linked web page appear in its own web page.

To see how to open a link as a separate web page, follow these steps:

1. From the Home screen, tap **Safari**. The Safari screen appears.
2. Tap the **Address** field. The virtual keyboard appears.
3. Tap the **Backspace** key, or tap the **X** that appears to the far right of the Address field to clear the contents of the Address field.
4. Type a website address such as **www.nostarch .com**, and tap the **Go** key on the virtual keyboard. Your chosen website appears.

5. Press and hold your finger over any link on the web page. After a few seconds, a menu appears as shown in Figure 11-3.
6. Tap the **Open in New Page** button. Your linked web page appears. (Tapping the Open button replaces the current web page with the linked page.)

FIGURE 11-3: A menu appears to let you open a link in a new page.

7. Tap the **Pages** icon. Notice that your linked web page appears as a separate thumbnail image.
8. Tap a web page to view it.

Emailing a Web Page Link

If you find a particularly interesting web page, you can email a link to the whole thing to someone (even your own email account that you can open on a regular computer). To email a web page link, follow these steps:

1. From the Home screen, tap **Safari**. The Safari screen appears.
2. Visit a website by typing an address, using a search engine, or visiting a previously stored bookmark.
3. Tap the **Action** icon (it looks like a square with a curved arrow pointing to the right). A menu appears, as shown in Figure 11-4.
4. Tap the **Mail Link to this Page**. An email message appears with a virtual keyboard.
5. Type an email address to receive your web page link. You may also want to type additional text as part of your message.
6. Tap **Send** to send your email message.

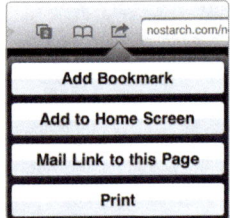

FIGURE 11-4: Emailing a link

Copying a Graphic Image from a Web Page

If you find a graphic image on a web page that you want to save, such as a picture accompanying a particularly interesting news story, you can save that image in the Photos app.

> ✳ NOTE: **Photographs and graphic images on other websites may be copyrighted.**

To copy and store a graphic image on a website, follow these steps:

1. From the Home screen, tap **Safari**. The Safari screen appears.
2. Visit your favorite website (by either typing the complete address such as **www.nostarch.com**, or by searching for it in the Search field).
3. Press and hold your finger over a graphic image that you want to save. A menu appears (see Figure 11-3).
4. Tap **Save Image**. Your iPad saves your chosen picture in the Photos app.

> ✳ NOTE: **If you tap the Copy button, you'll just copy the link to the graphic image but not the graphic image itself.**

Printing a Web Page

If you find a particularly interesting web page, you may not only want to bookmark it (see Chapter 12), but you may also want to print a copy, too. To print from an iPad, you need a wireless printer or a printer connected to your computer, although not all printers will work correctly with your iPad.

To print a web page, follow these steps:

1. From the Home screen, tap **Safari**. The Safari screen appears.
2. Visit your favorite website (by either typing the complete address such as **www.nostarch.com**, or by searching for it in the Search field).
3. Tap the **Action** icon (it looks like a square with a curved arrow). A menu appears, as shown earlier in Figure 11-4.
4. Tap the **Print** button. A Printer Options dialog appears, as shown in Figure 11-5.
5. Tap the **Printer** button to select a printer.
6. (Optional) Tap the minus (**–**) or plus (**+**) button to increase or decrease the number of copies to make.
7. Tap the **Print** button.

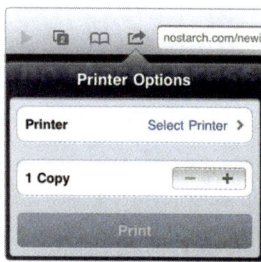

FIGURE 11-5: *Printing a web page*

Additional Ideas for Browsing the Internet

Browsing the Internet through Safari on your iPad is nearly identical to browsing web pages using a browser on your computer. Browsing the Internet on your iPad can be a great way to kill time; whenever you have a spare moment, you can look up sports scores, movie reviews, or the latest news from around the world.

With access to the Internet at your fingertips, you can browse for fun, for work, or for education. With Safari and an Internet connection, your iPad is a window to another world.

12

Using Bookmarks with Safari

If you frequently visit the same websites, you may tire of typing the same website addresses or search phrases each time you want to find those sites again. To make finding sites easier, you can create bookmarks.

As you browse, Safari automatically stores the websites you visit in a History window. This History window of recently visited websites can be handy when you want to find a site that you recently visited, but if you like a particular website, you might want to bookmark it so you can access it any time, at the tap of a finger, without having to peruse the History window.

In this chapter you'll learn how to create, display, and delete bookmarks of your favorite websites using Safari.

What You'll Be Using

To use bookmarks with Safari, you need to use the following:

► An Internet connection (Wi-Fi or 3G)

 The Safari app

 The Settings screen

Using the History Window

As you browse the Internet, Safari automatically keeps track of each website that you visit and stores each address in a History list going back the past week. Now if you remember visiting a particular site but don't recall how you found it, just visit the History window, find the website's name, and tap on its name to view that website.

Revisiting a Website Stored in the History Window

To see how the History window works, follow these steps:

1. From the Home screen, tap **Safari**. The Safari screen appears.
2. Tap the **Bookmark** icon (it looks like an open book). A Bookmarks window appears, as shown in Figure 12-1. It lets you find a previously viewed or saved website address.
3. Tap **History**. The History window lists all the websites you've recently visited, including those viewed in the past week, as shown in Figure 12-2.

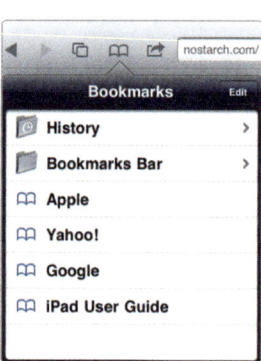

FIGURE 12-1: The Book-marks window

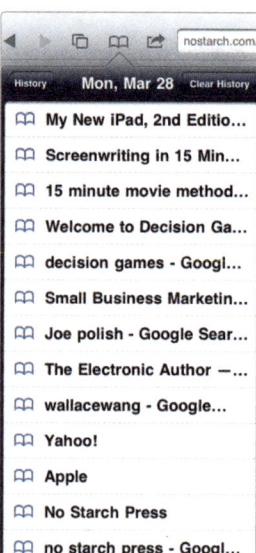

FIGURE 12-2: The History window

4. (Optional) Tap one of the day folders, such as a folder labeled *Friday* or *Monday*, to view the website addresses you visited on that particular day.
5. Tap a website to view that site.

Clearing the History Window

Since Safari automatically adds every website address you visit to its History window, that History window can get cluttered. If you know you won't need to visit any previously visited websites, you can clear this History window to make it look neater—or to cover your tracks. To clear the History window, follow these steps:

1. From the Home screen, tap **Safari**. The Safari screen appears.
2. Tap the **Bookmark** icon and then tap **History**. The History window appears.
3. Tap **Clear History**. A red Clear History button and gray Cancel button appear at the bottom of the History window.
4. Tap **Clear History** (or **Cancel**).

* **NOTE:** Clearing the History window wipes out the past few days worth of your previously visited websites. You cannot undo this action, so make sure you really want to clear your History window. You can also clear the History list in Safari via your iPad's settings, which you can access from the Home screen.

Adding and Managing Bookmarks

Safari comes with a list of bookmarks already created for you, but you'll probably want to add your own bookmarks to store your favorite websites. You can store a bookmark in three places.

First, you can store a bookmark within the Bookmarks window. This keeps your bookmark out of sight until you need it.

Second, you can store a bookmark in the Bookmarks Bar, which you can optionally hide or display at the top of the Safari screen. This makes your favorite bookmarks visible at all times. This is handy if you visit the same set of sites often.

Third, you can save your bookmark as an icon on your Home screen. This type of bookmark makes it easy to access your favorite websites with just a single touch from the Home screen, without even opening Safari.

Adding a Bookmark to the Bookmarks Window or Bookmarks Bar

To store a bookmarked website in the Bookmarks window, follow these steps:

1. From the Home screen, tap **Safari**. The Safari screen appears.
2. Visit your favorite website (either by typing the complete address such as **www.nostarch.com** or by searching for it in the Search field).
3. Tap the **Action** icon (it looks like a square with a curved arrow). A menu of options appears, as shown in Figure 12-3.
4. Tap the **Add Bookmark** icon. An Add Bookmark window appears (see Figure 12-4) with a virtual keyboard.

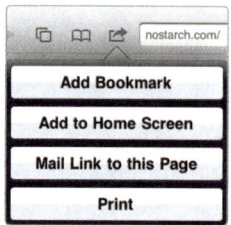

FIGURE 12-3: *The Action icon displays a menu of options for saving a bookmark.*

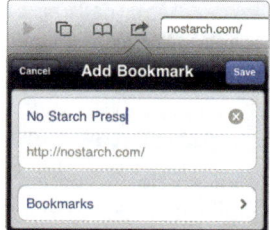

FIGURE 12-4: *You can type a descriptive name for your bookmark.*

5.   Edit the name of your favorite website as you want it displayed.

* **NOTE:** **Ideally, keep your website names short. Long website names take up more space if you store them in the Bookmarks Bar.**

6.   (Optional) Tap the **Bookmarks** icon, and tap either **Bookmarks** or **Bookmarks Bar**, as shown in Figure 12-5.
7.   Tap **Save**. Your bookmark gets saved in your chosen location either in the Bookmarks window or in the Bookmarks Bar.

FIGURE 12-5: *You can choose where to store a bookmark.*

Showing (or Hiding) the Bookmarks Bar

When you store bookmarks on the Bookmarks Bar, you can access them in two ways. First, you can access them through the Bookmarks window. Second, you can access them through the Bookmarks Bar, which appears at the top of Safari.

To save space, the Bookmarks Bar may not be visible, but you can make it visible by following these steps:

1.   From the Home screen, tap **Settings**. The Settings screen appears.
2.   Tap **Safari**. The Safari settings screen appears.
3.   Tap the **Always Show Bookmarks Bar**
     on/off switch to turn it *ON* (or *OFF* if you want to hide the Bookmarks Bar).
4.   Press the **Home** button.
5.   Tap **Safari**. The Safari screen appears, with (or without) the Bookmarks Bar.

Deleting and Rearranging Your Bookmarks

After you store several bookmarks, you may later want to rearrange or delete them. To rearrange or delete a bookmark, follow these steps:

1. From the Home screen, tap **Safari**. The Safari screen appears.
2. Tap the **Bookmark** icon (it looks like an open book). The Bookmarks window appears.
3. (Optional) Tap a folder, such as the *Bookmarks Bar* folder, to rearrange bookmarks in that folder.
4. Tap **Edit**. Red circles with white dashes appear to the left of each bookmark while three horizontal gray lines appear to the right of some bookmarks.

* **NOTE:** You cannot rearrange the default bookmarks already stored in the Bookmarks window, including the bookmarks for Apple, Google, and Yahoo! You can, however, delete them.

5. (Optional) Press and hold a fingertip over the icon with three horizontal gray lines to the right of a bookmark that you want to rearrange. Then slide your finger up or down to move the bookmark to a new location.
6. (Optional) Tap the red circle with the white dash to the left of a bookmark you want to delete. A red Delete button appears. (You can also delete bookmarks by swiping to the left or right.)
7. (Optional) Tap **Delete**.
8. Tap **Done**.

Saving a Website as a Home Screen Icon

To make accessing your favorite websites even faster, you can store a website as an icon on your Home screen. To do so, follow these steps:

1. From the Home screen, tap **Safari**. The Safari screen appears.
2. Visit your favorite website.
3. Tap the **Action** icon (it looks like a square with a curved arrow). A menu of options appears.
4. Tap **Add to Home Screen**. An Add to Home window and a virtual keyboard appear, as shown in Figure 12-6.
5. Type or edit a short descriptive name for your website.
6. Tap **Add**. Your chosen website appears as an icon on your Home screen.

FIGURE 12-6: *Storing a bookmarked site to your Home screen.*

✳ **NOTE:** You can delete a bookmarked icon from your Home screen just like an application: Hold your fingertip on the website icon until it starts wriggling and displays a Close icon in its upper-left corner. Then tap the Close icon (it looks like a big X), and press the Home button.

Creating Folders in the Bookmarks Window

The more bookmarks you add to the Bookmarks window, the more crowded it will get. To keep bookmarks organized, you can create folders and then store different bookmarks inside each folder. To create a bookmark folder, follow these steps:

1. From the Home screen, tap **Safari**. The Safari screen appears.
2. Tap the **Bookmark** icon (it looks like an open book). The Bookmarks window appears.
3. Tap **Edit**. A New Folder button appears in the upper-left corner of the Bookmarks window.
4. Tap **New Folder**. An Edit Folder window appears with a virtual keyboard, as shown in Figure 12-7.
5. Type a short descriptive name for your folder, and tap the **Done** key on the virtual keyboard. Your newly created folder appears in the Bookmarks window.
6. Tap **Done** in the bookmarks pane.

FIGURE 12-7: You can create and name a folder to store bookmarks.

✳ **NOTE:** If you open the Bookmarks window and tap the Edit button, you can rearrange, delete, or rename a folder. To rename a folder, just tap the Edit button, and then tap the folder name.

Additional Ideas for Bookmarking Favorite Websites

If you regularly visit certain websites, you can store these websites as icons on the Home screen and then organize all the website icons on a separate pane on the Home screen. That way, you can switch to that Home screen pane to see all your important websites.

If you share an iPad with others, create folders with each person's name, and then let each person store their own favorite websites in these separate, named folders. Then others don't have to wade through bookmarks of websites that they'll never visit in a million years.

By saving bookmarks, you can browse the Web without ever needing to type in a convoluted address again or dig through search engine listings—unless you want to find something new.

13

Setting Up an Email Account

To help you stay in touch with people around the world, you can set up one or more email accounts on your iPad. As long as you can access the Internet on your iPad, you'll be able to use Gmail, Yahoo!, MobileMe, AOL, Microsoft Exchange, or any other email account that you want.

What You'll Be Using

To set up and customize an email account, you need to use the following:

▶ An Internet connection (Wi-Fi or 3G)

 The Mail app

 The Settings screen

Setting Up an Email Account Automatically

If you use one of the more common email providers such as AOL, Yahoo!, Google, MobileMe, or Microsoft Exchange, your iPad can set up your email account almost automatically. All you have to do is type in your email address, and your iPad can figure out the correct settings.

To set up a MobileMe, Yahoo!, Google, AOL, or Microsoft Exchange email account, follow these steps:

1. From the Home screen, tap **Settings**. The Settings screen appears.
2. Tap **Mail, Contacts, Calendars**. The Mail, Contacts, Calendars settings screen appears, as shown in Figure 13-1.

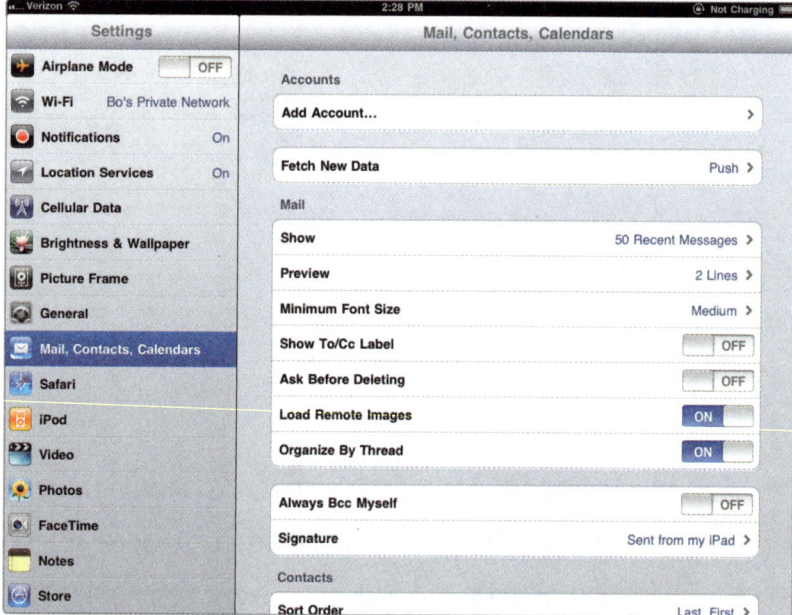

FIGURE 13-1: The Mail, Contacts, Calendars settings screen lets you define your email account settings.

3. Tap **Add Account**. The Add Account screen appears, as shown in Figure 13-2.

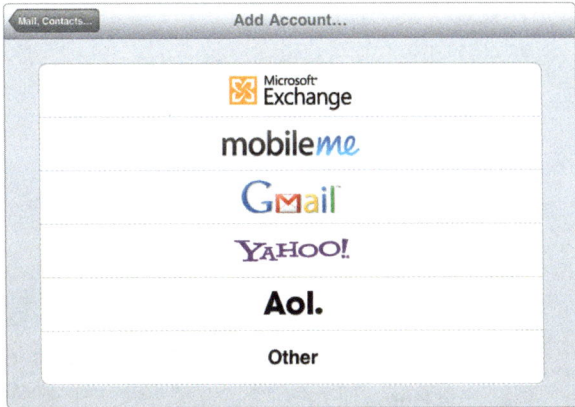

FIGURE 13-2: *You can choose from several popular email providers.*

* **NOTE:** **If you start the Mail app for the first time without setting up an account, you'll be prompted with the same options shown in Figure 13-2.**

4. Tap the button of your email provider. A screen and virtual keyboard appears where you can type your name, email address, password, and an optional description of your account, as shown in Figure 13-3. Write carefully! The name listed here will be visible on emails you send from your iPad.

FIGURE 13-3: *The initial email account setup screen*

5. Type your name, email address, password, and optional description of your account, and tap **Next** in the upper-right corner. A dialog may appear, letting you include Mail, Calendars, and Notes from that account, as shown in Figure 13-4.

6. Tap the on/off buttons for **Mail**, **Calendar**, and **Notes**, and tap the **Save** button.

7. Press the **Home** button. The Home screen appears.

8. Tap **Mail**. If you're currently connected to the Internet, your iPad will retrieve any messages for that email account.

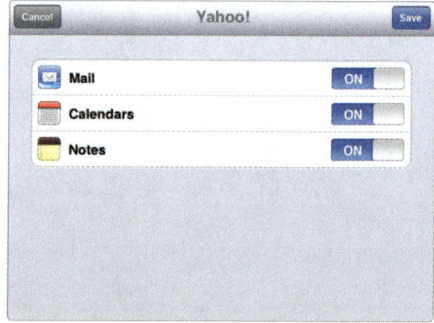

FIGURE 13-4: *You can include notes and calendars with an email account.*

✳ **NOTE:** If you don't have an email address yet, you can get a free one by visiting *http://www.gmail.com/* or *http://mail.yahoo.com/*.

Setting Up an Email Account Manually

If you need to set up an email account that isn't from one of the more popular providers, you'll need to type some additional information such as your incoming and outgoing mail server settings. (If you have no idea what these settings are, you'll need to get them from your email provider or your Internet service provider.)

To set up an email account manually, follow these steps:

1. From the Home screen, tap **Settings**. The Settings screen appears.

2. Tap **Mail, Contacts, Calendars**. The Mail, Contacts, Calendars settings screen appears (shown earlier in Figure 13-1).

3. Tap **Add Account**. The Add Account screen appears (shown earlier in Figure 13-2).

4. Tap **Other**. The Other screen appears, as shown in Figure 13-5.

5. Tap **Add Mail Account**. A New Account window appears with the virtual keyboard.

6. Type your name, email address, password, and description of your email account, and tap **Next**. The New Account window appears, as shown in Figure 13-6.

7. Scroll down and type your host name, username, and password for your incoming and outgoing mail servers.

8. Tap **Save**. A New Account window appears where you can type information for your incoming and outgoing mail server, as shown in Figure 13-7.

9. Tap the **IMAP** or **POP** tab.

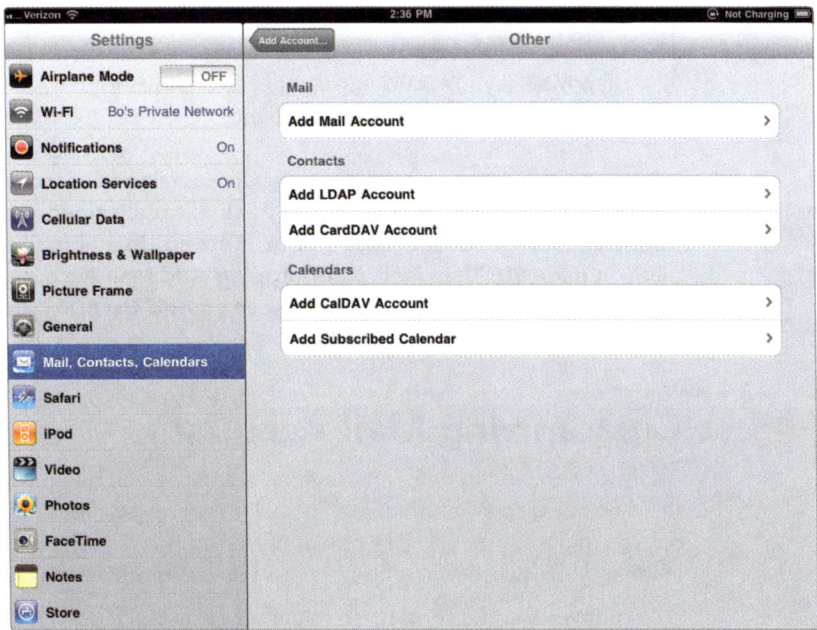

FIGURE 13-5: The Other screen lets you define email settings manually.

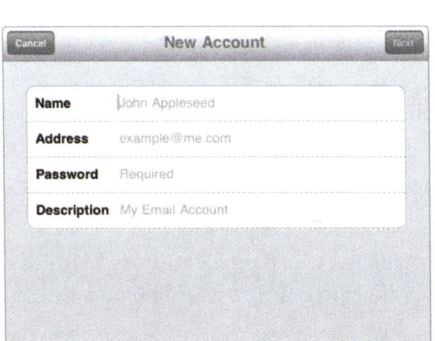

FIGURE 13-6: The New Account window lets you define a name, email address, password, and an optional description.

FIGURE 13-7: You need to type in your incoming and outgoing mail server information.

10. Type the Incoming Mail Server and Outgoing Mail Server information.
11. Press the **Home** button. The Home screen appears.
12. Tap **Mail**. If you're currently connected to the Internet, your iPad will retrieve any messages for that email account.

* *NOTE:* **You may later want to set up a Contacts and Calendars account with your email account so you can keep track of appointments and contact information. Just repeat steps 1–4 of "Setting Up an Email Account Manually" on page 90. Then instead of tapping Add Mail Account, tap one of the Contacts or Calendars options, such as Add CardDAV Account or Add CalDAV Account.**

Customizing Mail Accounts

After you have set up one or more email accounts, you might want to customize the way they display information. These customizing options aren't necessary, but you might want to choose one or more settings to make your email account uniquely your own. Some of the options you can modify are as follows:

▸ **Show**   Defines how many messages to display

▸ **Preview**   Defines how many lines of each message to display

▸ **Minimum Font Size**   Defines the size of text in each message

▸ **Show To/Cc Label**   Displays the To and Cc labels in the preview of your list of messages

▸ **Ask Before Deleting**   Makes you verify that you really want to delete a message

▸ **Load Remote Images**   Turns on (or off) the ability to display images in an email message (turn this setting off to save bandwidth)

▸ **Organize By Thread**   Turns on (or off) the ability to show related messages and replies

▸ **Always Bcc Myself**   Sends a copy of each message to yourself so you know it was sent

▸ **Signature**   Lets you define a message to appear at the end of every message you send

▸ **Default Account**   Defines which email address Mail uses when you send a message such as via clicking a Contact Us link on a web page

To customize your email account settings, follow these steps:

1. From the Home screen, tap **Settings**. The Settings screen appears.
2. Tap **Mail, Contacts, Calendars**. The Mail, Contacts, Calendars settings screen appears (shown earlier in Figure 13-1).

3. (Optional) Tap **Show**. When the Show screen appears, tap an option such as **25 Recent Messages** or **75 Recent Messages**, and tap **Back** to return to the Mail, Contacts, Calendars screen.

4. (Optional) Tap **Preview**. When the Preview screen appears, tap an option such as **3 Lines** or **5 Lines**, and tap **Back** to return to the Mail, Contacts, Calendars screen.

5. (Optional) Tap **Minimum Font Size**. When the Minimum Font Size screen appears, tap an option such as **Small** or **Medium**, and tap **Back** to return to the Mail, Contacts, Calendars screen again.

6. (Optional) Tap the **Show To/Cc Label** on/off switch.

7. (Optional) Tap the **Ask Before Deleting** on/off switch.

8. (Optional) Tap the **Load Remote Images** on/off switch.

9. (Optional) Tap the **Organize By Thread** on/off switch.

10. (Optional) Tap the **Always Bcc Myself** on/off switch.

11. (Optional) Tap **Signature**. When the Signature screen appears, type the message that you want as your email signature, and tap **Back** to return to the Mail, Contacts, Calendar screen again. By default, your signature will be "Sent from my iPad." Simply delete this message if you want to have no signature.

12. (Optional) Tap **Default Account**. When the Default Account screen appears, tap the email account you want to define as the default account.

13. Press the **Home** button.

Additional Ideas for Setting Up and Customizing Email Accounts

Since you can set up multiple email accounts, consider creating one account for work and a second one for personal use. That way, you won't accidentally send a flippant message about your vacation to your boss or a serious message about work to your nine-year-old nephew.

After you've set up one or more email accounts, consider customizing your signature to display or advertise your website, your business, or your own unique skills. For example, if you're a carpenter or a doctor, your signature could publicize your line of work such as "The Most Honest Carpenter in Denver" or "The Doctor That Children Trust." The more free advertising you can get through email signatures, the more exposure you'll get, which will be better for you.

If email is important to you, you can read and write messages on your iPad and never lose contact with anybody. Now all you have to worry about is giving out your email address sparingly only to those people you trust. Otherwise you'll risk getting overrun with unsolicited messages.

14

Sending and Reading Email

After you have set up at least one email account on your iPad, you can read messages that you've retrieved and write new messages to send to others. As you receive messages from others, you may want to move them to different folders or just delete them altogether.

In this chapter you'll learn how to read, write, and organize email on your iPad.

What You'll Be Using

To read, write, and organize email, you need to use the following:

▸ An Internet connection (Wi-Fi or 3G)

 The Mail app

Reading Email

Each email account you set up on your iPad contains multiple folders for storing messages. When you receive messages, they get stored in the *Inbox* folder. If you have set up multiple email accounts, you'll have a single inbox that displays new mail for all accounts called *All Inboxes*, as well as an individual *Inbox* for each account, as shown in Figure 14-1.

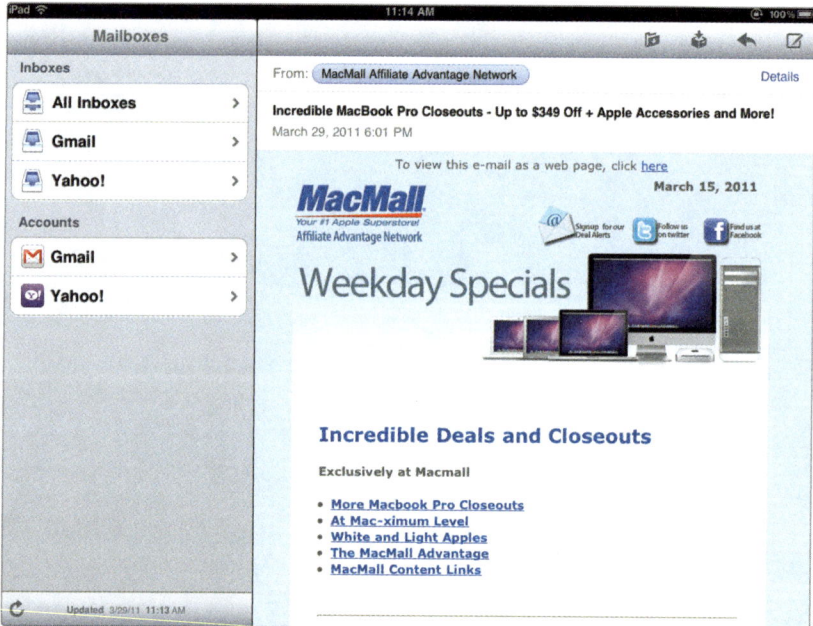

FIGURE 14-1: *If you want to read* Drafts, Sent Mail, *or any other folder, you'll want to tap the email address under Accounts.*

To read your messages stored in an email account, follow these steps:

1. From the Home screen, tap **Mail**. The Mail screen appears, displaying what you last viewed.
2. Tap the **Back** button that appears in the upper-left corner of the screen. If you have set up multiple email accounts, a list of your email accounts appears.

3. (Optional) Tap the email account under Inboxes that you want to use, or just tap **All Inboxes** to view all mail sent to all accounts. If you have set up only one email account, you can skip this step.

4. Tap the **Inbox** folder. A list of messages appears.

5. Tap the message you want to read. Your message appears in the right pane of the screen, as shown in Figure 14-2.

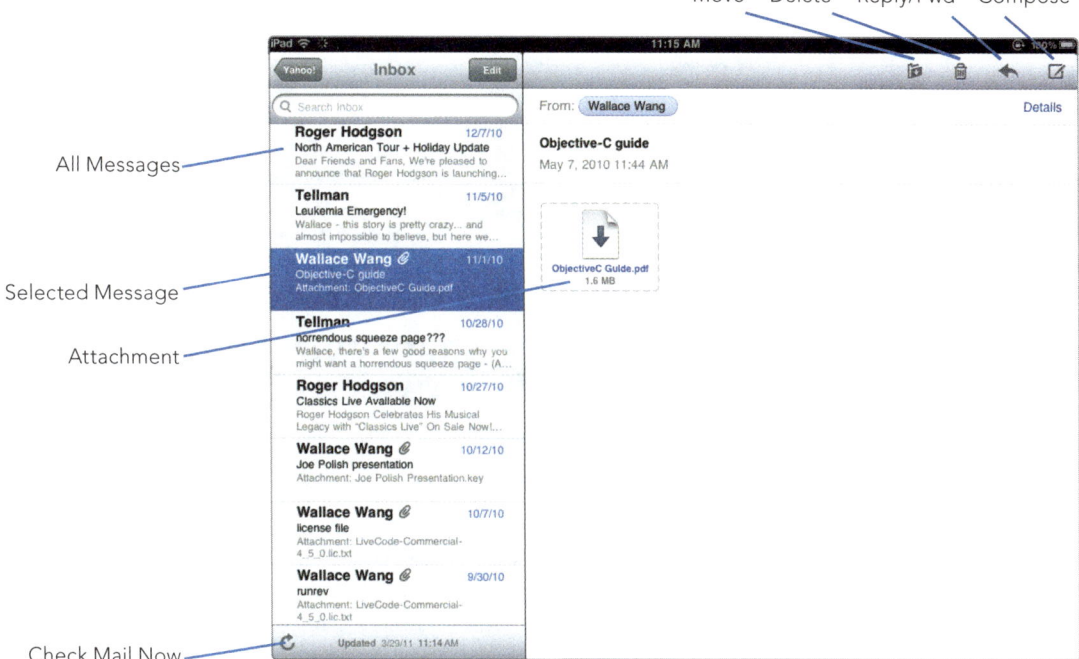

FIGURE 14-2: *The* Inbox *folder contains your messages.*

Moving a Message to a Folder

Since your *Inbox* folder constantly receives messages, you may want to organize them in different folders that you can create through your email provider. By moving messages to different folders, you can stay organized. In addition, moving messages also lets you retrieve deleted messages from the *Trash* folder.

Moving a Single Message

To move a single message to a different folder, follow these steps:

1. While using the Mail app, tap the **Move** icon (it looks like a folder) that appears in the upper-right corner of the screen. A list of folders appears in the left pane, as shown in Figure 14-3.

2. Tap a folder where you want to store the currently displayed message, or tap **Cancel**.

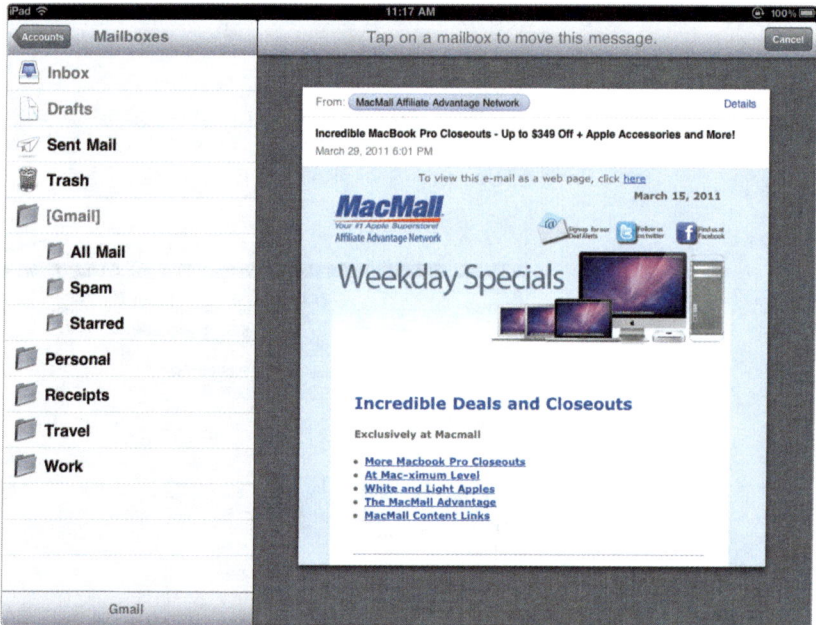

FIGURE 14-3: *Tapping the Move icon displays a list of folders where you can choose to store the currently displayed message.*

3. (Optional) If you just want a message moved out of your *Inbox*, you can just Archive it or Delete it entirely. To archive or delete a single message, swipe the subject line of the message to the right, and tap the red **Archive** or **Delete** button that appears. You'll see Archive or Delete (not both) depending on the email service provider.

Moving (or Deleting) Messages

To move multiple messages to a different folder (or delete multiple messages instead), follow these steps:

1. Follow all the steps in "Reading Email" on page 96 to view any message.
2. Tap the **Edit** button that appears in the upper-right corner of the Inbox window. Small circles appear to the left of each message, as shown in Figure 14-4.
3. Tap the circle to the left of each message that you want to move or delete. A checkmark appears in the circle.
4. Tap the **Delete** or **Move** button at the bottom of the Inbox window. (If you tap the Move button, you'll need to tap a folder displayed in the Inbox window to choose which folder to move your selected messages in.)

✳ **NOTE:** Instead of a Delete button, you may see an Archive button with certain email accounts, such as Gmail.

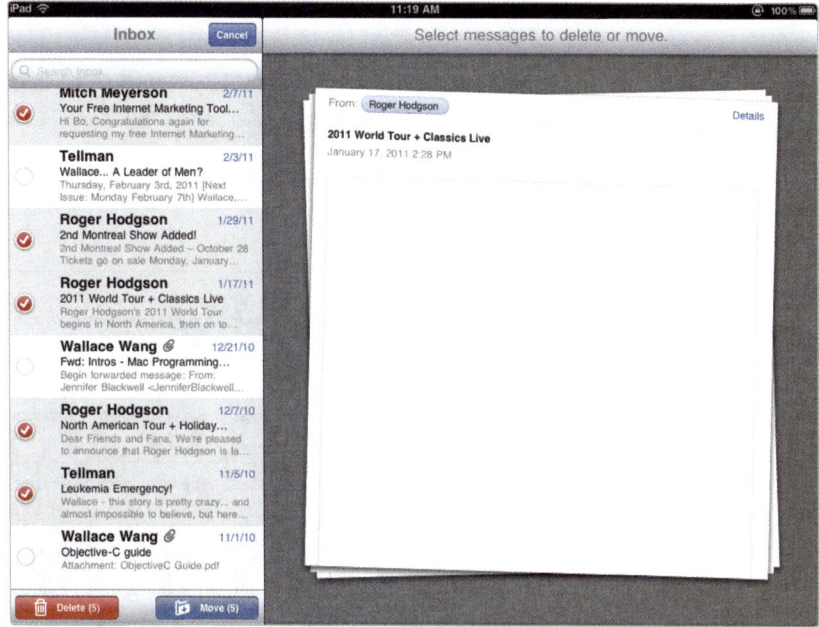

FIGURE 14-4: *Tapping the Edit button lets you select multiple messages to move or delete.*

Replying to, Forwarding, or Printing an Email Message

The simplest way to write a message is to reply to an existing message that you've already received. That way, you can send the message back to the sender's email address to provide a little context with your response without having to type it all over again. Another option is to forward a message. This lets you send a received message to someone else. If you have a wireless printer, you can also print a message so you have a copy you can review later.

Replying to a Message

To reply to a message, follow these steps:

1. Follow all the steps in "Reading Email" on page 96 to view the message to which you want to reply.
2. Tap the **Reply** icon (it looks like an arrow pointing to the left and appears at the upper right of the screen). A menu appears listing Reply, Reply All, Forward, and Print options, as shown in Figure 14-5.

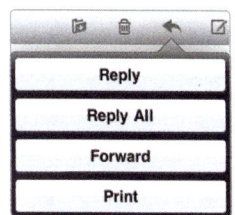

FIGURE 14-5: *Tapping the Reply icon displays Reply, Reply All, Forward, and Print buttons.*

3. Tap **Reply**. A message window appears along with a virtual keyboard, as shown in Figure 14-6.

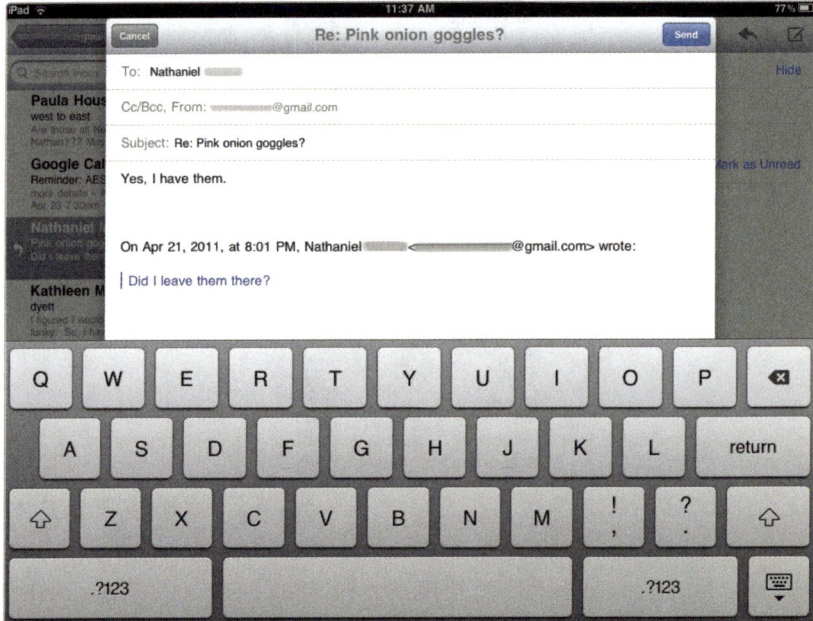

FIGURE 14-6: *The message window already includes the recipient's email address.*

4. (Optional) Type any additional text that you want to add to the message.
5. Tap **Send**. Your iPad sends your message.

Forwarding a Message

Forwarding a message can be handy when you want to resend something that somebody sent you, such as a joke or interesting picture. To forward a message, follow these steps:

1. Follow all the steps in "Reading Email" on page 96 to view the message that you want to forward.
2. Tap the **Reply** icon (it looks like an arrow pointing to the left and appears at the upper right of the screen). A menu appears listing a Reply, Reply All, Forward, and Print options (shown earlier in Figure 14-5).
3. Tap **Forward**. If the message contains a file attachment, a window may pop up asking if you want to include or not include the file attachment with your forwarded copy of the message, as shown in Figure 14-7.

4.   Tap **Include** or **Don't Include**. A message window appears with a virtual keyboard.

5.   Tap the **To** field, and type an email address.

* **NOTE:** **If you tap the plus sign icon that appears in the far right of the To field, a Contacts window pops up, allowing you to tap the name of a person whose email address you've already stored in the Contacts app.**

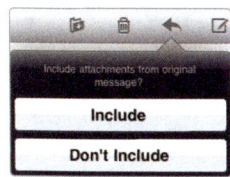

FIGURE 14-7: *Forwarding a message with a file attachment*

6.   Tap **Send**. Your iPad sends your message.

Printing a Message

If you have a wireless printer or a compatible printer connected to your computer, you may be able to print an email message wirelessly through your computer. To print a message, follow these steps:

1.   Follow all the steps in "Reading Email" on page 96 to view the message that you want to forward.

2.   Tap the **Reply** icon (it looks like an arrow pointing to the left and appears at the upper right of the screen). A menu appears listing Reply, Reply All, Forward, and Print options (shown earlier in Figure 14-5).

3.   Tap the **Print** button.

Writing a New Message

Rather than reply or forward a message, you may want to create a new message to send to someone. To create a new message, follow these steps:

1.   While using the Mail app, tap the **New Message** icon (it looks like a square with a pencil writing on it that appears at the upper right of the screen). A New Message window appears with a virtual keyboard.

2.   Tap the **To** field, and type an email address.

* **NOTE:** **If you tap the plus sign icon that appears in the far right of the To field, a Contacts window pops up, allowing you to tap the name of a person's whose email address you've already stored in the Contacts app.**

3.   Tap the **Subject** field, and type a subject for your message.

4.   Tap the text field, and type your message.

5.   Tap **Send**. Your iPad sends your message.

Deleting Messages

The more messages you receive, the more you'll likely need to delete messages to keep your *Inbox* folder from overflowing with too many messages. To delete messages, you can delete them individually or select multiple messages and delete them all at once.

To delete a message, follow these steps:

1. Follow all the steps in "Reading Email" on page 96 to view the message you want to delete.
2. Tap the **Delete** icon at the top of the screen. The currently displayed message gets moved to the Trash folder.
3. (Optional) To delete multiple messages, tap the **Edit** button to display radio buttons to the left of each message. Tap the radio button of each message you want to delete and then tap the **Trash** button at the bottom of the screen.

* *NOTE:* **To permanently delete messages, you'll need to delete all the messages stored in the *Trash* folder.**

Searching Email

After you've received multiple messages, you may lose track of all of them. One way to deal with this flood of information is to constantly move messages into their own folders. Since this takes constant effort, you may find it easier just to search for a particular message instead.

You can search for text that appears in the From, To, or Subject fields, or you can search for text that appears in any of those three fields. This lets you search for messages that you received from a specific email address, messages that you sent to a particular email address, messages with certain types of subjects, or all three (the From, To, and Subject fields).

To search for a messages stored in an email account, follow these steps:

1. While using the Mail app, tap a folder that contains the messages you want to find. A list of messages appears.
2. Tap the **From**, **To**, **Subject**, or **All** button at the top of the folder window.
3. Tap the **Search** field. A virtual keyboard appears at the bottom of the screen, as shown in Figure 14-8.
4. Type a word or phrase. As you type, the folder window displays only those messages that match your search criteria.
5. Tap the message you want to read.

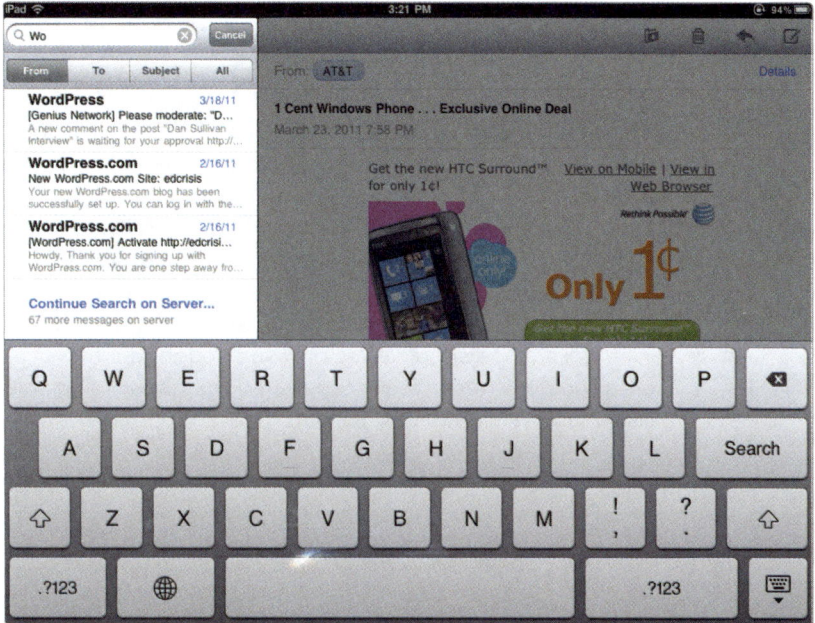

FIGURE 14-8: *As you type in the Search field, all nonmatching messages disappear from view.*

Viewing Multiple Email Accounts

If you have set up two or more email accounts, you can choose to view messages within one account or view all of your messages at once. To view all your messages, follow these steps:

1. From the Home screen, tap **Mail**. The Mail screen appears, displaying what you last viewed.
2. Tap the **Back** button that appears in the upper-left corner of the screen to display the Mailboxes left panel, as shown in Figure 14-9.
3. Tap **All Inboxes**. The right panel displays messages from all your email accounts.
4. (Optional) Tap the **Mailboxes** button in the upper-left corner to return to the previous screen. Then tap an account name under Accounts. Your *Inbox*, *Drafts*, *Sent*, and other folders for that account appear.

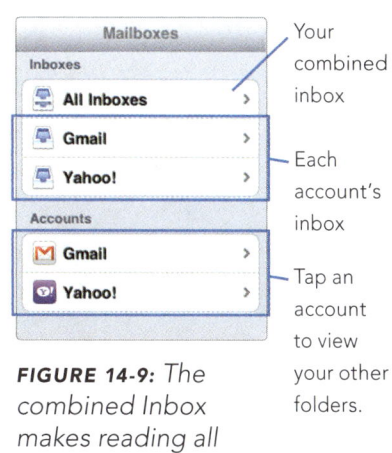

FIGURE 14-9: *The combined Inbox makes reading all incoming mail easy.*

Your combined inbox

Each account's inbox

Tap an account to view your other folders.

Additional Ideas for Reading, Writing, and Organizing Messages

After you've read a message, you may want to store it in another folder right away or delete it to keep your *Inbox* folder easy to manage. If you allow a flood of messages to fill your *Inbox* folder, it will be harder to find the one message you really want.

The Search feature can help you find a particular message, but to ensure that this Search feature works, train yourself to type descriptive words or phrases in the Subject field of all your outgoing messages. That way, you'll be able to search for a particular message using the Subject field.

Take time periodically to browse through your messages and weed out the ones you don't need. The less cluttered your *Inbox* folder, the easier it will be to find what you need when you need it.

PART 4

Video, Music, Photos, and Ebooks

15

Transferring Songs, Videos, and Other Stuff to Your iPad

You can think of your iPad as an independent computer, but it's really an extension of a desktop or laptop computer. Since you probably already have important data stored on another computer, you need to learn how to transfer files to your iPad so you can use those files wherever you go.

To transfer files from your computer to your iPad, you'll need to use the iTunes program. Every Macintosh comes with iTunes, but if you have a Windows computer, you'll need to download and install iTunes directly from the Apple website (*http://www.apple.com/itunes/*).

What You'll Be Using

To transfer files to your iPad, you need to use the following:

▶ The iPad's USB cable   iTunes on your computer

 The iBooks app

Importing Files to iTunes on Your Computer

Before you can transfer files to your iPad from your computer, you must store those files in the iTunes program on your computer. You can buy music and movies directly from iTunes on your computer, or you can get them from another source. For example, you can get a copy of an audio file from a friend or download it from another source, such as Amazon.com. Most people capture photographs using a digital camera or a mobile phone, which they can then transfer to their computer.

* **NOTE:** **You can also buy and download songs directly to your iPad using the iTunes app on your iPad. In most cases, movies and TV shows are too big to download directly to your iPad, so you'll first need to download them on your computer and then transfer them to your iPad from the iTunes program on your computer, like you're doing in this section.**

No matter where you get your photo, audio, ebook, and video files, you must make sure that any files you import into iTunes are stored in file formats that iTunes (and your iPad) can recognize. Table 15-1 lists the most popular file formats that iTunes supports for each type of file.

Table 15-1: Common File Formats Recognized by the iPad

File Type	iPad-Compatible File Format
Photo	BMP, JPG, GIF, PSD, TIF, SGI, and PNG
Audio	MP3, AAC, WAV, MOV, AIFF, WAV, Apple Lossless, and AA
Ebook	EPUB and PDF
Video	MPEG-4 and MOV

* **NOTE:** **To convert files into one of the file formats recognized by the iPad, you may need a special audio/video file conversion program, such as Audacity (*http://audacity.sourceforge.net/*) or Handbrake (*http://handbrake.fr/*). Programs such as iPhoto or Photoshop Elements can convert graphic images to a compatible file format for your iPad. Programs such as iMovie and Premiere Elements can convert video to different video formats as well. Flip ahead to "Converting Files to EPUB Format" on page 116 for hints on converting ebooks.**

To import an audio or video file into the iTunes program on your computer, follow these steps:

1. Run the iTunes program on your computer.
2. Choose **File ▸ Add to Library** (Mac OS X) or **File ▸ Add File to Library** (Windows). An Add to Library dialog appears.
3. Click the file that you want to import into iTunes, and click **Choose** (or **Open**). Your chosen file gets loaded into iTunes. Depending on the type of file you chose, your file may appear in a different iTunes category, such as Music or Movies.

✳ **NOTE:** Alternatively, you can simply drag your files from Finder or Windows Explorer into iTunes. With photographs, you don't need to import them directly into iTunes. Instead, you can store them in iPhoto (on a Macintosh) or in any folder.

Transferring Music to Your iPad

The most common type of audio files you can store in iTunes and transfer to your iPad are songs, audio lectures, and voice memos (which are typically recorded from an iPhone). You'll probably find the bulk of your audio files stored in the Music category.

To transfer music and other audio files to your iPad, follow these steps:

1. Connect your iPad to your computer using the USB cable that came with your iPad.
2. Run the iTunes program on your computer.
3. Click the name of your iPad in the Devices category in the left pane of the iTunes window.
4. Click the **Music** tab to view the options for synchronizing audio files to your iPad.
5. Check (or uncheck) the **Sync Music** checkbox.
6. Click the **Entire music library** or **Selected playlists, artists, albums, and genres** radio button. If you choose Selected playlists, artists, albums, and genres, you'll see additional checkboxes for selecting all your playlists, artists, albums, or genres stored in iTunes, as shown in Figure 15-1.
7. (Optional) Click any additional checkboxes to select specific playlists, artists, albums, or genres.
8. (Optional) Select (or clear) the **Include music videos** checkbox.
9. (Optional) Select (or clear) the **Include voice memos** checkbox.
10. (Optional) Select (or clear) the **Automatically fill free space with songs** checkbox. This option analyzes the songs you've selected and tries to guess similar songs that you did not select to be transferred to your iPad. Then it stores these additional songs on your iPad, filling up the remaining storage space.
11. Click **Apply**. The Sync button appears.
12. Click **Sync** (if your iPad doesn't start synchronizing automatically).

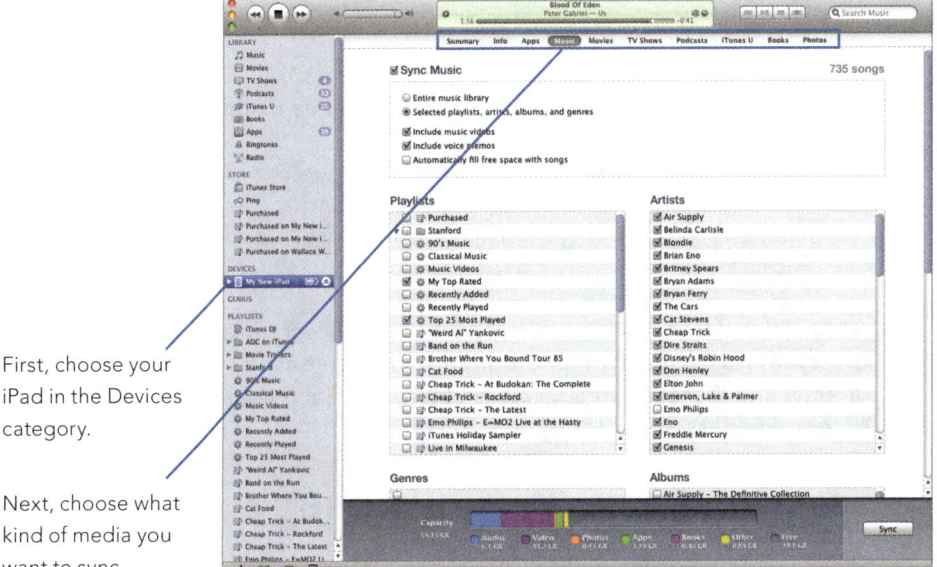

First, choose your iPad in the Devices category.

Next, choose what kind of media you want to sync.

FIGURE 15-1: *Additional checkboxes appear to let you select playlists, artists, genres, or albums.*

Synchronizing Podcasts

Podcasts can consist of multiple episodes; some podcasts are audio only, while others are video. Since it's possible to download podcasts directly to your iPad or on your computer, it's possible that you could download a podcast episode to your iPad and a newer episode of that same podcast on your computer. When you connect your iPad to your computer, iTunes is smart enough to synchronize the different podcast episodes together so both your computer and your iPad contain identical podcast episodes.

When synchronizing podcasts, you need to choose not only which podcasts to transfer, but also which episodes of that podcast to synchronize. You can select individual episodes, or you can automatically sync episodes based on criteria, such as all unplayed episodes or only the most recent episodes.

To synchronize podcasts with your iPad, follow these steps:

1. Connect your iPad to your computer with the USB cable, and run the iTunes program on your computer.
2. Click the name of your iPad in the Devices category, and then click the **Podcasts** tab. The Podcasts screen appears.
3. Check (or uncheck) the **Sync Podcasts** checkbox. If you uncheck the Sync Podcasts checkbox, you won't be able to choose any other options. If you check the Sync Podcasts checkbox, you'll be able to select which podcasts and which episodes to transfer, as shown in Figure 15-2.

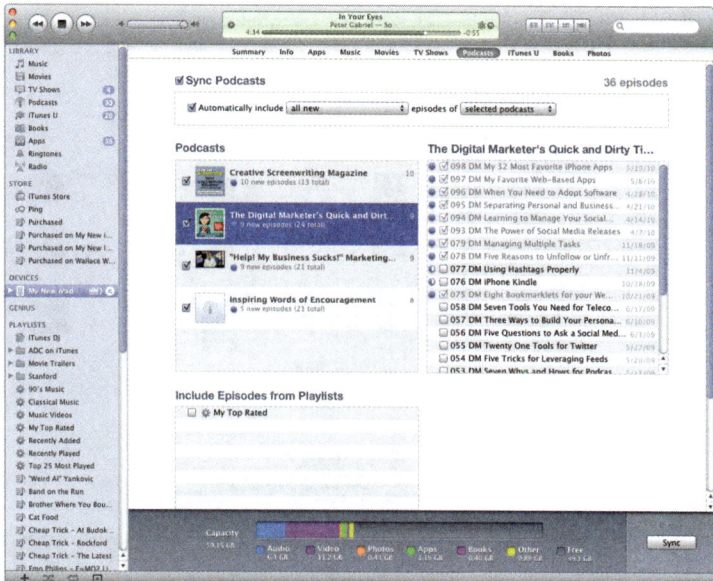

FIGURE 15-2: The Podcasts tab lists all stored podcasts available on your computer.

4. (Optional) Check the **Automatically include** checkbox, and select an option in the pop-up menu to choose the podcasts to transfer, such as all unplayed podcasts or the most recent podcasts. Then select an option in the episodes of pop-up menu to transfer all podcasts or selected podcasts. If the Automatically include checkbox is unchecked, you can click each podcast and individually select episodes from each podcast.
5. (Optional) Click **Sync** to start transferring your selected podcasts to your iPad.

Transferring Movies and TV Shows to Your iPad

To transfer movies and TV shows to your iPad, follow these steps:

1. Connect your iPad to your computer with the USB cable, and run the iTunes program on your computer.
2. Choose your iPad in the sidebar, and then click the **Movies** tab. A list of your stored movies appears, as shown in Figure 15-3.
3. Check (or uncheck) the **Sync Movies** checkbox.
4. (Optional) Check the **Automatically include** checkbox, and select an option in the pop-up menu to choose movies based on how many recent or unwatched movies you want to transfer, as shown in Figure 15-4. If the Automatically include checkbox is unchecked, icons representing all your movies appear, letting you select individual movies.

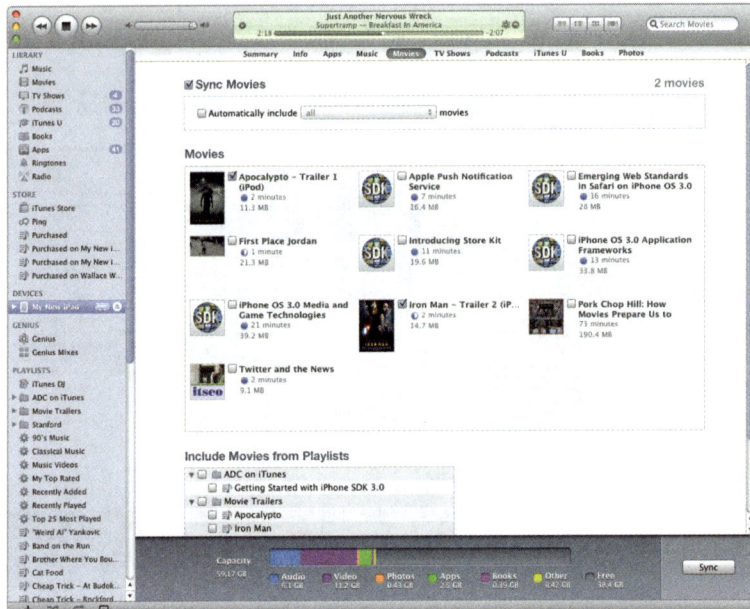

FIGURE 15-3: The Movies tab lets you select any movies to transfer.

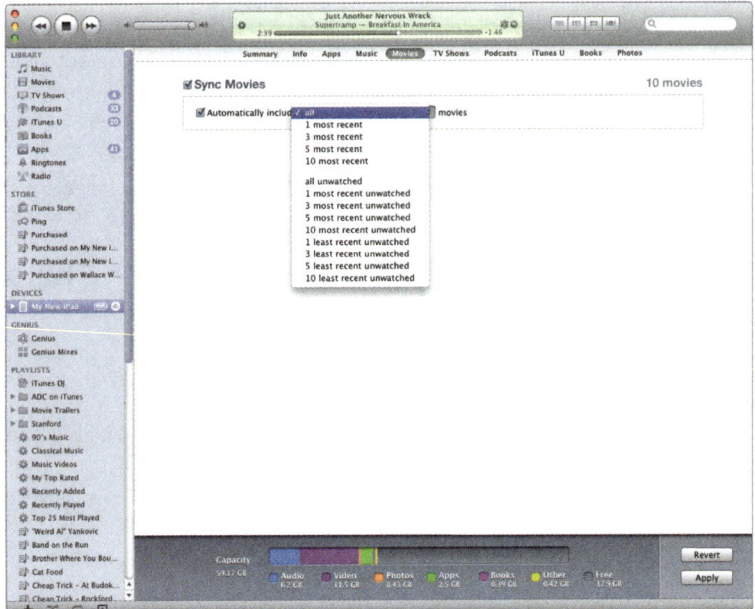

FIGURE 15-4: The Automatically include pop-up menu lets you choose to transfer recent or unwatched movies.

5. (Optional) Click **Apply** to start transferring your selected movies to your iPad.
6. Click the **TV Shows** tab.
7. Check (or uncheck) the **Sync TV Shows** checkbox. If you clear the Sync TV Shows checkbox, you won't be able to choose any other options. If you select the Sync TV Shows checkbox, you'll be able to select which TV shows and which episodes to transfer, as shown in Figure 15-5.

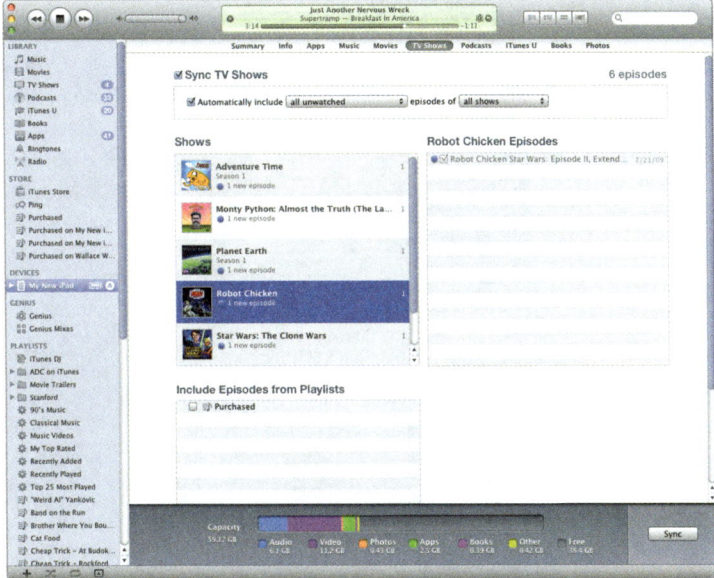

FIGURE 15-5: *The TV Shows tab lists all stored TV shows available on your computer.*

8. (Optional) Check the **Automatically include** checkbox, and select an option like **all unwatched** in the first pop-up menu. Then choose **all shows** or **selected shows** in the episodes of second pop-up menu.
9. (Optional) If the Automatically include checkbox is clear, you can click each TV show and individually select episodes from that show.
10. (Optional) Click **Apply** to start transferring your selected TV shows to your iPad.

Synchronizing Photos

The iPad can take pictures on its own, but you can transfer the digital photos you've already taken onto your iPad, too. Synchronizing your photos between your iPad and your computer also gives you a backup of any photos taken with your iPad.

To synchronize photos, follow these steps:

1. Connect your iPad to your computer using the USB cable.
2. Run iTunes on your computer.

3. Click the name of your iPad in the Devices category.
4. Click the **Photos** tab. The Photos screen appears.
5. Check (or uncheck) the **Sync Photos from** checkbox.
6. Click the **Sync Photos from** pop-up menu, and choose a program to synchronize your photographs (such as iPhoto or Photoshop Elements) or a folder where you store your photographs on your computer (such as the *Pictures* folder).
7. Click the **All photos, albums, events, and faces** or **Selected albums, events, and faces** radio button. (If you click the Selected albums, events, and faces radio button, you can check the checkboxes of different albums, as shown in Figure 15-6.)

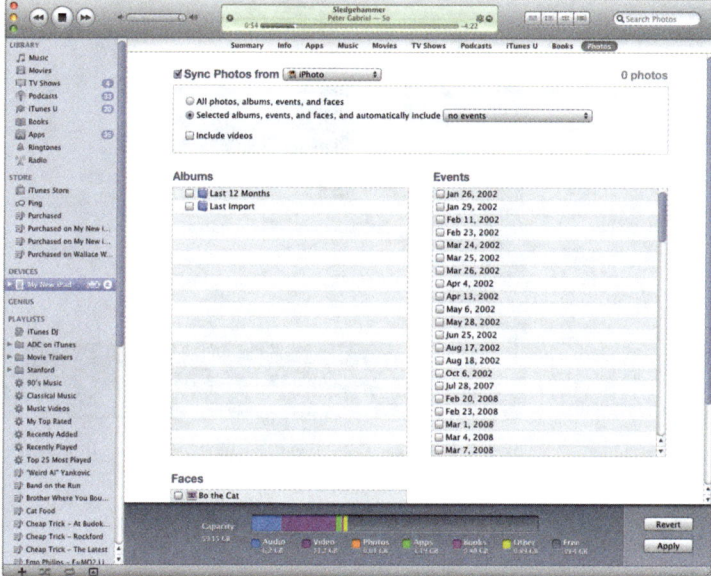

FIGURE 15-6: *The Photos tab lets you synchronize pictures with your iPad.*

8. (Optional) Check the checkboxes of individual photo albums that you want to synchronize with your iPad.
9. Click **Apply**.

Importing Ebooks into Your iPad

To read ebooks on your iPad, you need to install the free iBooks app, which you can download from the App Store. The iBooks app can display ebooks stored in the EPUB or PDF file formats. To install the iBooks app, follow these steps:

1. From the Home screen, tap **App Store**. The App Store screen appears.
2. Tap in the Search field in the upper-right corner of the screen. The virtual keyboard appears at the bottom of the screen.

3. Type **iBooks**, and tap **Search**. The iBooks icon appears on the screen.
4. Tap **FREE** next to the iBooks app. The FREE button turns into an INSTALL APP button. (If you see the word *INSTALLED* next to the iBooks icon, that means you already have iBooks installed on your iPad.)
5. Tap **INSTALL APP**. A dialog may appear, asking that you type your iTunes account password. After you type your password, the iPad downloads and installs the iBooks app.

Importing Ebooks and Audiobooks into iTunes

If you already have an audiobook or ebook stored on your computer, you just need to import it into iTunes, just like you would a song or video. To import a file into iTunes, follow these steps:

1. Run iTunes on your Mac or PC.
2. Choose **File ▸ Add to Library** (Mac OS X) or **File ▸ Add File to Library** (Windows). An Add to Library dialog appears.
3. Click the file that you want to import into iTunes, and click **Choose** (or **Open**). Your chosen file gets loaded into the Books library in iTunes.

* *NOTE:* **Alternatively, you can simply drag your files from Finder or Windows Explorer directly into iTunes.**

Transferring Ebooks and Audiobooks from iTunes to Your iPad

Once you have some ebooks or audiobooks in iTunes on your computer, you can transfer them to your iPad. To transfer your files, follow these steps:

1. Connect your iPad to your computer using the USB cable.
2. Run iTunes on your computer.
3. Click the name of your iPad in the Devices category.
4. Click the **Books** tab. The Books screen appears, listing all your stored EPUB and PDF books, as shown in Figure 15-7.
5. Check (or uncheck) the **Sync Books** checkbox.
6. Click the **All books** or **Selected books** radio button. (Choosing the Selected books radio button allows you to select EPUB and PDF books individually.)
7. (Optional) Click the pop-up menu under the Books heading and choose **Books and PDF files**, **Only Books**, or **Only PDF files**.
8. (Optional) Click the second pop-up menu and choose **Sort by Title** or **Sort by Author**.
9. (Optional) If you chose the Selected books radio button, check the check-boxes of the books you want to transfer.
10. (Optional) Check (or uncheck) the **Sync Audiobooks** checkbox, and click the **All audiobooks** or **Selected audiobooks** radio button. (If you choose the Selected audiobooks radio button, you'll be able to select audiobooks individually.)
11. Click **Apply** to start synchronizing your EPUB files and audiobooks with your iPad.

FIGURE 15-7: *The Books tab lists all the available EPUB and PDF books stored on your computer.*

Converting Files to EPUB Format

If you have non-EPUB or non-PDF documents (such as Microsoft Word *.doc/.docx* files) that you want to store on your iPad, you have several choices. You can use the iWork app to open and view these files (see Chapter 29 for details). Or you can convert the file to the EPUB file format. Some websites that offer free EPUB conversion are 2EPUB (*http://www.2epub.com/*), EPUB 2 Go (*http://www.epub2go.com/*), and ePubConverter (*http://www.epubconverter.org/*).

✱ **NOTE: Converting any file into another file format, such as a Microsoft Word file into the EPUB file format, may not always be accurate. This could mean text is formatted incorrectly or pictures may be missing.**

If you'd rather not hassle with converting files, you can download free EPUB books from sites such as ePubBooks.com (*http://www.epubbooks.com/*), Project Gutenberg (*http://www.gutenberg.org/*), and Google Books (*http://books.google.com/*). Many classic books are freely available for download because they are in the public domain.

Rather than convert files to EPUB format, you might find it easier to convert files to a PDF file instead. On a Macintosh, you can choose the Print command to convert any file (such as a word processor or spreadsheet file) into a PDF file. On a Windows PC, you may need to use PDF creation software, such as Adobe Acrobat, to convert files to PDF.

* NOTE: If your *.doc* or *.docx* file is small enough, you can also just email it to yourself and open the attachment in the Mail app.

If you're ready to learn how to read ebooks and navigate the iBooks app, flip ahead to Chapter 19.

Synchronizing Contacts

On the iPad, contact information gets stored in the Contacts app. If you're using a Macintosh, this information is probably already stored in your Address Book program. If you're using a Windows computer, this contact information is likely in Microsoft Outlook or Windows Live Mail.

In addition, you can also store and synchronize contact information that you may have saved in Google Contacts or Yahoo! Address Book. Syncing means that any new contact you add to your address book of choice will automatically appear in your iPad (and vice versa).

To synchronize your contact information, follow these steps:

1. Connect your iPad to your computer using the USB cable.
2. Run iTunes on your computer.
3. Click the name of your iPad in the Devices category.
4. Click the **Info** tab. The Info screen appears.
5. Check (or uncheck) the **Sync Address Book Contacts** checkbox, as shown in Figure 15-8.

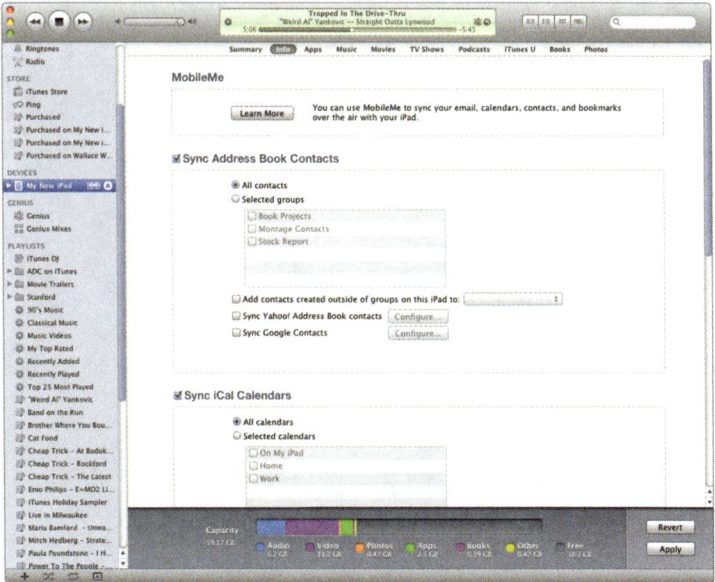

FIGURE 15-8: *The Info tab lets you choose the contact information to synchronize with your iPad.*

6. Click the **All contacts** or **Selected groups** radio button. (If you click the Selected groups radio button, you can check the checkboxes of different contact groups you may have created on your computer.)

7. (Optional) Check the **Add contacts created outside of groups on this iPad** checkbox. Then use the pop-up menu to define which group to store these contacts in.

8. (Optional) Check the **Sync Yahoo! Address Book contacts** checkbox. Then click **Configure**.

9. (Optional) Check the **Sync Google Contacts** checkbox. Then click **Configure**.

10. Click **Apply**.

Synchronizing Appointments

Appointments can help keep you on schedule so you know where you have to be and when. On the iPad, all this information gets stored in the Calendar app. If you're using a Macintosh, this information gets synchronized into your iCal program. If you're using a Windows computer, this contact information gets synchronized into Microsoft Outlook. To synchronize appointments, follow these steps:

1. Connect your iPad to your computer using the USB cable.

2. Run iTunes on your computer.

3. Click the name of your iPad in the Devices category.

4. Click the **Info** tab. The Info screen appears.

5. Check (or uncheck) the **Sync iCal Calendars** checkbox, as shown in Figure 15-9.

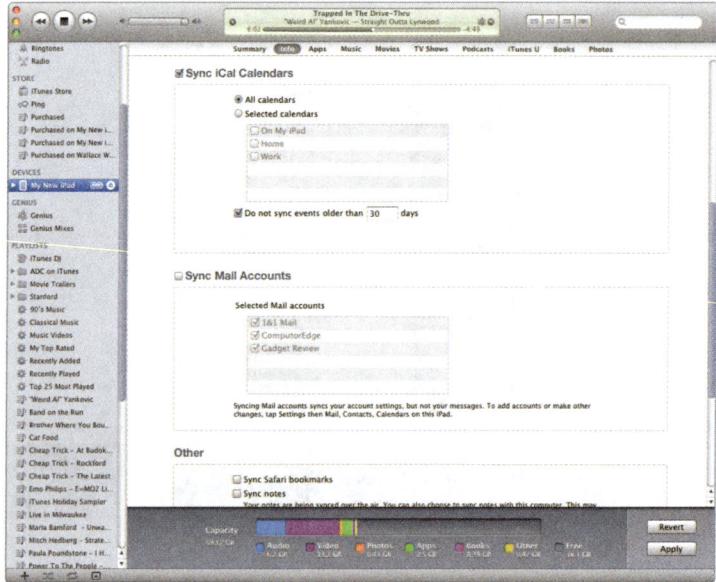

FIGURE 15-9: *Synchronizing your calendars with your iPad*

6. Click the **All calendars** or **Selected calendars** radio button. (If you click the Selected calendars radio button, you can check the checkboxes of different calendars, such as Home or Work.)

7. (Optional) Check (or uncheck) the **Do not sync events older than** checkbox. Then click in the **days** text box and type the number of days, such as **30**.

8. Click **Apply**.

Synchronizing Mail, Notes, and Bookmarks

Most people rely on email to stay in touch with friends and business associates. Since staying in touch through email can be crucial for many people, you may want to synchronize your email accounts between your computer and your iPad.

Synchronizing email affects only your account settings, not the actual messages. Synchronized settings let you access your email from either your computer or your iPad without having to retype all those cryptic mail account settings.

After you've synchronized email account settings on your computer and iPad, you'll be able to read and access the same messages on either device. This lets you read a message on your iPad while you're on the road, then return back to your computer to read and respond to that message on your computer.

On the iPad, you can synchronize email account settings from the Mail app and the Mail program (Macintosh) or Microsoft Outlook or Windows Live Mail (Windows).

If you often get good ideas and need to jot them down, you could scribble them on the nearest scrap of paper. However, it might be better to store them in the Notes app on your iPad and then synchronize those notes to the Mail program on a Macintosh or Microsoft Outlook on Windows. Notes act like miniature word processor documents for storing text.

Finally, you may have a group of favorite bookmarks that you'd like to transfer between your iPad's Safari browser and your computer web browser. By keeping your favorite bookmarks synchronized, you'll be able to visit your favorite websites whenever you need them.

To synchronize email, notes, and browser bookmarks, follow these steps:

1. Connect your iPad to your computer using the USB cable.

2. Run iTunes on your computer.

3. Click the name of your iPad in the Devices category.

4. Click the **Info** tab. The Info screen appears.

5. Scroll down the Info screen.

6. Check (or uncheck) the **Sync Mail Accounts** checkbox, as shown in Figure 15-10.

7. (Optional) Check (or uncheck) the checkboxes of the email accounts whose settings you want to synchronize with your iPad.

8. (Optional) Check (or uncheck) the **Sync Safari bookmarks** checkbox.

9. (Optional) Check (or uncheck) the **Sync notes** checkbox.

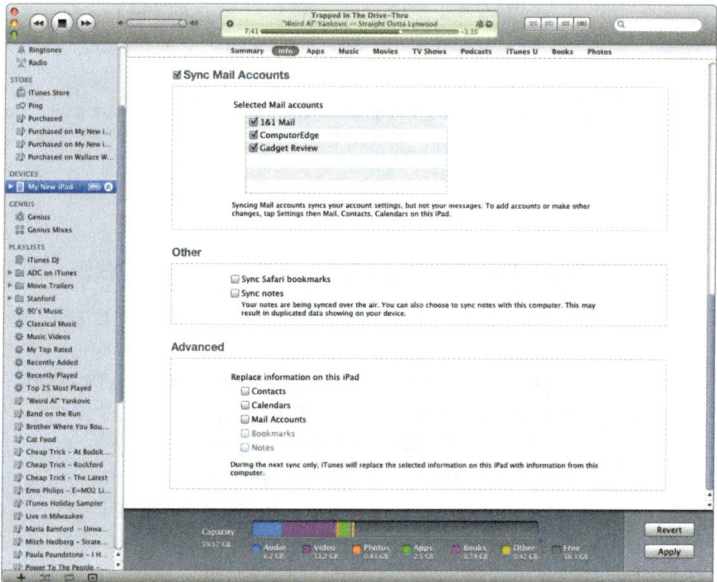

FIGURE 15-10: *The Info tab lets you choose information to synchronize with your iPad, such as email account settings, browser bookmarks, or notes.*

10. (Optional) Check (or uncheck) the checkboxes in the Advanced category to define whether you want to erase information stored on your iPad and replace it with information from your computer.

11. Click **Apply**.

Additional Ideas for Syncing Data

You can freely erase and transfer different audio, video, and ebook files to your iPad, so don't think you need to cram everything from your computer onto your iPad. You can transfer a handful of audio or video files from your computer that you want to hear or watch for that day and then pick an entirely different batch of audio or video files to use the next day.

If you're learning a foreign language, you can store audio files of that language in the iTunes program on your computer and then transfer them to your iPad so you can hear them wherever you go. You can load motivational lectures as audio files and take them with your iPad, too.

16

Shopping on iTunes and the iBookstore

Many people have audio CDs that they can store in iTunes on their computer and then transfer these music files to their iPad. It's also easy to download music files from other online services, such as Amazon.com, and transfer them into iTunes.

However, one of the simplest ways to add new content to your iPad is through Apple's online stores. If you want to buy music, movies, TV shows, or audiobooks, you can use the iTunes Store.

If you want to buy new ebooks, you can visit the iBookstore. With so many ways to get the latest movies, TV shows, hit songs, and best-selling books, you'll never run out of ways to keep yourself entertained with your iPad.

＊ *NOTE:* **To purchase anything from one of Apple's online stores, you'll have to set up a free iTunes account.**

What You'll Be Using

To browse and shop online, you need to use the following:

▸ An Internet connection (Wi-Fi or 3G)

 The iBooks app

 The iTunes app

Shopping for Music, Movies, TV Shows, and Audiobooks

Shopping online on the iTunes Store is like getting lost in a huge shopping mall. With so many options available, it's easy to feel overwhelmed by the sheer number of choices. To help you navigate your way around iTunes, iTunes lets you choose separate Music, Movies, TV Shows, and Audiobooks categories. Within each category, you can choose to view the latest featured products or the top sellers. For even more help locating what you want, you can choose different genres.

＊ *NOTE:* **Somewhat confusingly, iTunes on your Mac or PC is a full-fledged music player where you can also buy music. But on the iPad, you play music through the iPod App. iTunes on the iPad is how you'll buy new media.**

To see how you can browse and shop at the iTunes Store, follow these steps:

1. From the Home screen, tap **iTunes**. The iTunes screen appears.
2. Tap **Music** at the bottom of the iTunes screen. The iTunes screen displays available songs.
3. Tap the **Featured** tab at the top of the iTunes screen, as shown in Figure 16-1. The Featured screen displays new and noteworthy selections.
4. Tap **Movies** at the bottom of the iTunes screen to see some of the currently available movies you can rent or buy.
5. Tap **TV Shows** at the bottom of the iTunes screen to see some of the currently available TV show episodes you can buy.
6. Tap **Audiobooks** at the bottom of the iTunes screen to see some of the currently available audiobooks you can buy.
7. Tap the **Top Charts** tab at the top of the iTunes screen. The iTunes screen lists the top sellers in your chosen category (music, movies, TV shows, or audiobooks), as shown in Figure 16-2.
8. Tap **Music**, **Movies**, or **TV Shows** at the bottom of the iTunes screen.
9. Tap the **Genius** tab at the top of the iTunes screen. Apple's Genius examines the music, movies, or TV shows currently stored on your iPad and tries to suggest similar items that you might also enjoy, as shown in Figure 16-3.

FIGURE 16-1: *The iTunes screen displays an ever-changing list of avail-able songs.*

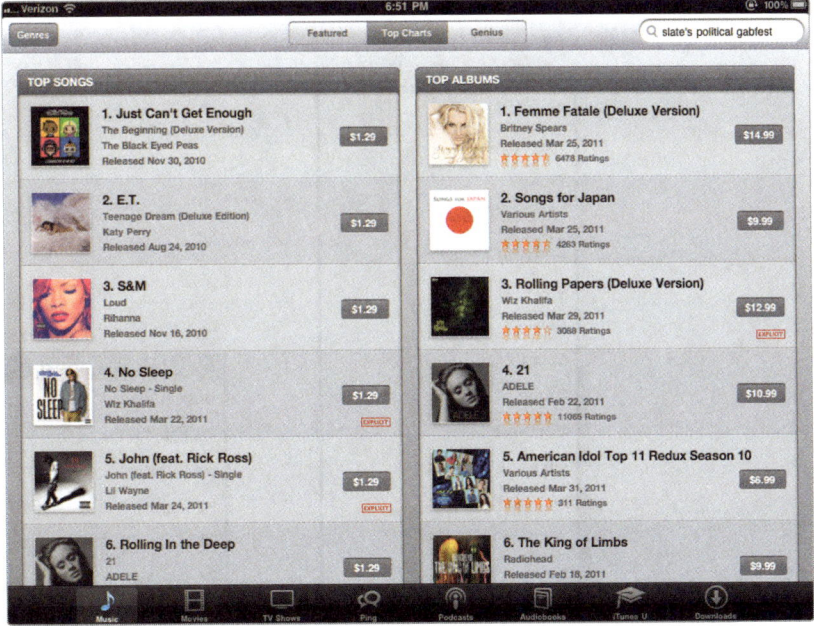

FIGURE 16-2: *The Top Charts tab shows the best sellers for each category.*

FIGURE 16-3: *The Genius screen offers suggestions based on the current items stored on your iPad.*

10. Tap **Genres** in the upper-left corner of the screen. A menu appears, as shown in Figure 16-4.

11. Tap the **Search** field in the upper-right corner of the iTunes screen. A virtual keyboard appears.

12. Type the name of an artist. As you type, a list of possible options appears, as shown in Figure 16-5.

13. Tap a suggested option, or finish typing and tap the **Search** key on the virtual keyboard. The iTunes Store displays products that match your search criteria.

FIGURE 16-4: *Looking for items within a certain genre*

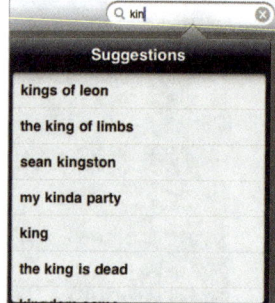

FIGURE 16-5: *As you type, iTunes tries to guess what you want to find.*

Shopping for iBooks

If you want to find the latest best sellers, you could rush to your nearest bookstore and carry around a handful of bulky books that weigh more than your iPad. A better alternative is to download the ebook version of those books directly on your iPad through the iBooks app.

✳ **NOTE:** You must download and install the free iBooks app before you can browse the iBookstore. See Chapter 15 for instructions on installing it.

To browse the iBookstore, follow these steps:

1. From the Home screen, tap **iBooks**. The iBooks screen appears with all your currently stored books on a shelf. (If you were reading an ebook, the iBooks screen will show you the last page you read. To view the iBooks main screen, just tap the Library button in the upper-left corner of the screen.)
2. Tap **Store** at the upper-left corner of the screen. The iBooks screen flips around to reveal the iBookstore.
3. Tap **Featured** at the bottom of the iBookstore screen to see the latest ebooks available, as shown in Figure 16-6.

FIGURE 16-6: *The iBookstore screen*

4. Tap **NYTimes** at the bottom of the screen to see the latest *New York Times* best sellers in the fiction and nonfiction categories.
5. Tap **Top Charts** at the bottom of the iBookstore screen to see the most popular free and paid ebooks.

6. Tap **Browse** at the bottom of the iBookstore screen to see a list of authors and their books available on the iBookstore, as shown in Figure 16-7.

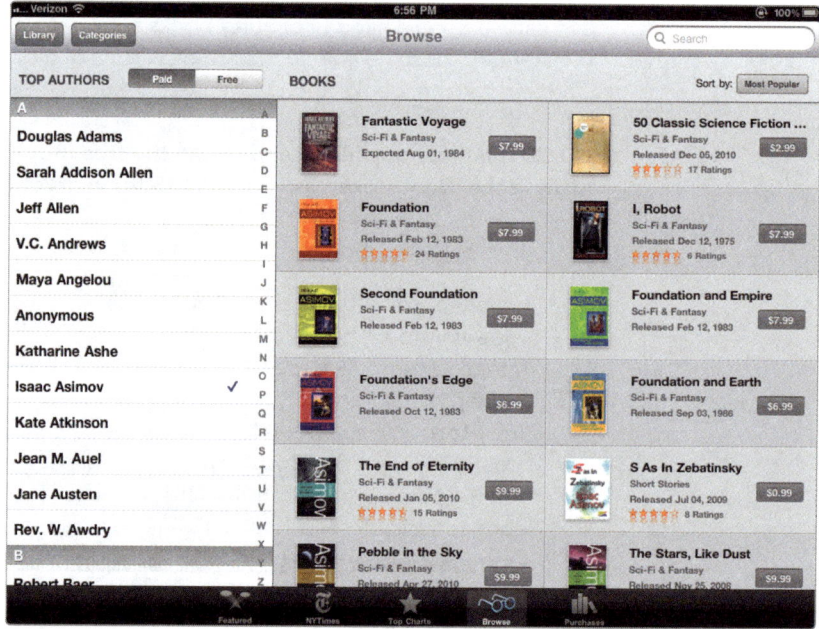

FIGURE 16-7: *You can browse for books based on the author's name.*

7. Tap **Purchases** at the bottom of the iBookstore screen to see all the ebooks you've downloaded and purchased.
8. Tap **Library** in the upper-left corner of the screen to return to your bookshelf on the iBooks screen.

Additional Ideas for Shopping Online

Buying audio, video, and ebooks through one of Apple's online stores represents the most convenient way to load new content onto your iPad. Although most people naturally seem to gravitate toward the latest releases, don't overlook the huge library of older products that you might find interesting as well.

Browse through iTunes using the Genius feature, and iTunes can analyze your current music library to determine which songs by other artists you might be interested in hearing. By exploring similar but different artists who you may never have heard before, you can expand your audio and video library without wasting your money randomly guessing which artists you might like next.

For ebooks, just remember that for every latest best seller, there are probably dozens of similar books that have been written, and those older books are probably much less expensive than the latest best seller. Many classics are now in the public domain and are totally free.

17

Listening to Music and Other Audio Files

If you have an iPod or other portable digital music player, you can put it aside because your iPad essentially duplicates all the features of an iPod (except for the smaller size). Besides listening to music, you can also listen to podcasts, audiobooks, or even iTunes University lectures.

Before you can play any audio files, you'll need to load them into your iPad, as explained in Chapters 15 and 16.

What You'll Be Using

To listen to music and other audio files on your iPad, you need to use the following:

 iTunes on your computer   The iPod app

Playing a Song in Different iPod Modes

The iPod app lets you choose one or more songs and play them on your iPad. When playing a song, you have three options:

▶ **Full screen mode**   Displays album art on the screen.

▶ **Browsing mode**   Displays album art as a thumbnail image while letting you browse in the iPod app.

▶ **Background mode**   Plays audio in the background while you run another app, such as Safari, Mail, or Contacts.

To see how to switch the iPod app into different modes, follow these steps:

1. From the Home screen, tap **iPod**. The iPod screen appears.
2. Tap **Music** in the Library category in the left pane of the iPod window. A complete listing of your songs appears in the right pane.
3. Tap on a song that you want to hear. The Full screen mode appears, displaying the album art that the song came from.
4. Tap the screen. Controls appear at the top and bottom of the screen, as shown in Figure 17-1.
5. Tap **Return** (it looks like an arrow in a circle, pointing to the left) in the lower-left corner of the screen. The album art of the currently playing song shrinks to a thumbnail image in the bottom-left corner of the screen, as shown in Figure 17-2. This is the Browsing mode, which lets you browse through the iPod app.
6. Press the **Home** button. The Home screen appears while your song continues playing in the background.
7. Press the **Home** button twice. A list of app icons appears at the bottom of the screen.
8. Swipe these icons to the right until you see the rewind, pause, play, and fast-forward, as shown in Figure 17-3.
9. Tap **iPod** to return to the iPod screen (or tap the screen to leave the music playing in the background).

FIGURE 17-1: Tapping the screen in Full screen mode displays the Return button in the bottom-left corner.

FIGURE 17-2: In Browsing mode you can hear and control your song while browsing through the iPod app.

FIGURE 17-3: *In Background mode, you can control a song through a miniature iPod window while running another app, such as Safari.*

Choosing a Song

All your songs get stored in the Music category in the iPod app. Since you might have hundreds of songs stored on your iPad, you need to know all the different ways to find a particular song so you can find what you want to hear as quickly as possible.

To find a song stored on your iPad, follow these steps:

1. From the Home screen, tap **iPod**. The iPod screen appears.
2. (Optional) If you have music already playing, the album art will appear. Tap the screen to display controls, and then tap the **Return** icon (it looks like a left-pointing arrow) in the bottom-left corner of the screen.
3. Tap **Music** in the Library category in the left pane of the iPod window. A complete listing of your songs appears in the right pane.
4. Tap **Songs** at the bottom of the iPod screen.
5. Scroll up or down to see your list of songs.
6. Tap a letter, such as *D* or *T*, displayed on the index that appears on the far right of the iPod window (see Figure 17-4). The iPod window lists all songs that begin with the letter you tapped.
7. Tap **Artists** at the bottom of the iPod screen. The iPod screen displays an alphabetical list of artists, as shown in Figure 17-4.
8. Tap the name of a recording artist. A list of albums from that artist appears, as well as songs from each album, as shown in Figure 17-5.

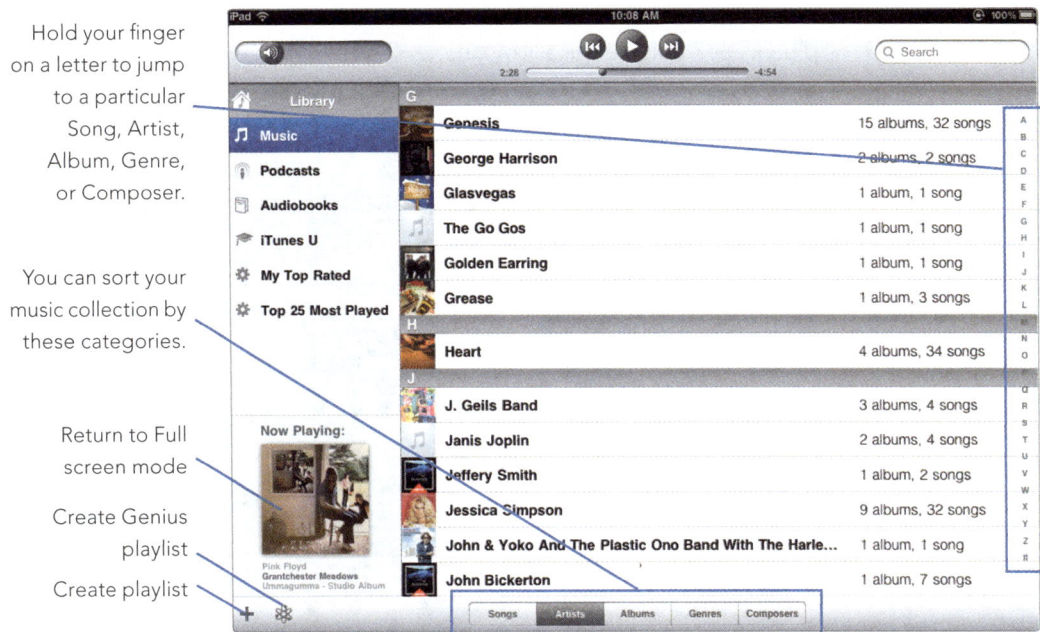

Hold your finger on a letter to jump to a particular Song, Artist, Album, Genre, or Composer.

You can sort your music collection by these categories.

Return to Full screen mode

Create Genius playlist

Create playlist

FIGURE 17-4: *The Artists tab lets you find songs from a specific recording artist.*

FIGURE 17-5: *A list of songs organized by album from a specific recording artist*

9. Tap **Albums** at the bottom of the iPod screen. The iPod screen displays your album covers alphabetically by title, as shown in Figure 17-6.

FIGURE 17-6: *The Albums tab*

10. Tap an album cover. A window appears that lists all the songs from that album that are stored on your iPad, as shown in Figure 17-7.

FIGURE 17-7: *Tap a cover to view the songs on that album.*

11. Tap **Genres** at the bottom of the iPod screen. The iPod screen displays different genre icons.
12. Tap a genre icon. A window appears, listing all the songs within that genre that are stored on your iPad.
13. Tap **Composers** at the bottom of the iPod screen. An alphabetical list of composers of songs stored on your iPad appears.
14. Tap a composer name. A list of albums and songs by that composer appears.
15. Press the **Home** button to return to the Home screen.

Controlling Your Music

When you first tap a song or other audio file, the iPad's screen displays a large version of the album art. This makes your iPad more colorful to look at (while showing you which audio file is currently playing) but also gives you a few more controls to manipulate your audio file. You can control the iPod app from this screen, or you can go back to browsing for the next song.

To control your music as you play a song, do the following:

1. Find a song or audio file you want to play and tap it, as discussed in "Choosing a Song" on page 130. The song's album art appears on screen. If you don't have the album art, a set of music notes appears.
2. Tap the image. Controls appear, as shown in Figure 17-8.

Repeat Volume slider Playhead slider Rewind Play/Pause Forward Shuffle

Return   Genius Playlist   Album/Episode List

FIGURE 17-8: *Tapping the full-screen image of an audio file displays controls.*

3. Try using the following controls:

▸ **Repeat**   Tap once to make a playlist loop, tap a second time to make a single song loop endlessly, and tap a third time to turn off the repeat feature entirely.

▸ **Volume slider**   Drag this left and right to adjust the volume.

▸ **Playhead slider**   Drag this left and right to play different parts of the audio file. If you drag your finger down the screen as you drag left and right, you'll lower the "scrubbing rate," which will allow you to speed up or slow down so you can find a particular spot in a song or lecture.

▸ **Rewind**   Hold to rewind the currently playing audio file, or tap to play the previous audio file in a list.

▸ **Play/Pause**   Tap to pause or resume playing of an audio file.

▸ **Forward**   Hold to fast-forward through the currently playing audio file, or tap to play the next audio file in a list.

▸ **Shuffle**   Tap once to shuffle your audio list; tap a second time to turn shuffle off.

▸ **Album/Episode List**   Tap once to view all the songs or episodes for that album, podcast, or iTunes U course, as shown in Figure 17-9.

▸ **Genius Playlist**   The iPod app will use the currently playing song to create a new playlist of similar songs stored on your iPad.

FIGURE 17-9: *When you tap the Album/Episode List button, the list of songs or episodes from an album, podcast, or iTunes U course appears.*

▶ **Return**   Tap once to display the iPod screen with the audio file's image shrunk to a thumbnail image in the bottom-left corner of the screen. You can go back to browsing and choose your next song from here, as discussed in "Choosing a Song" on page 130.

Finding a Podcast, Audiobook, or iTunes U Course

Podcasts and iTunes U courses work similarly. You can have multiple podcasts or iTunes U courses, and within each podcast or iTunes U course, you can have multiple episodes. To learn how to find a podcast, audiobook, or iTunes U course stored on your iPad, follow these steps:

1. From the Home screen, tap **iPod**. The iPod screen appears.
2. Tap **Podcasts** in the Library category in the left pane of the iPod window. A list of stored podcasts appears, as shown in Figure 17-10.

FIGURE 17-10: *The Podcasts category lists all the podcasts stored on your iPad.*

3. Tap a podcast. A list of episodes for that podcast appears.
4. Tap **Audiobooks** in the Library category in the left pane of the iPod window. A list of stored audiobooks appears.
5. Tap **iTunes U** in the Library category in the left pane of the iPod window. A list of iTunes U courses appears.
6. Tap an iTunes U course. A list of episodes for that course appears.

Searching for Any Audio File

Rather than search through individual categories, such as the Music or Podcasts libraries, you might find it easier just to search for a particular audio file by typing part or all of the recording artist's name, song title, or album name.

To search for any audio file stored in your iPad, follow these steps:

1. From the Home screen, tap **iPod**. The iPod screen appears.
2. Tap the **Search** field that appears in the upper-right corner of the iPod screen. A virtual keyboard appears, as shown in Figure 17-11.

Hide Keyboard key

FIGURE 17-11: *Searching for a particular audio file*

3. Type a word or phrase. As you type, the iPod app displays a list of matching items. Tap the one you want to play.
4. Tap the **Hide Keyboard** key at the bottom right of the virtual keyboard.

Additional Ideas for Listening to Audio Files

With the iPad, you have your choice of blasting your audio files through the iPad's speakers or plugging in headphones and listening to your audio files in private. However you choose to enjoy your audio files, your iPad can help you take your audio files wherever you go and enjoy listening to them at any time.

If you suddenly need to access the iPod app, don't forget you can press the Home button twice and swipe to the left to view the iPod controls, or just tap the orange iPod icon and jump into the full app.

18

Watching Videos

Although you can watch some videos through the iPod app (such as iTunes U courses or podcasts stored as video files), you may not want to wade through the mix of audio and video files stored in the iPod app. When you just want to watch video, you can use the Videos or YouTube app and turn your iPad into a portable viewing device.

In this chapter you will learn how to watch and control video files stored on your iPad, stored only on your computer, or stored in YouTube's video library collection.

What You'll Be Using

To watch video files on your iPad, you need to use the following:

 The Videos app   The YouTube app

Choosing a Video File

To see how to find a video file stored on your iPad, follow these steps:

1. From the Home screen, tap **Videos**. The Videos screen appears.
2. Tap the **Movies** tab at the top of the screen. Thumbnail images of movie posters appear, as shown in Figure 18-1.

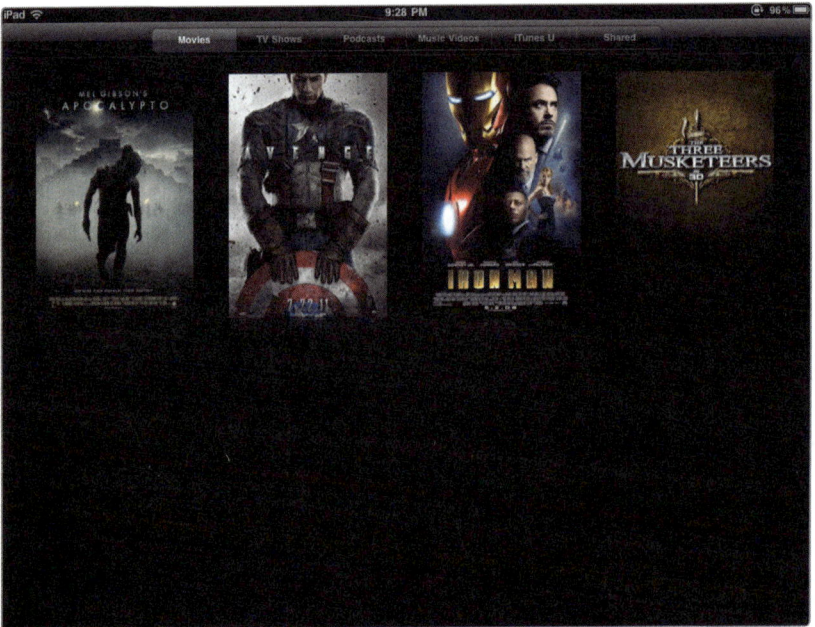

FIGURE 18-1: *The Movies tab in the Videos app shows your stored movies.*

3. Tap the **TV Shows** tab at the top of the screen. Thumbnails of your TV shows appear. Tapping the **Podcasts**, **Music Videos**, and **iTunes U** tabs will display thumbnails of your files in the same way.
4. Tap a thumbnail image to start watching that video.

Viewing a Video File

When you're watching a video file, you can display controls by tapping the screen once. The controls appear at the top and bottom of the screen, as shown in Figure 18-2. If you don't use any of the displayed controls after a few seconds, they disappear again. You can also hide the controls by tapping the screen once while they are displayed.

Playhead slider   Full Screen

Rewind   Volume slider   Play/Pause   Forward

FIGURE 18-2: *Tapping a playing video displays controls at the top and bottom of the screen.*

The available controls are as follows:

▶ **Playhead slider** Drag this left and right to play different parts of the video file.

▶ **Full Screen** Tap to expand the video to fill the entire screen; tap a second time to shrink the video slightly.

▶ **Rewind** Tap to rewind to the beginning of a video file or play the previous video file in a list. If you hold your finger over the rewind button, you can quickly skip back through a video.

▶ **Volume slider** Drag this left and right to adjust the volume.

- ▶ **Play/Pause**   Tap to pause or resume playing of a video file.
- ▶ **Forward**   Tap to play the next video file in a list. If you hold your finger over the forward button, you can quickly jump ahead in a video.

✳ *NOTE:* **To skip backward or forward in a video at different speeds, hold your finger over the Playhead slider until a Hi-Speed Scrubbing message appears underneath the Playhead slider, as shown in Figure 18-3. Slide your finger down away from the Playhead slider. As you move your finger down, the Hi-Speed Scrubbing message changes into Half Speed Scrubbing, Quarter Speed Scrubbing, and Fine Scrubbing. When your desired speed appears, slide your finger left or right to rewind or fast forward through your video.**

FIGURE 18-3: *Sliding your finger down lets you choose different scrubbing rates to change the speed that you can scroll backward or forward.*

To see how to control a video, follow these steps:

1. Follow the steps in "Choosing a Video File" on page 138 to find a video you want to play.
2. Tap the image that represents the video you want to play. A list of episodes appears in the left side of the screen, as shown in Figure 18-4.
3. Tap **Play**. Your chosen episode starts playing, filling the entire screen.

FIGURE 18-4: *Viewing a list of episodes for a video*

4. Tap the screen once to display controls at the top and bottom of the screen.
5. Drag the **Playhead** slider to view a different part of the video.
6. Drag the **Volume** slider to adjust the volume.
7. Tap **Play/Pause** to pause and play the video.
8. Tap and hold **Rewind**. Your video plays backward.
9. Tap and hold **Forward**. The video advances and then stops when you release.
10. Tap **Full Screen**. The video expands to fill the screen.
11. Tap **Full Screen** again. The video shrinks slightly.
12. Tap **Done**.

Choosing a YouTube Video

For those times when you want to watch something for just a few minutes, you can browse the massive selection of videos available on YouTube. On your iPad, you can access YouTube directly without going through your browser at all. All you need is a reliable and (preferably) fast Internet connection, and you'll be ready to watch short video clips whether you're standing in line or sitting down.

Before you start browsing YouTube's massive library of videos, make sure you have a reliable Internet connection. If you have a weak Internet connection, you may spend your time staring at a screen that appears frozen but occasionally lurches forward to display a few additional frames before grinding to a halt once more.

After you're satisfied that your Internet connection is reliable, you can browse through YouTube by following these steps:

1. From the Home screen, tap **YouTube**. The YouTube screen appears.
2. Tap **Featured** at the bottom of the screen. Thumbnail images of videos that YouTube is promoting that day appear, as shown in Figure 18-5.

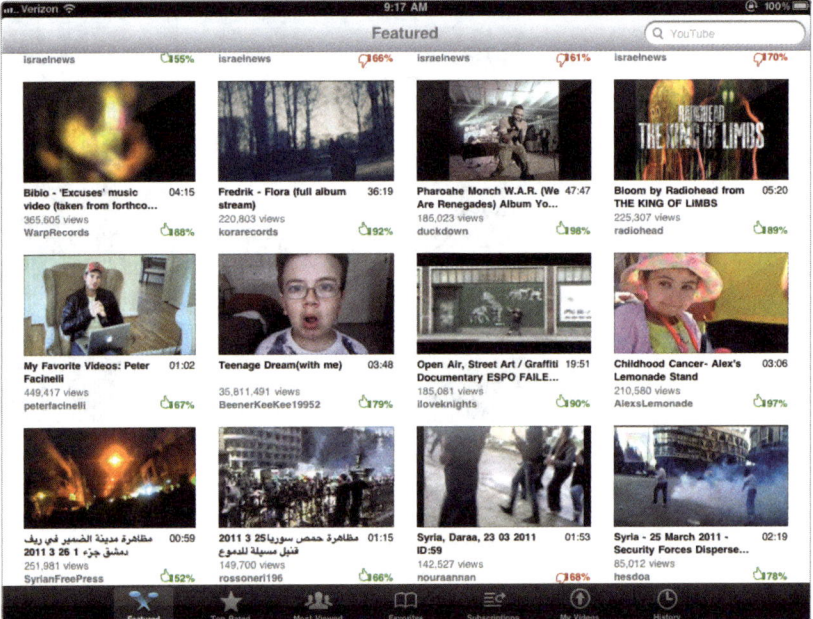

FIGURE 18-5: *Tapping the Featured icon displays the latest featured YouTube videos.*

3. Tap **Top Rated** at the bottom of the screen. Thumbnail images of the highest-rated videos appear.
4. Tap the **Today**, **This Week**, or **All** tab at the top of the screen to view just today's top-rated videos, the past week's top-rated videos, or all top-rated videos.
5. Tap **Most Viewed** at the bottom of the screen. Thumbnail images of the most viewed videos appear.
6. Tap the **Today**, **This Week**, or **All** tab at the top of the screen to view just today's most viewed videos, the past week's most viewed videos, or all of the most viewed videos.
7. Tap **History** at the bottom of the screen. Thumbnail images of the last videos you've seen appear.
8. (Optional) Tap **Clear** at the upper-left corner of the screen to remove this list of videos you've watched.

Viewing a YouTube Video

When you're watching a video file, you can display controls by tapping the screen once to display controls at the top and bottom of the screen, as shown in Figure 18-6.

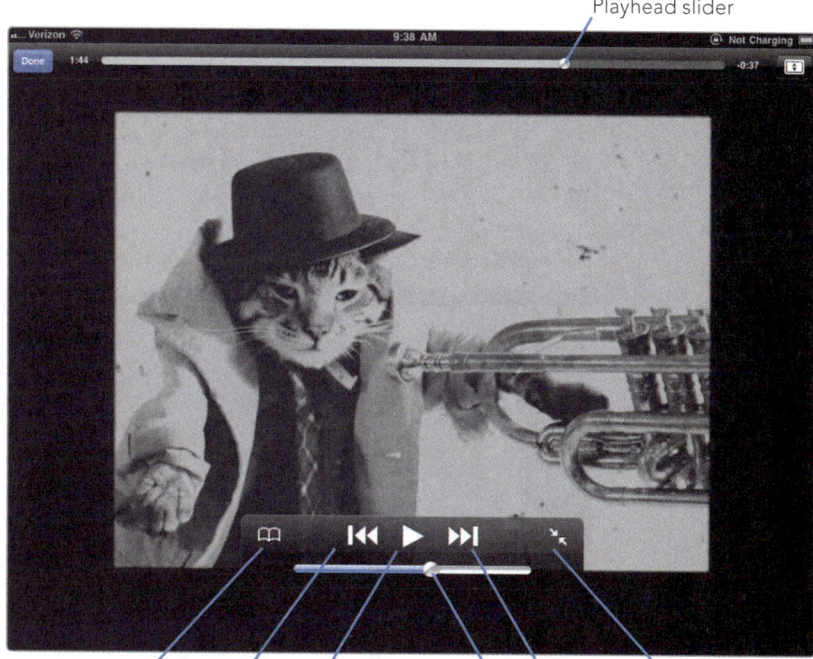

Playhead slider

Bookmark/Add   Rewind   Play/Pause   Volume slider   Forward   Full Screen/Shrink

FIGURE 18-6: *Tapping a playing video displays the controls.*

The available controls are as follows:

▸ **Playhead slider**   Drag this left and right to play parts of the video.

▸ **Bookmark/Add**   Tap to store this video in your Favorites list.

▸ **Rewind**   Tap to rewind to the beginning of the video or play the previous video in a list. If you hold your finger over the rewind button, you can quickly skip back through a video.

▸ **Play/Pause**   Tap to pause or resume playing of a video.

▸ **Volume slider**   Drag this left and right to adjust the volume.

▸ **Forward**   Tap to play the next video in a list. If you hold your finger over the forward button, you can quickly jump ahead in a video.

▸ **Full Screen/Shrink**   Tap to expand the video to fill the screen; tap a second time to shrink the video slightly.

To see how to control a video, follow these steps:

1. Follow the steps in "Choosing a YouTube Video" on page 141 to find a video you want to play.
2. Tap the image that represents the video you want to play. Your chosen video appears on the full screen and displays controls briefly, as shown in Figure 18-6. After a few seconds, the controls disappear.
3. Tap anywhere on the screen to display the controls again. Notice that when the video appears on part of the screen, the Add, Share, Like, Dislike, and Flag icons appear at the top of the video.
4. Tap **Shrink**. The video shrinks to fill part of the screen, as shown in Figure 18-7. Tap the small screen, and you can Add, Share, Like, Dislike, or Flag a video.
5. Tap **Full Screen**. The video expands to fill the entire screen.

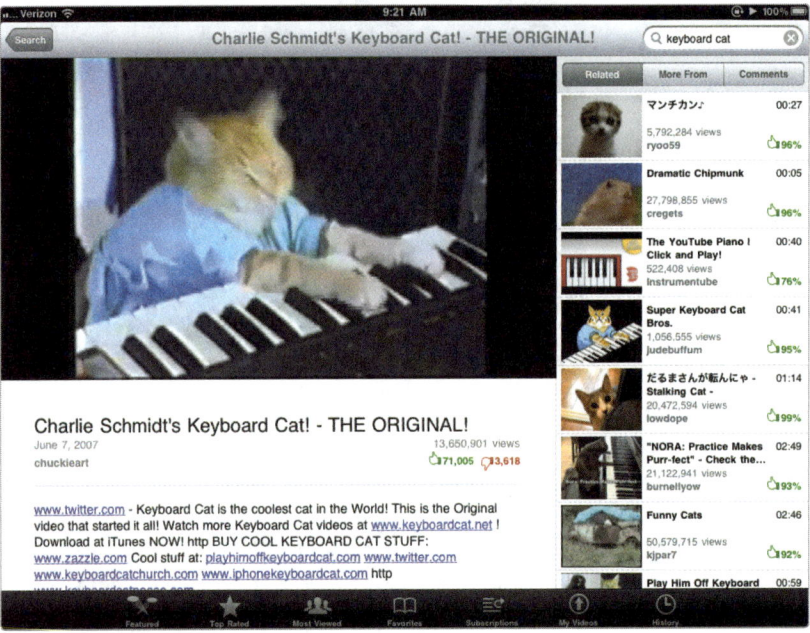

FIGURE 18-7: *Tapping the Shrink button lets you find related videos and read the video's description and comments.*

Searching for a YouTube Video

Since YouTube contains thousands of videos, you probably don't want to spend your time browsing through each one. To find a specific type of video, you can type a descriptive word or phrase and let YouTube show you only those videos that match your search criteria.

To search for a YouTube video, follow these steps:

1. From the Home screen, tap **YouTube**. The YouTube screen appears.
2. Tap the **Search** field that appears in the upper-right corner of the screen. The virtual keyboard appears.
3. Type a descriptive word or phrase, and tap the **Search** key on the virtual keyboard. (To clear any text in the Search field, tap **Close** in the far right of the Search field, or tap the **Backspace** key on the virtual keyboard.) YouTube displays a list of videos matching your search criteria.

Additional Ideas for Watching Videos

By loading educational podcasts or iTunes U courses, you can improve your current work skills or develop new ones. For the intellectual challenge, download video iTunes U courses on topics that interest you so you can turn your iPad into a portable educational tool.

Bring along a pair of headphones or ear buds so you can watch a video on your iPad without disturbing others (although others will likely disturb you so they can see how the iPad works).

To avoid cramming too many videos onto your iPad, you can store videos on your PC or Mac and then stream your video to your iPad. This lets you watch videos on your iPad without having to store them on your iPad.

To stream videos, you need a Wi-Fi network. On your computer, open iTunes, click the Advanced menu, and choose the Turn On Home Sharing option. You'll need to get a free Apple ID to turn on this feature, but then you'll be able to watch videos on your iPad without going through the hassle of transferring those video files between your iPad and your computer.

To get even more out of watching YouTube videos, visit YouTube's website (*http://www.youtube.com/*) and create an account for free. With a free YouTube account, you can upload your own videos (and view them using the My Videos icon), create video playlists (and view them through the Favorites icon), or subscribe to certain YouTube video creators.

19 Reading Ebooks

For those who love to read, an iPad can become an indispensable device since you can cram thousands of different books into an iPad without the drawbacks of the physical weight or bulk of these books. With ebooks, you can read the latest best sellers, the best from classic literature, or anything in between.

To read ebooks on your iPad, you'll need to download the free iBooks app from the App Store. After you install the iBooks app, you can start downloading and reading ebooks directly from Apple's iBookstore.

What You'll Be Using

To read ebooks on your iPad, you need to use the following:

 The iBooks app

Opening (and Closing) an Ebook

The iBooks app displays all your ebooks as books on a virtual shelf. If you start stuffing iBooks full of ebooks, you may need to scroll down to see the rest of your ebooks.

To open an ebook, follow these steps:

1. From the Home screen, tap **iBooks**. The iBooks screen appears, as shown in Figure 19-1.

FIGURE 19-1: *The iBooks virtual shelf*

2. Tap the **Collections** button and choose **Books** or **PDFs**.
3. Tap the image of the book that you want to read. Your chosen ebook opens with animation that mimics the opening of a real book.

✱ **NOTE: Your ebook opens to the last page you viewed before exiting the iBooks app.**

4. Flip your iPad to view both landscape and portrait modes. In landscape mode, the ebook appears as two pages. In portrait mode, the ebook appears as one page, as shown in Figure 19-2. (PDF files only appear as a single page in both portrait and landscape mode.)

5. Tap the screen, and tap **Library** in the upper-left corner of the screen. The virtual bookshelf screen reappears. You can now choose another book to read.

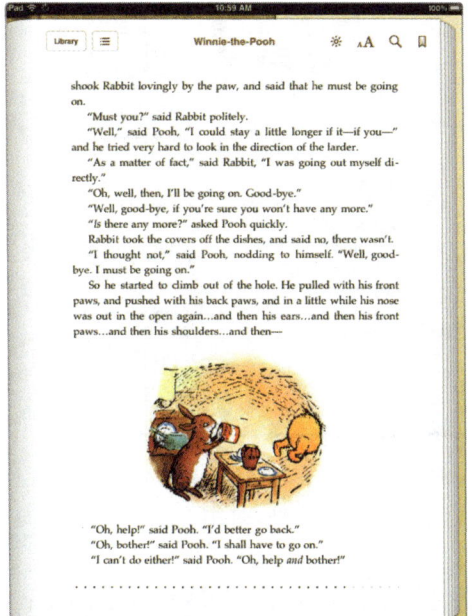

FIGURE 19-2: *Viewing an ebook in portrait and landscape modes.*

Turning the Pages of an Ebook

In addition to simply paging through your ebook, you can also jump to a new page by using bookmarks or the table of contents.

Turning One Page at a Time

While reading an ebook, you'll spend most of your time turning pages one at a time. If you want to turn to the next page, place your finger on the right margin and swipe your finger to the left. If you want to see the previous page, place your finger on the left margin and swipe your finger to the right. Either swiping motion curls the page as if you were turning a real book page, as shown in Figure 19-3.

You can also just tap the right margin (to view the next page) or the left margin (to view the previous page).

To turn pages when viewing a PDF file, just swipe your finger to the left (to view the next page) or to the right (to view the previous page).

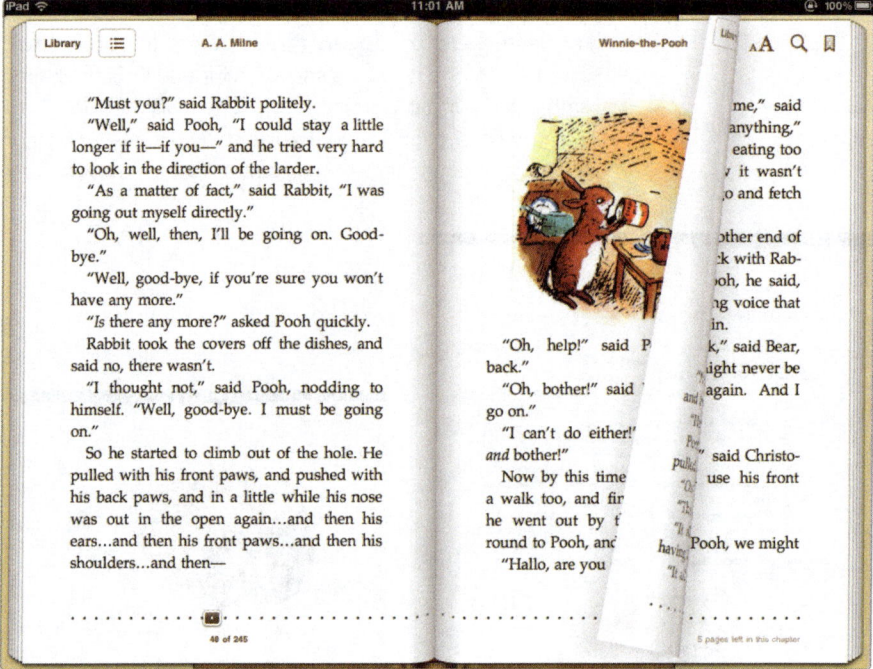

FIGURE 19-3: *Swiping to turn a page animates the page to curl back.*

Jumping to Specific Chapters

To jump to a particular chapter, you'll need to view the table of contents and then tap the chapter you want to read. (These steps do not work when displaying PDF files.) To jump to a specific chapter in an ebook, follow these steps:

1. While you're reading a book in iBooks, a Table of Contents icon appears in the upper-left corner of the screen, as shown in Figure 19-4.

FIGURE 19-4: *Most controls for the iBooks app are at the top of the page.*

2. Tap the **Table of Contents** icon. The Table of Contents page appears, as shown in Figure 19-5.
3. Tap the chapter or section that you want to view.

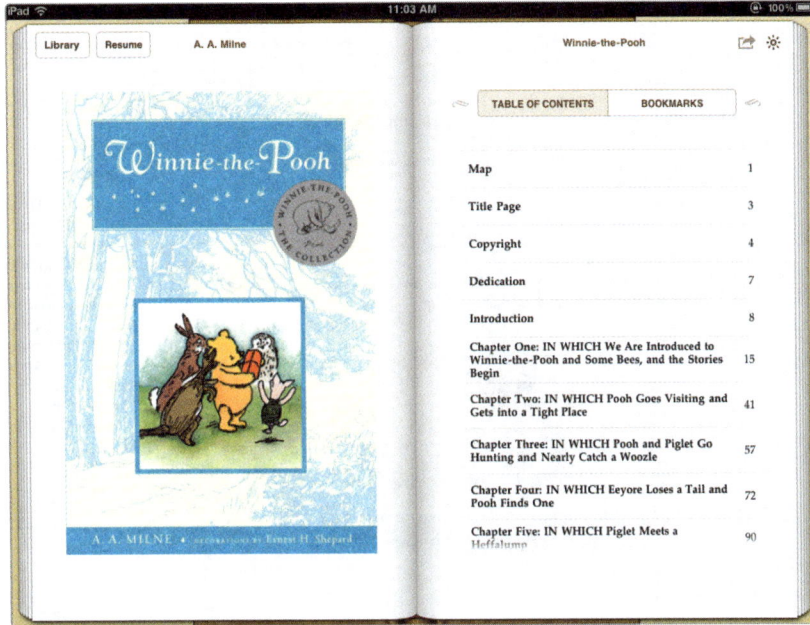

FIGURE 19-5: *Tap a chapter title in the table of contents, and you'll go to the first page of that chapter.*

Jumping to Any Page in an Ebook

Rather than turn pages one at a time or jump to specific chapters or sections in an ebook, you might just want to jump to a certain page in your ebook. To jump to any page in an ebook, follow these steps:

1. While reading an ebook in iBooks, flip through several pages, and tap a page.
2. Notice that the bottom of the screen displays the current page number, the total number of pages in the ebook, and how many pages are left in that particular chapter. In addition, a line of dots appears at the bottom of the screen, which represents the pages of the ebook. A current page icon (it looks like a brown square over one of the dots) can show you the relative position of the currently displayed page compared to the total number of pages in the ebook, as shown in Figure 19-6.
3. Place your finger over the current page icon and slide it left or right over the row of dots. As you slide the current page icon, a pop-up appears, telling you the current chapter (or section) and page number.
4. Lift your finger off the screen to view a page. Your chosen page now appears.

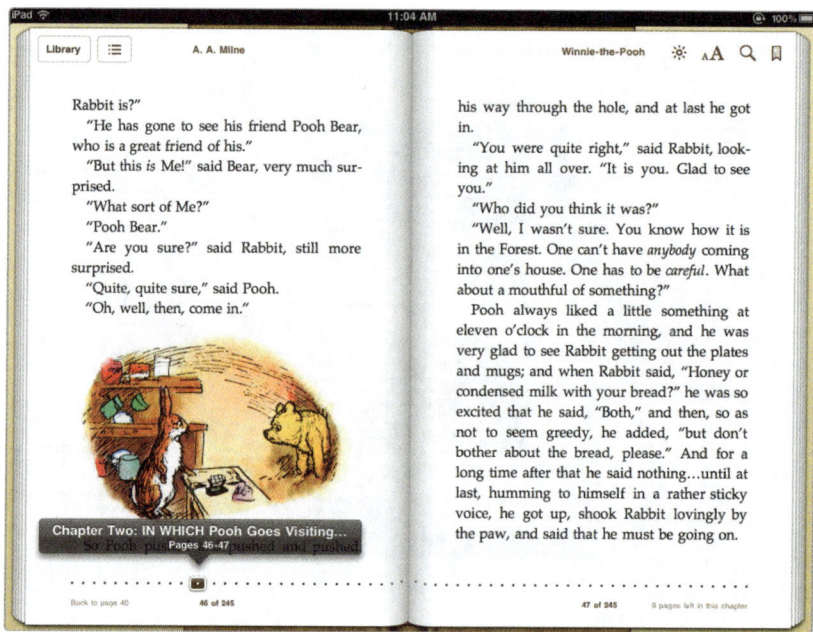

FIGURE 19-6: *The bottom of the screen lets you select a specific page.*

✳ **NOTE:** Ebooks in the iBooks app don't have set page numbers like a physical book. A book's pagination depends on the font choices and the orientation of your iPad (portrait or landscape).

Jumping to Any Page in a PDF File

When you're reading a PDF file, you can jump to another page by following these steps:

1. While reading a PDF file in iBooks, tap the page. Controls appear at the top and bottom of the page, as shown in Figure 19-7.
2. (Optional) Tap a thumbnail of a page at the bottom of the screen. Your chosen page appears.
3. (Optional) Tap the **Display Thumbnails** icon in the upper-left corner of the screen. Multiple pages appear in rows and columns on the screen, as shown in Figure 19-8. Tap the page you want to view, and that page appears on the screen.

Display Thumbnails   Action   Brightness   Search   Bookmarks

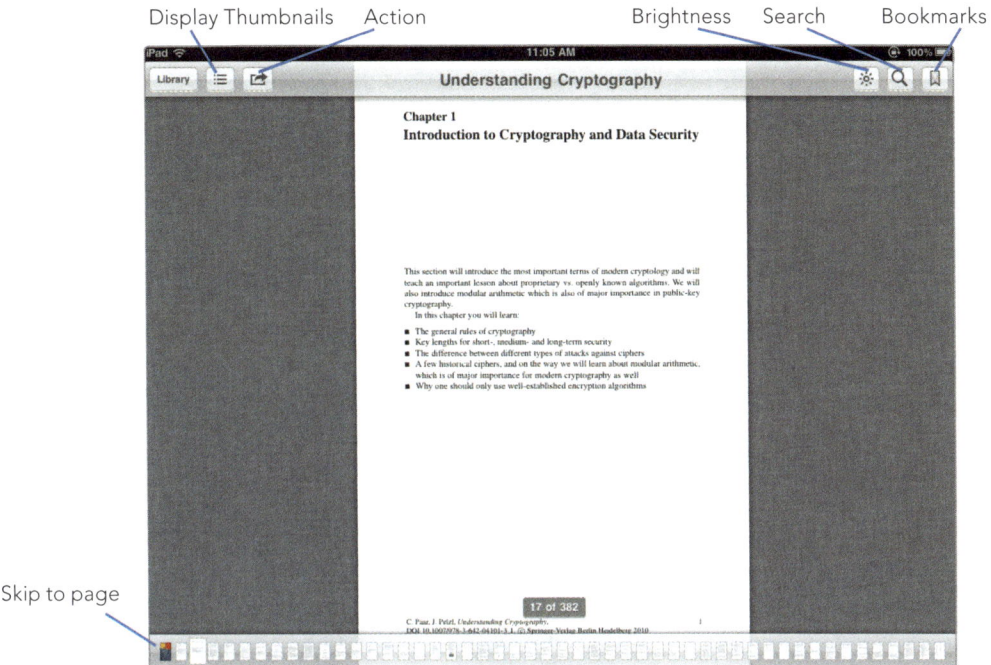

FIGURE 19-7: *Tapping the screen displays controls at the top and bottom of the screen.*

Skip to page

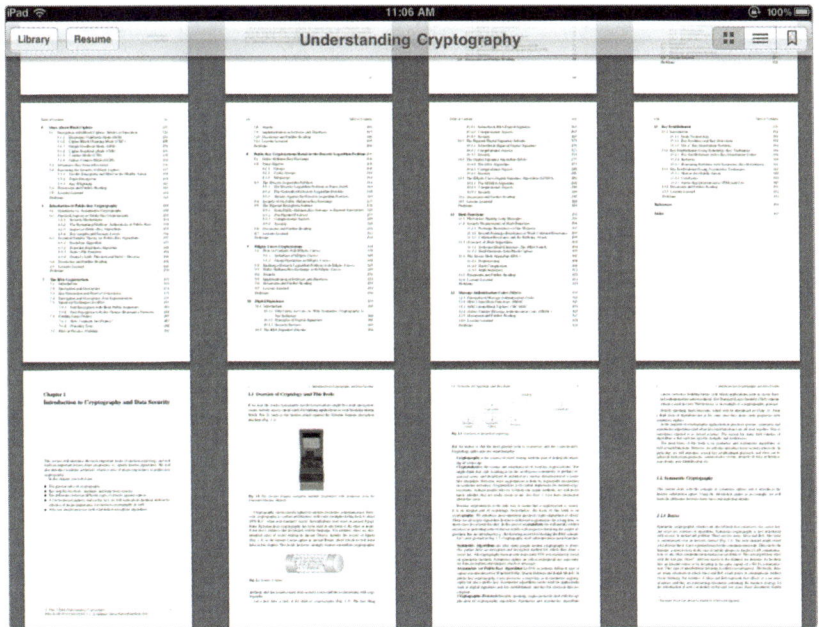

FIGURE 19-8: *Thumbnail images let you scroll through all the pages of a PDF file.*

Searching for Text

One huge advantage that ebooks have over paper books is the ability to search for specific text within the book.

To search for text in an ebook or PDF file, follow these steps:

1. From the Home screen, tap **iBooks**. The iBooks screen appears (shown earlier in Figure 19-1).
2. Tap the image of the book you want to read. Your chosen ebook opens.
3. Tap the **Search** icon (it looks like a magnifying glass that appears in the upper-right corner of the screen). A Search field appears along with a virtual keyboard.
4. Type the word or phrase you want to find, and tap the **Search** key on the virtual keyboard. A listing of where that text appears in the book is displayed, as shown in Figure 19-9. Scroll down to see more instances of your search term.

FIGURE 19-9: *A list appears, showing pages that contain the word or phrase you typed. Note that you can also search for your word on Wikipedia or the Web at large using Google—tapping either button will launch Safari.*

5. Scroll through this list, and tap the page that you want to view. Your chosen page appears with your word or phrase highlighted, as shown in Figure 19-10.

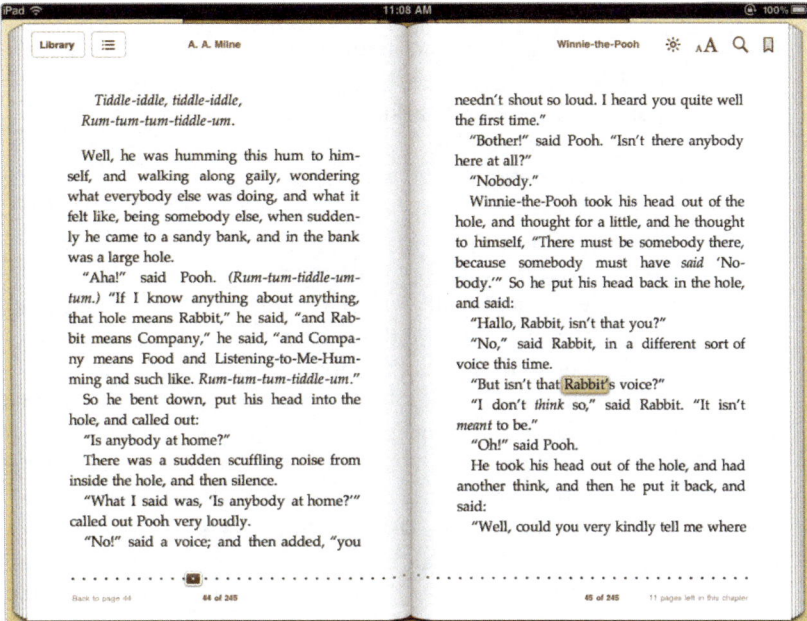

FIGURE 19-10: *Matching text appears highlighted on the page.*

Using Bookmarks

With a paper book, it's easy to stuff multiple bookmarks in various places in a book so you can find certain pages again. With an ebook, you can't stuff a piece of paper in between its pages, but you can place multiple bookmarks.

Creating a Bookmark

To create a bookmark, follow these steps:

1. While reading an ebook in iBooks, open to a page that you want to bookmark.
2. Tap the **Bookmark** icon in the upper-right corner of the screen. The Bookmark icon changes to red to show that you have placed a bookmark.

Jumping to and Deleting a Bookmark

After you have created one or more bookmarks, you can view and jump to them at any time or remove the bookmark altogether. To use and remove your bookmarks, follow these steps:

1. While using iBooks, tap the image of the book that you want to read that contains a bookmarked page. (If you want to find a bookmark in a PDF file, skip to step 5.)

2. For an ebook stored under the Books category, tap the **Table of Contents** icon that appears in the upper-left corner of the screen. The table of contents of your ebook appears.

3. Tap the **Bookmarks** button that appears at the top of your Table of Contents page. A list of bookmarked pages appears, as shown in Figure 19-11.

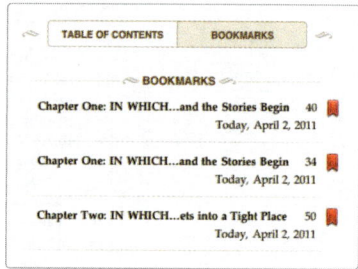

4. Tap the bookmarked page that you want to view. (If you tap the red Resume button in the top-right corner of the Table of Contents page, you can jump to the last page you viewed.) Your chosen bookmarked page appears.

FIGURE 19-11: *The table of contents can also list all your bookmarked pages.*

5. (Optional) To view bookmarks in a PDF file, tap the **Display Thumbnails** icon in the upper-left corner of the screen. All the pages of your PDF file appear in rows and columns. Scroll up or down, and then tap on the page that contains a red bookmark in the upper-right corner of the page, as shown in Figure 19-12.

6. (Optional) To delete a bookmark, jump to that bookmarked page, and then tap the red Bookmark icon in the upper-right corner of the page. When the Bookmark icon no longer displays red, then your bookmark no longer exists.

Red bookmark image

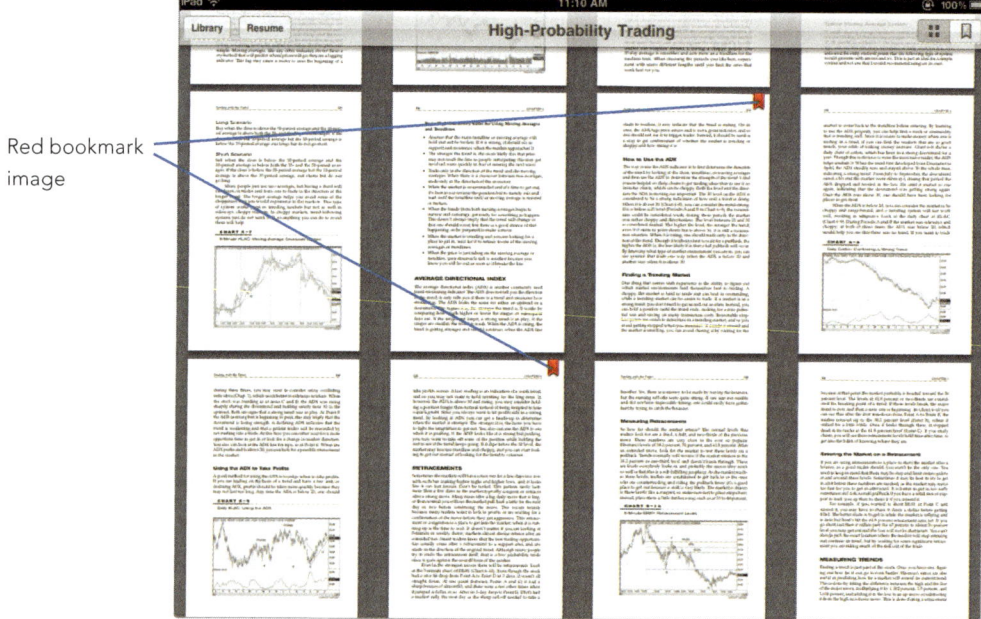

FIGURE 19-12: *You can identify bookmarked pages in a PDF by the red bookmark image that appears in the upper-right corner of the page.*

Making Ebooks Easier to Read

If you find that the text is hard to read with a paper book, you either have to buy a magnifying glass, get a special large-print version of the book, or just do nothing and suffer. Fortunately with ebooks, you can modify the text to make it more readable by adjusting the font, font size, and screen brightness.

✳ **NOTE: You cannot change the font or font size of a PDF file, but you can change the brightness of the screen.**

To see how to change the font, font size, and screen brightness of an ebook, follow these steps:

1. From the Home screen, tap **iBooks**. The iBooks screen appears (shown earlier in Figure 19-1).
2. Tap the image of the book you want to read.
3. Flip to any page in the ebook. In the upper-right corner of the screen, the Brightness and Font icons appear, as shown earlier in Figure 19-4. (If you do not see these icons, tap the screen until they appear.)
4. Tap the **Brightness** icon. A Brightness slider appears, as shown in Figure 19-13.
5. Slide the Brightness slider left and right to change the brightness of the screen.
6. Tap the **Font** icon. A Fonts menu appears, as shown in Figure 19-14.
7. Tap the **Shrink** icon (it looks like a small *A*) or **Enlarge** icon (it looks like a big *A*). Each time you tap the Shrink or Enlarge icon, the text in your ebook changes size.
8. Tap the **Fonts** button icon. A list of fonts appears, as shown in Figure 19-15.
9. Tap a different font such as **Cochin** or **Verdana**. Your entire ebook text changes to your chosen font.
10. Tap anywhere on the page to make the Font menu disappear.

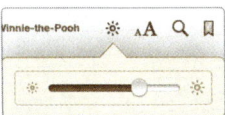

FIGURE 19-13: *The Brightness slider*

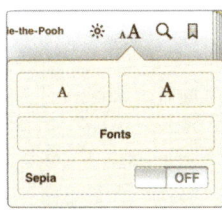

FIGURE 19-14: *The Fonts menu*

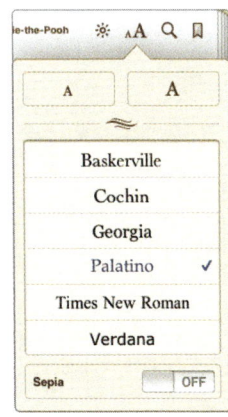

FIGURE 19-15: *The list of fonts*

Additional Ideas for Reading Ebooks

There's a saying that goes, "Leaders are readers." With iBooks, you can easily carry and read all types of books to help you become a better person, whether you want to read for work, pleasure, or education.

If you purchased Amazon's Kindle or Barnes & Noble's NOOK and bought Kindle or NOOK ebooks, download the free Kindle or NOOK app for your iPad, and you can transfer and read all your Kindle or NOOK ebooks on your iPad. Now your investment in all those ebooks won't be a waste of money when you wind up carrying your iPad everywhere and leaving your old reader to collect dust in a closet.

If you also read ebooks on your iPhone or computer, you can sync your iBooks across devices. Just click Sync when prompted by iBooks, as shown in Figure 19-16. To change your ebook synchronization options, tap the Settings icon from the Home screen and tap iBooks (under the Apps category on the left-hand side) to view your iBooks synchronization options.

FIGURE 19-16: *Apple will sync your iBooks and bookmarks between devices.*

As ebooks grow in popularity, you can expect to find more choices covering a wide variety of topics, so you should never run out of reading material, unless your iPad runs out of battery power first.

20

Photos, Videos, and FaceTime

The latest version of the iPad includes a front- and back-facing camera for capturing still or video images and videoconferencing with your friends and family. Apple calls their videoconferencing system FaceTime, and you'll be able to video chat with anyone who has a new iPad, iPhone, iPod touch, or even just a Mac with a webcam. If you capture stills or videos, you can transfer them to your computer to edit them, or use apps like Photoshop Express (photos) or iMovie (videos) to edit them directly on your iPad. As long as you have your iPad with you, you can capture pictures wherever you go.

What You'll Be Using

To learn how to take photos and video with your iPad, you need to use the following:

 The Photo Booth app   The Settings screen

 The Camera app   The FaceTime app

Taking Pictures

Your iPad comes with an app called Camera, which lets you take still or video images using the front- or back-facing camera. To see how to take pictures, follow these steps:

1. From the Home screen, tap **Camera**. The Camera screen appears, as shown in Figure 20-1.

Choose front- or back-facing camera

Still/Video

Record

Photos

FIGURE 20-1: *The Camera screen*

2. Tap the **Camera** button in the upper-right corner of the screen. Tapping this button switches between the front- and back-facing cameras.
3. Slide the **Still/Video** slider in the lower-right corner of the screen. When the slider appears to the left, the iPad's cameras capture still images. When the slider appears to the right, the iPad's cameras capture video.

4. Tap the **Record** button in the bottom middle of the screen to capture a still image or start recording a video. (You will need to tap the Record button a second time to stop recording video.)

5. Tap the **Photos** button in the lower-left corner of the screen to view your captured still or video images. (This is equivalent to tapping the Photos icon on the Home screen.) Tap the **Done** button in the Photos app when you want to return back to the Camera app.

* **NOTE:** Your iPad's camera is not very high resolution, so if you plan to print your photos, you may want to use a different camera for special occasions. The iPad's camera is best suited for taking videos.

Using Photo Booth

Your iPad comes with an app called Photo Booth, which mimics those coin-operated photography machines at amusement parks and shopping malls. With Photo Booth, you can take a regular picture or a distorted image using either the front- or back-facing camera.

To see how to capture bizarre images using Photo Booth, follow these steps:

1. From the Home screen, tap **Photo Booth**. The Photo Booth screen appears, displaying several different visual effects, as shown in Figure 20-2.

2. Tap a visual effect, such as Light Tunnel or Mirror. Your chosen visual effect appears, as shown in Figure 20-3.

3. Tap the **Camera** button in the lower-right corner of the screen. Tapping this button switches between the front- and back-facing cameras.

4. Tap the **Record** button in the middle bottom of the screen to capture a still image.

5. Tap the **Effects** button in the lower-left corner of the screen to view different visual effects (see Figure 20-2).

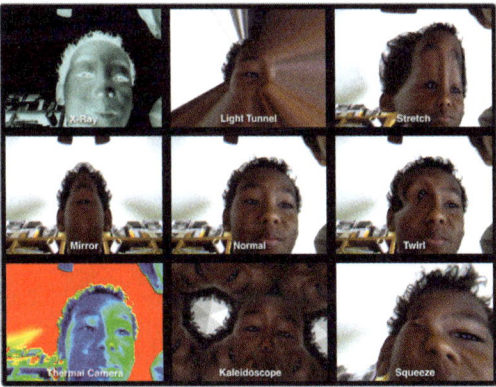

FIGURE 20-2: Photo Booth displays different visual effects you can use.

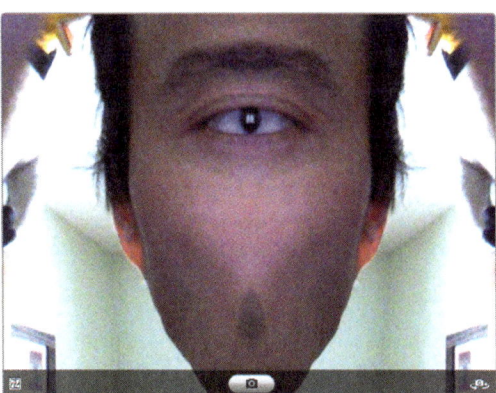

FIGURE 20-3: Photo Booth lets you turn ordinary images into bizarre creations.

Setting Up FaceTime

Perhaps one of the more practical uses for the iPad's cameras is to chat with someone through a videoconference using FaceTime. To use FaceTime, both you and the other person need an iPad, iPhone, iPod touch, or a Mac with a webcam, and Wi-Fi access.

To call someone who has an iPhone, you simply need that person's iPhone number. To call someone who has an iPad, iPod touch, or Mac, you need to use that person's email address, which they have assigned as their FaceTime ID.

Before you can make a FaceTime call, you must assign an email address to your iPad's FaceTime account. To define one or more email addresses, follow these steps:

1. From the Home screen, tap **Settings**. The Settings screen appears. (If you start FaceTime without setting up an account, you'll be prompted to enter an existing Apple ID.)
2. Tap **FaceTime**. The FaceTime screen appears, as shown in Figure 20-4.
3. If you already have an Apple ID and password, type that in the user name and password text fields. Otherwise tap the **Create New Account** button to display a dialog where you can define a user name, as shown in Figure 20-5.

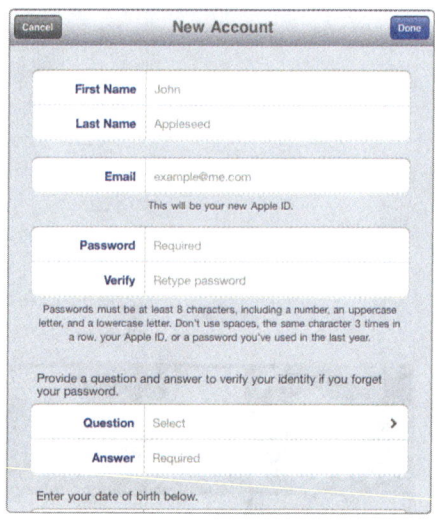

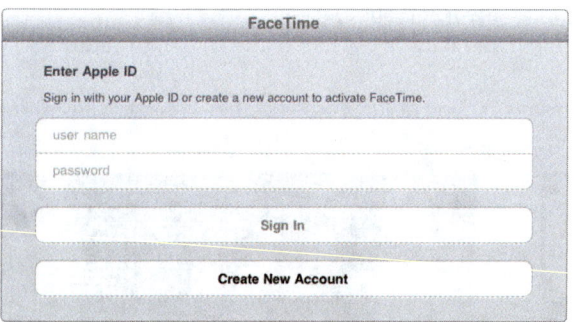

FIGURE 20-4: *Setting up a FaceTime account*

FIGURE 20-5: *Defining a FaceTime account*

4. Type your name, email address, password, and other information to create a FaceTime account. Then tap **Done**. Another screen appears where you can define an email address for your FaceTime account, as shown in Figure 20-6.

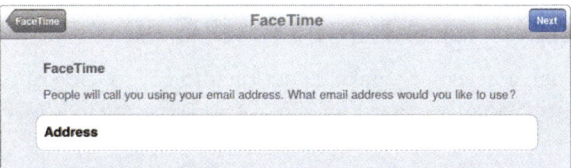

FIGURE 20-6: *Defining an email address for your FaceTime account*

5.   Type an email address that you want others to use when they contact you for a FaceTime chat. Tap **Next** to display the FaceTime screen again, as shown in Figure 20-7.

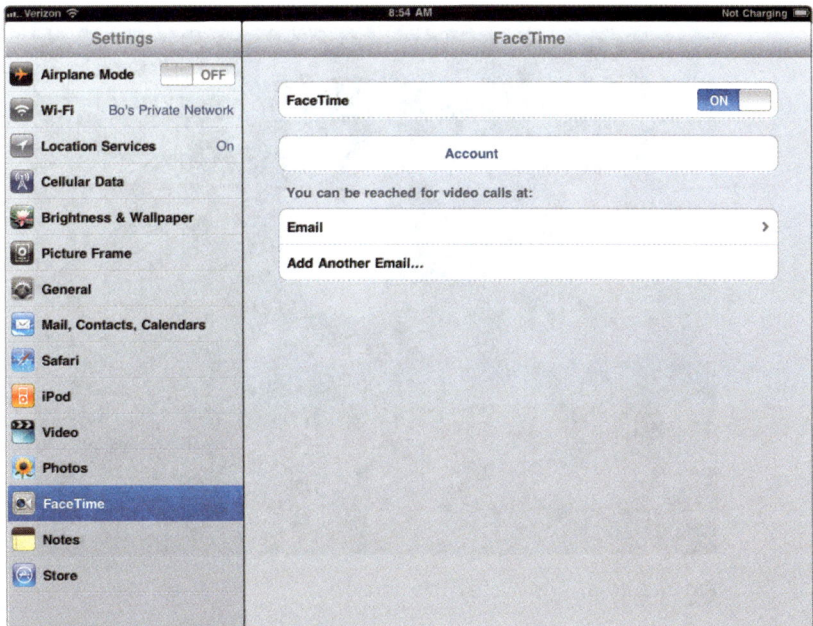

FIGURE 20-7: *The FaceTime screen lets you control your FaceTime account.*

6.   (Optional) Tap the FaceTime on/off switch to turn FaceTime on or off, or tap the **Add Another Email** button if you want to associate your FaceTime account with two or more email addresses. At this point, anyone else can contact you through FaceTime by using the email address you assigned to your FaceTime account.

* **NOTE:** To set up FaceTime on your Mac, install the FaceTime app through the Mac App Store.

Making a FaceTime Call

When you want to make a FaceTime to call to someone else who uses a Macintosh, iPad, iPhone, or iPod touch, make sure you are in a Wi-Fi hotspot and then follow these steps:

1. From the Home screen, tap the **FaceTime** icon. The FaceTime screen appears, using the front-facing camera so you can see how you will look to others, as shown in Figure 20-8.
2. (Optional) If you have already used FaceTime on your iPad, you can tap the Favorites or Recents icons in the bottom-right corner of the screen to connect with someone you chatted with before.
3. Tap the plus sign in the upper-right corner of the screen to define a new FaceTime contact. A New Contact window appears, as shown in Figure 20-9.

FIGURE 20-8: *The FaceTime screen*

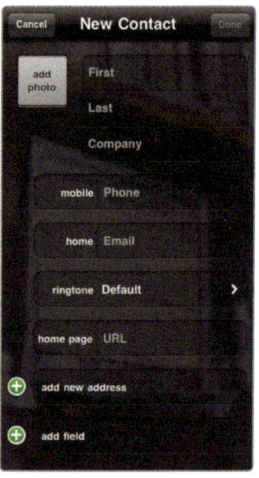

FIGURE 20-9: *The New Contact window*

4. Type a name and an iPhone phone number or email address associated with someone else's FaceTime account and tap the **Done** button. Your saved name and FaceTime contact information appears.
5. Tap the iPhone number or email address to start a FaceTime videoconference. Your face appears as a thumbnail image in the corner of the screen while the other person's face fills the screen, as shown in Figure 20-10.
6. (Optional) Tap the **Mute** or **Switch Camera** icons to shut off the volume or switch the view of your iPad from the front-facing to the back-facing camera.
7. Tap the **End** button when you want to stop your FaceTime videoconference.

FIGURE 20-10: *The FaceTime screen lets you chat through video.*

Additional Ideas for Using the iPad's Cameras

If you're in a meeting or class, you can turn on the iPad's camera to record notes jotted down on a chalkboard or whiteboard, or take pictures or video of a slide-show presentation.

If you like using videoconferencing but need to reach people who don't have FaceTime, then you can use Skype instead. Skype works nearly the same as FaceTime, allowing you to make audio or video conferences with almost anyone. Best of all, Skype can run on a Windows or Linux PC, which you can't call through FaceTime.

Finally, don't forget that while the iPad's cameras may not offer the sharpest resolution, they're still available anywhere you take your iPad. If you get in a car accident, use your iPad to take pictures of the accident scene. If everyone takes their iPad with them everywhere they go, maybe one day we'll finally get a decent picture of a UFO or Bigfoot that isn't blurry or out of focus.

21 Viewing, Using, and Sharing Photographs

If you own a digital camera (or a mobile phone with a digital camera), you probably already have dozens of digital photographs scattered all over your computer.

To get photographs into your iPad, you'll need to synchronize them using iTunes (see Chapter 15) or buy Apple's optional camera connection kit, which lets you plug a digital camera into an iPad through a USB port or through a Secure Digital (SD) card. No matter how you get your pictures into your iPad (or even if you just take photos with the iPad itself), you'll be able to view and use them in different ways.

Remember, you aren't just limited to storing digital photographs in your iPad. You can store any type of graphic image that's in the JPEG, TIF, PNG, or GIF file format. That means you can store artwork that someone has created using a program, such as Photoshop or Corel Painter or engineering drawings created by a computer-aided design (CAD) program.

In this chapter you will learn how to view pictures (digital photographs, graphic images, and so on) on your iPad.

What You'll Be Using

To view and share pictures on your iPad, you need to use the following:

 The Photos app   The Settings screen

Viewing Pictures

The Photos app provides several ways to view your pictures:

▶ **Photos**   Lists every picture individually for you to choose

▶ **Albums**   Groups pictures into categories

▶ **Events**   Groups pictures based on the date they were captured

▶ **Faces**   Organizes pictures based on the people in them

▶ **Places**   Organizes pictures based on where they were taken

✳ *NOTE:* **To take advantage of the Faces feature covered in this chapter, you'll need to use iPhoto or Aperture (on a Macintosh) to tag pictures with each person's face. If you're using a Windows computer, you won't be able to use the Faces feature. No matter what type of computer you use, you'll be able to use the other features because most digital cameras capture the date a picture was taken and some of the newest ones can even identify the location where a picture was taken.**

To see all the different ways of viewing your pictures, make sure you have loaded some pictures into your iPad, and then follow these steps:

1.   From the Home screen, tap **Photos**. The Photos screen appears.
2.   Tap the **Photos** tab at the top of the screen. Thumbnail images of all your pictures appear, as shown in Figure 21-1.
3.   Tap any picture. Your chosen picture expands to fill the screen.
4.   Tap the screen to display controls at the top and bottom of the screen, as shown in Figure 21-2. (After a few seconds, these controls automatically disappear.) Notice the thumbnail images of pictures that appear at the bottom of the screen.
5.   Tap the screen to display the controls, and tap **All Photos** in the upper-left corner of the screen to return to the Photos screen.

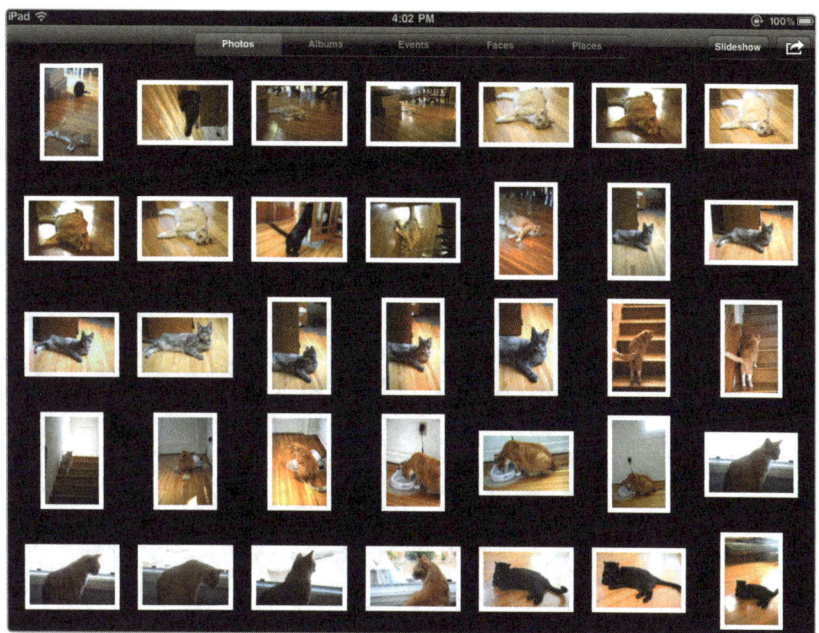

FIGURE 21-1: *The Photos tab displays all your stored pictures.*

FIGURE 21-2: *Tapping a picture displays controls at the top and bottom of the screen.*

6. Tap the **Albums** tab at the top of the screen. Thumbnail images of your photo albums appear.

7. Tap any thumbnail. All the pictures stored in your album appear on the screen. You may need to scroll up and down to see them all.

8. Tap **Albums** at the upper-left corner of the screen to return to the Photos screen.

9. Tap the **Events** tab at the top of the screen. Thumbnail images of all different dates appear, showing pictures stored on each date, as shown in Figure 21-3.

FIGURE 21-3: *The Events tab displays all pictures organized by the time they were captured.*

10. Tap any event. All the pictures stored in your album appear on the screen. You may need to scroll up and down to see them all.

11. Tap **Events** at the upper-left corner of the screen to return to the Photos screen.

12. Tap the **Faces** tab at the top of the screen. Thumbnail images of all your defined faces (using iPhoto or Aperture) appear.

13. Tap any face. All the pictures that contain that person's face appear on the screen. You may need to scroll up and down to see them all.

14. Tap **Faces** at the upper-left corner of the screen to return to the Photos screen.

15. Tap the **Places** tab at the top of the screen. A map with red pins appears, showing the locations where you captured pictures, as shown in Figure 21-4.

16. Tap a pin to view photos taken at that location.

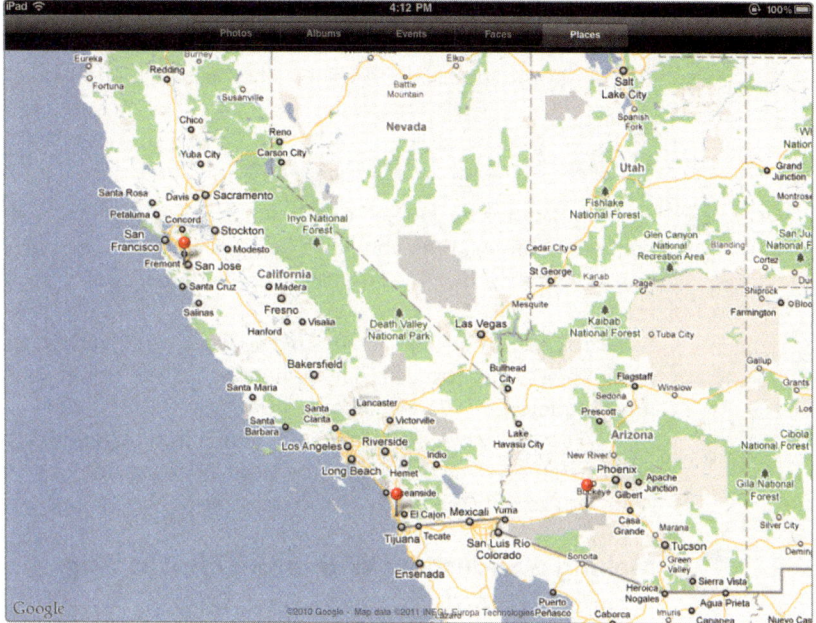

FIGURE 21-4: *The Places tab uses pins to show locations where you have taken pictures.*

Navigating Through Pictures

Being able to find and view all the different ways your iPad has organized your pictures is the first step to looking at them, but once you've chosen a particular way to find a picture (Photos, Albums, Events, Faces, or Places), you need to learn how to navigate your way through multiple pictures. To view your pictures, you can choose the following commands:

▶ **Tap** Selects a picture from a group of thumbnail images of multiple pictures

▶ **Swipe** Displays the next or previous picture in a group

▶ **Slide** Lets you scroll through multiple images quickly

To see how these three ways of navigating through groups of pictures work, follow these steps:

1. From the Home screen, tap **Photos**. The Photos screen appears.
2. Tap the **Photos** tab at the top of the screen. Thumbnail images of all your pictures appear (shown earlier in Figure 21-1).
3. Tap a picture to view it. Your chosen picture appears on the screen.
4. Swipe your finger left or right to see the next or previous picture.
5. Tap the screen to make thumbnail images of all the pictures appear at the bottom of the screen, as shown earlier in Figure 21-2.

6. Tap and hold any thumbnail image and slide your finger left or right to quickly scroll through your pictures.

7. Lift your finger off the screen when you've found a picture you want to view.

Creating a Slideshow

Viewing pictures by yourself can be fun, but it may be more enjoyable to show your pictures to others. With your iPad, you can create a slideshow to display pictures one at a time, with various transitions between each picture or even background music.

You can create a slideshow in two ways. First, you can create a slideshow within the Photos app. This can be handy for showing off your latest vacation pictures or pictures of your child's birthday party.

A second way to create a slideshow is to turn your iPad into an electronic picture frame, which can display pictures when you're not using your iPad, such as when you've put your iPad in a recharging dock.

Making a Slideshow Within the Photos App

Creating a slideshow within the Photo app can be handy for impromptu presentations. To create a slideshow, follow these steps:

1. From the Home screen, tap **Photos**. The Photos screen appears.

2. Tap a tab at the top of the screen, such as **Photos** or **Albums**. If you choose the Photos tab, thumbnail images of all your pictures appear (shown earlier in Figure 21-1). Otherwise, different groups of your pictures appear, which you'll need to tap to display all the pictures stored inside.

3. Tap **Slideshow** in the upper-right corner of the screen. A Slideshow Options window appears, as shown in Figure 21-5.

4. (Optional) Tap the **Play Music** on/off switch. If you turned the switch to read *ON*, tap the **Music** button to choose from a list of the songs you have stored in the iPod app.

5. Tap **Transitions** and then tap a transition, such as **Cube** or **Ripple**.

6. Tap **Start Slideshow**. Your slideshow starts playing using all the pictures stored in the group you selected earlier. The slideshow automatically ends after it has displayed all of your pictures or when you tap the screen.

FIGURE 21-5: *The Slideshow Options window*

Turning Your iPad into an Electronic Picture Frame

Apple sells an optional recharging dock where you can prop up your iPad in a base that holds it upright. If you have this optional dock or if you just like the idea of propping your iPad up while it's plugged in, you can turn your iPad into an electronic picture frame and display pictures stored in the Photos app.

To turn your iPad into an electronic picture frame, follow these steps:

1. From the Home screen, tap **Settings**. The Settings screen appears.
2. Tap **Picture Frame**. The Picture Frame screen appears, as shown in Figure 21-6.

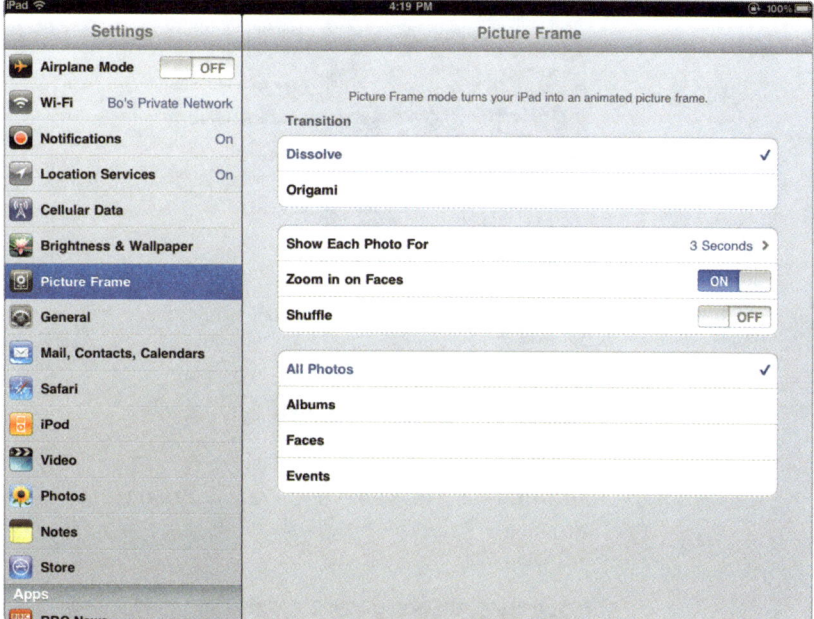

FIGURE 21-6: *The Picture Frame screen lets you define how to display pictures.*

3. Tap a transition in the Transition category, such as **Dissolve** or **Origami**.
4. Tap the **Zoom in on Faces** on/off switch.
5. Tap the **Shuffle** on/off switch.
6. Tap **All Photos**, **Albums**, **Faces**, or **Events**. If you choose Albums, Faces, or Events, an additional list of items appears at the bottom of the screen, as shown in Figure 21-7. (You may need to scroll down to see all the listed items.)
7. If you chose Albums, Faces, or Events in the previous step, tap one or more listed items to check (or uncheck) which groups of photos you want to display as part of your electronic picture frame.
8. Press the **Sleep/Wake** button at the top of your iPad to put it to sleep.
9. Press the **Sleep/Wake** button at the top of your iPad to wake it up. The Picture Frame icon appears at the bottom-right corner of the screen, as shown in Figure 21-8.
10. Tap the **Picture Frame** icon. Your picture frame settings now display a slideshow of your chosen pictures.

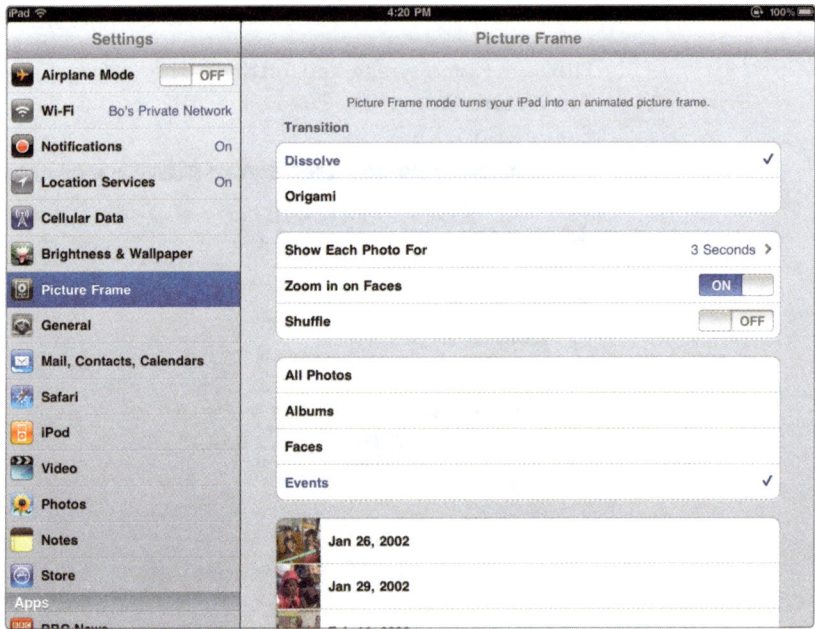

FIGURE 21-7: *You can selectively choose which groups of pictures to display.*

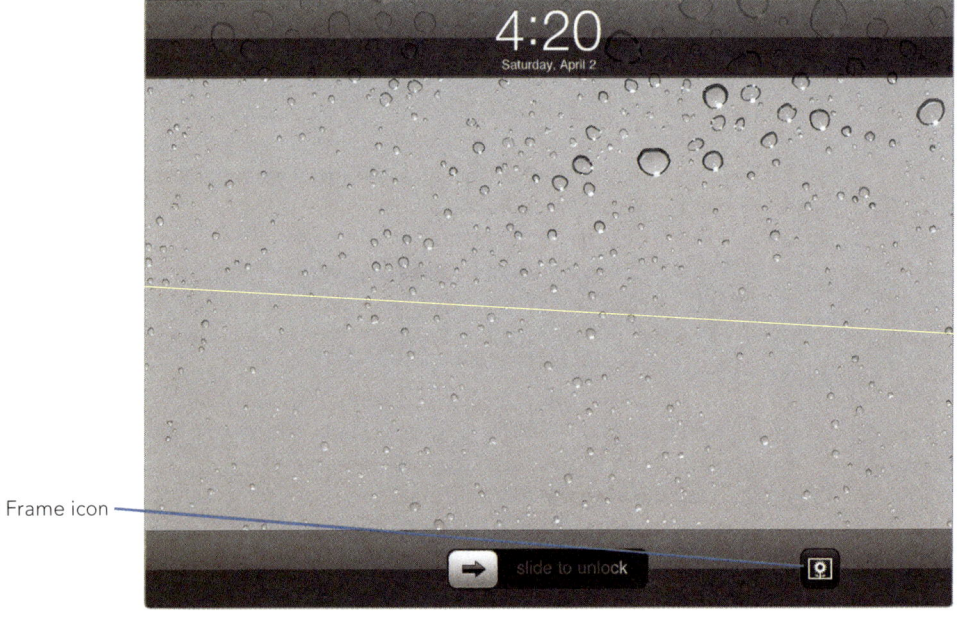

Picture Frame icon

FIGURE 21-8: *The Picture Frame icon lets you turn on (or off) your picture frame.*

11. Tap the screen to pause your picture frame slideshow. The slider and Picture Frame icon appear again.

12. Tap the **Picture Frame** icon again to turn off the picture frame slideshow.

Sending Pictures by Email

Before you can send a picture by email, you need to set up an email account and make sure your iPad has an Internet connection. After you have set up an email account, you can email single pictures or send a whole group of photos.

Sending a Single Picture by Email

To send a single picture by email, follow these steps:

1. From the Home screen, tap **Photos**. The Photos screen appears.

2. Tap one of the tabs at the top of the screen (**Photos**, **Albums**, **Events**, **Faces**, or **Places**). If you tap Photos, you'll see thumbnail images of all your pictures. If you choose any of the other options, you'll need to choose an album, event, face, or place to view thumbnail images of your pictures.

3. Tap a picture that you want to send. Your chosen picture fills the screen.

4. Tap the screen to display controls at the top and bottom of the screen. Then tap the **Send** icon that appears in the upper-right corner of the screen. A menu appears, as shown in Figure 21-9.

5. Tap **Email Photo**. An email message appears with the virtual keyboard at the bottom of the screen, as shown in Figure 21-10. Your chosen photo is included as an attachment.

6. Tap the **To** text field, and type an email address to receive your photo. (If you tap the plus sign icon to the far right of the To text field, a Contacts window appears, letting you choose a name of someone whose email address you have already stored in the Contacts app.)

FIGURE 21-9: *The Send icon displays a menu of different ways to share your picture.*

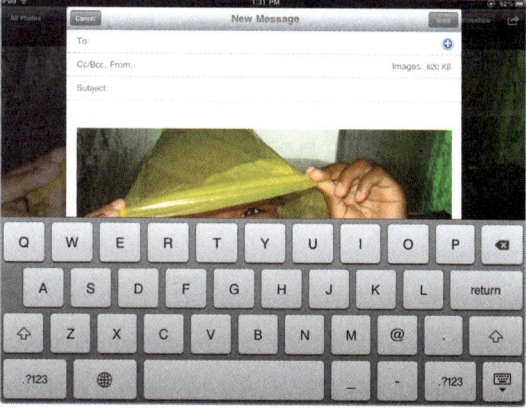

FIGURE 21-10: *A blank email message appears that includes your chosen photo as a file attachment.*

7. (Optional) Tap the **Subject** and **Message** text fields to type a subject and any text you want to send along with your photo.
8. Tap **Send** to send your email message with your chosen photo.

Sending Multiple Pictures by Email

If you want to send someone two or more pictures, it's easier to send a group of pictures as a file attachment by following these steps:

1. From the Home screen, tap **Photos**. The Photos screen appears.
2. Tap one of the tabs at the top of the screen (**Photos**, **Albums**, **Events**, **Faces**, or **Places**). If you tap Photos, you'll see thumbnail images of all your pictures. If you choose any of the other options, you'll need to choose an album, event, face, or place to view thumbnail images of your pictures.
3. Tap the **Send** icon in the upper-right corner of the screen. Email and Copy buttons appear in the upper-left corner of the screen. (If you tapped the Photos tab, you'll also see a red Delete button next to the Copy button.)
4. Tap one or more pictures that you want to send by email. Each time you select a picture, a check mark appears to let you know which pictures you've already selected, as shown in Figure 21-11.
5. Tap **Email** in the upper-left corner of the screen.

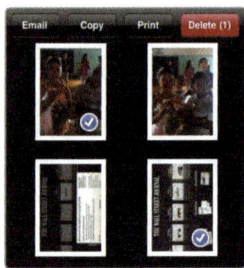

FIGURE 21-11: *A check mark identi-fies which pictures you have selected.*

* *NOTE:* **Instead of tapping the Email button, you can tap the Copy button to copy a picture, which you can later paste into another app, such as Pages or Keynote. You can also tap the Print but-ton to print your selected photos if you have a wireless printer that works with your iPad.**

6. An email message appears with the virtual keyboard at the bottom of the screen (shown earlier in Figure 21-10).
7. Tap the **To** text field, and type an email address to receive your photos. (If you tap the plus sign icon to the far right of the To text field, a Contacts win-dow appears, letting you choose the name of someone whose email address you have already stored in the Contacts app.)
8. (Optional) Tap the **Subject** and **Message** text fields to type a subject and any text you want to send along with your photos.
9. Tap **Send** to send your email message with your chosen photos.

Assigning a Picture to a Contact

When you start storing names and other personal information about people in the Contacts app, you might also want to store a picture of that person (or a picture that best represents that person) in the Contacts app.

To assign a picture to a name in the Contacts app, follow these steps:

1. From the Home screen, tap **Photos**. The Photos screen appears.
2. Tap one of the tabs at the top of the screen (**Photos**, **Albums**, **Events**, **Faces**, or **Places**). If you tap Photos, you'll see thumbnail images of all your pictures. If you choose any of the other options, you'll need to choose an album, event, face, or place to view thumbnail images of your pictures.
3. Tap a picture. Your chosen picture fills the screen.
4. Tap the screen to display the Send icon in the upper-right corner of the screen.
5. Tap the **Send** icon. A menu appears (shown earlier in Figure 21-9).
6. Tap **Assign to Contact**. The All Contacts window appears, as shown in Figure 21-12.
7. Tap a name. The Choose Photo window appears, as shown in Figure 21-13.
8. Move or resize your picture. When you're happy with the size and position of the picture, tap **Use**. Now if you open the Contacts app and choose this person's name, you'll see your chosen picture.

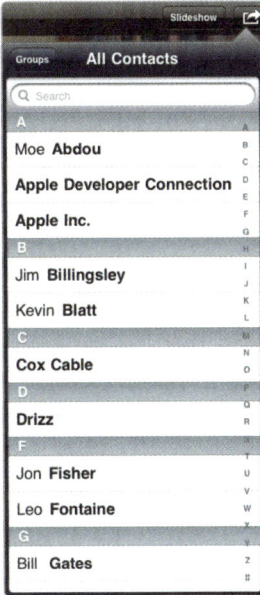

FIGURE 21-12: *An All Contacts window lets you assign your current picture to a name.*

FIGURE 21-13: *The Choose Photo window lets you adjust the position and size of your currently displayed picture.*

Viewing and Trimming Videos

You can also view the videos you take with the iPad's camera in the Photos app. Just select the video you want to see, press the big play button, and you can relive the magic. You can also trim the beginning or end of a long video. To trim a video you've just taken with your iPad, follow these steps:

1. From the Home screen, tap **Photos**. The Photos screen appears.
2. Tap the **Photos** tab at the top of the screen. Thumbnail images of all your pictures and videos appear.
3. Tap the video you want to trim. Your chosen video fills the screen.
4. Tap the screen once so that the controls are visible, as shown in Figure 21-14.

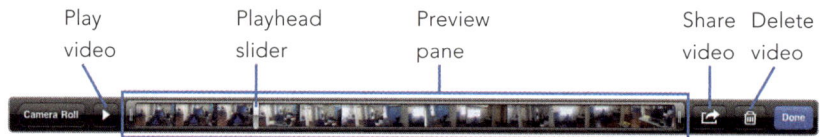

FIGURE 21-14: *The Video controls in the Photos app*

5. Tap the preview pane to enable the yellow trim box, and then drag the ends of the box to your desired start and end points, as shown in Figure 21-15.

FIGURE 21-15: *Press and hold either end of the preview pane for fine-grained control when trimming a video.*

6. Preview your new, slightly shorter video using the Play button. When you're satisfied, tap **Trim**.

Additional Ideas for Using Your Pictures

With so many different types of pictures that you can store on your iPad—from digital photographs to artwork created or modified with programs such as Photoshop or Corel Painter—you can use your iPad as a portable picture frame or a storage device before sending your pictures to others by email.

Taking, viewing, organizing, and sharing pictures may not be the only reason you got an iPad, but it's one of many ways you can make your iPad more useful.

PART 5

Organizing Yourself

22 Jotting Down Notes

Since ideas can be so fleeting and precious, it's important to capture them as quickly as possible. With your iPad, you can jot down ideas, notes, or entire letters and reports.

The iPad comes with a Notes app that mimics a yellow notepad so you can type ideas for an upcoming project, a daily to-do list, or a rough draft of a report you need to write later. Once you've written some notes on your iPad, you can email them to yourself (or someone else).

What You'll Be Using

To type and manage notes on your iPad, you need to use the following:

 The Notes app

Typing a Note

Depending on how you hold your iPad (portrait or landscape mode), the Notes app either displays a single yellow notepad (portrait mode) or a yellow notepad on the right with a list of all your notes displayed on the left (landscape mode), as shown in Figure 22-1.

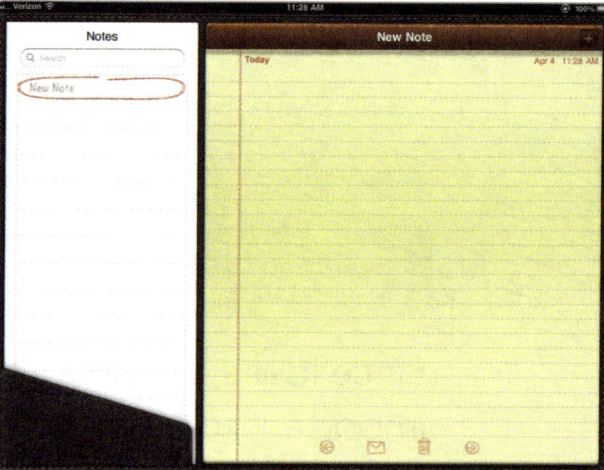

FIGURE 22-1: *The Notes app in portrait mode and landscape mode*

To type a note, follow these steps:

1. From the Home screen, tap **Notes**. If you haven't created any notes yet, you'll just see a blank yellow notepad screen.
2. Tap the position on the notepad where you want to place the cursor. A magnifying glass appears, letting you precisely place the cursor by sliding your finger on the screen. (If you haven't created any notes yet, just tap the notepad to place the cursor.) The virtual keyboard appears at the bottom of the screen.

3. Type some text. Notice that the first few words you type also appear in the Notes window, as shown in Figure 22-2. (If you are holding the iPad in portrait mode, you'll need to tap the **Notes** button in the upper-left corner to see the Notes window, as shown in Figure 22-3.) When you're done typing, you can tap the key in the bottom-right corner to hide the virtual keyboard.

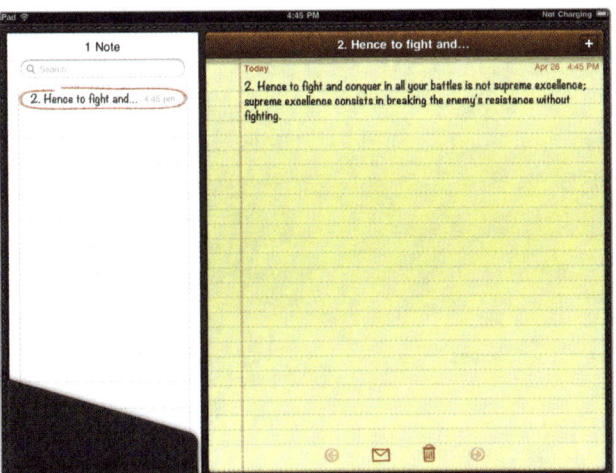

FIGURE 22-2: *The Notes window appears on the left side in landscape mode.*

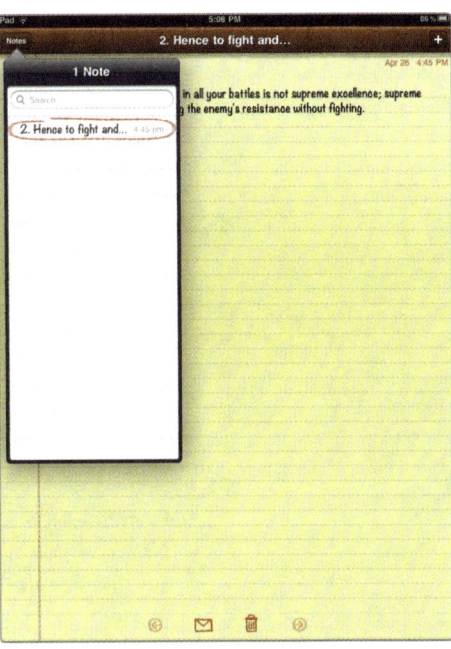

FIGURE 22-3: *The Notes window appears in portrait mode only when you tap the Notes button.*

✳ *NOTE:* **To make your notes easier to find, consider typing a short, descriptive heading as the first line of text in each note. This descriptive heading will appear in the Notes window to help you identify the contents of each note, as shown in Figure 22-4.**

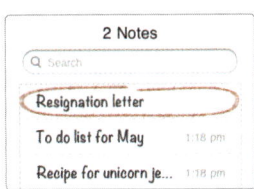

FIGURE 22-4: *Descriptive text makes the contents of each note easier to identify.*

Creating New Notes

The Notes app lets you store text on a single page, where each page represents another note.

To create new notes, follow these steps:

1. From the Home screen, tap **Notes**. The Notes screen appears.
2. Tap the plus sign that appears in the upper-right corner of the screen. A new blank page appears with the virtual keyboard at the bottom of the screen so you can start typing your new note.

Navigating Through Your Notes

Over time, you may wind up with dozens of notes. Since you may have created each note at different times, there won't be any logical order to the way your notes are organized. To find a note, you can scroll through notes one at a time, jump to a specific note using the Notes window, or search for text that appears in specific notes.

To see all three methods of searching notes, make sure you have created a handful of notes, and then follow these steps:

1. From the Home screen, tap **Notes**. The Notes screen appears.

2. Tab the **Previous** or **Next** arrow icons at the bottom of the note, as shown in Figure 22-5. (If an arrow is dimmed, that means you're viewing either the first or last note.) Another note appears with the animation of a real page flipping.

FIGURE 22-5: The bottom of each note displays Previous, Send, Trash, and Next icons.

3. Tap a note that appears in the Notes window. (If you're holding your iPad in portrait mode, you'll need to tap the Notes button in the upper-left corner of the screen to see the Notes window, as shown earlier in Figure 22-3.)
4. Tap the **Search** field at the top of the Notes window. The virtual keyboard appears at the bottom of the screen.
5. Type a word or phrase that you know appears in one of your notes. The Notes window lists only those notes that contain that word or phrase.
6. Tap **Clear** (it looks like an X inside a gray circle at the far right of the Search field) to display all your notes in the Notes window again.

Sending a Note by Email

After you've written a note, you may want to send it to yourself or to someone else. To transfer a note out of your iPad, you can email it by following these steps:

1. From the Home screen, tap **Notes**. The Notes screen appears.
2. Find a note that you want to send using any of the methods explained in the previous section.

3. Tap the **Send** icon (it looks like an envelope) at the bottom of the note. An email message and the virtual keyboard appear on the screen.
4. Tap the **To** text field, and type an email address. (If you tap the plus sign at the far right of the To text field, you can pick a name stored in your Contacts app.)
5. Tap the **Subject** text field, and type a subject for your message.
6. Tap the message text field where the text from your note appears, and type new text or modify the existing text.
7. Tap **Send**.

Deleting a Note

After you've created a few notes, you may find that you no longer need some of them. To delete a note, follow these steps:

1. From the Home screen, tap **Notes**. The Notes screen appears.
2. Find a note that you want to delete using any of the methods explained in "Navigating Through Your Notes" on page 184.
3. Tap the **Trash** icon at the bottom of the note. A red Delete Note button appears, as shown in Figure 22-6.

FIGURE 22-6: *Tapping the Trash icon displays a Delete Note button.*

✳ *WARNING:* **Make sure you really want to delete a note, because you can't retrieve it later.**

4. Tap **Delete Note** (or tap anywhere on the screen to make the Delete Note button disappear). If you tap the Delete Note button, your currently displayed note disappears.

Additional Ideas for Typing Notes

One of the simplest and most productive tools is to write down your goals for each day. Most people write their to-do list of goals on a piece of paper, but you can write them in the Notes app so you can constantly review them while you're using your iPad.

Another handy use for the Notes app is to write drafts of email messages. By using the Notes app, you can store your draft and modify it over time. When you're done writing, just email this note, and all your text automatically appears in the message text field of your email. As long as you have your iPad with you, you'll always have a way to jot down notes at any time, anywhere.

23 Keeping Contact Information

Since the iPad is so small and light, you'll probably wind up taking it with you almost everywhere you go. When you're travelling, you'll often need to look up someone's address, phone number, or email address. Storing all this information on your computer is a start, but synchronizing this information to your iPad gives you the ability to search your list of contacts wherever you happen to be. (If you've already stored contact information on your computer, such as in the Address Book program on a Macintosh or Microsoft Outlook on a Windows computer, you can transfer that data to your iPad as explained in Chapter 15.)

To store your valuable contact information on your iPad, you'll use the Contacts app. Besides storing text information, the Contacts app can also include a picture of each person so you'll remember what that person looks like. And if you want to email your friend or even find driving directions to his house or business, it's just a click away.

What You'll Be Using

To store and manage contact information on your iPad, you need to use the following:

 The Contacts app

Viewing Contact Information

The Contacts app mimics a paper address book. The left side of the screen displays your list of names, and the right side shows a single person's contact information, as shown in Figure 23-1.

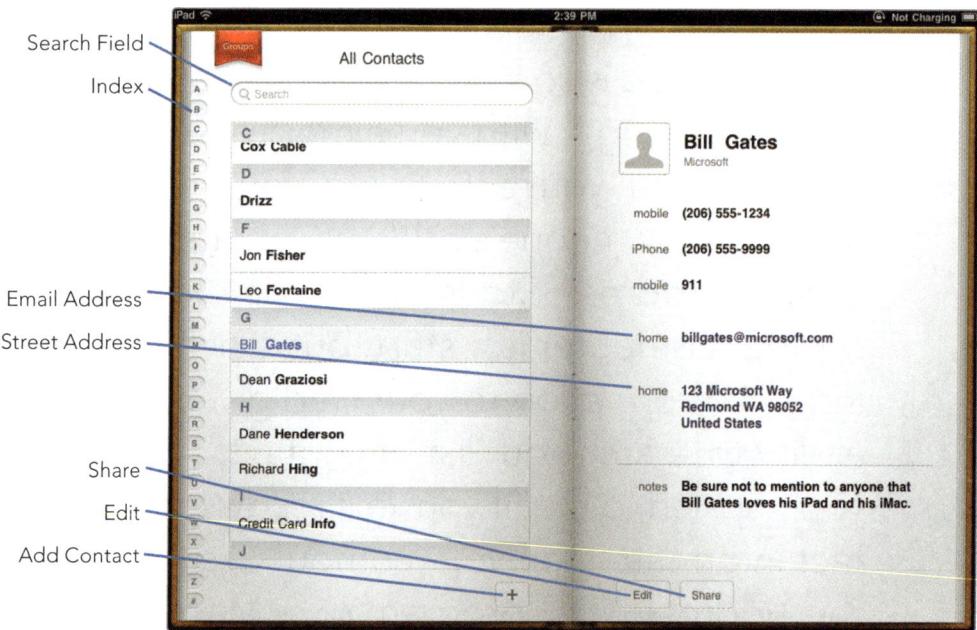

FIGURE 23-1: *The Contacts app mimics a paper address book.*

Besides displaying a list of names and more detailed information about a single person, the Contacts screen also displays various controls to help you find or do something with your contact information:

▶ **Index** Appears on the left side of the screen and lets you jump to any contact by last name.

- **Search field**   Lets you type part of a name to find it.
- **Email address**   Lets you tap a displayed email address to send a message.
- **Street address**   Lets you tap a displayed street address to see its location on the Maps app.
- **Edit button**   Lets you edit the currently displayed contact information.
- **Share button**   Lets you send the currently displayed contact information to someone by email.

To find a particular name stored in the Contacts app, you can scroll up and down your list of names. For a short list of names, this may be all you need, but if you have a long list of names, you can tap the index that appears along the left side of the screen. Just tap a letter, such as *D* or *T*, to find all last names that begin with *D* or *T*, respectively. You can even search your address book if you just know part of someone's name.

To view your contact information, follow these steps:

1. From the Home screen, tap **Contacts**. The Contacts screen appears, displaying the last name you viewed.
2. Scroll through your list of names on the left side of the screen. (You can flick your finger to scroll quickly or just slide your finger up or down slowly to scroll much slower.)
3. Tap a name. The information for your contact appears in the right side of the screen (shown in Figure 23-1).
4. Tap in the **Search** field. The virtual keyboard appears.
5. Type part of a name. As you type, a list of matching names appears.
6. Tap the name of the contact information you want to view.

✳ *NOTE:* **If you have organized your contacts into groups using the Address Book program on a Macintosh, you can view those groups by tapping the red Groups button (it looks like a red ribbon bookmark) that appears in the upper-left corner of the screen.**

Adding a New Contact

When you're travelling with your iPad, you may meet someone and want to store that person's information into the Contacts app. (Later you can synchronize this contact information with your computer as explained in Chapter 15.) To add a new contact, follow these steps:

1. From the Home screen, tap **Contacts**. The Contacts screen appears.
2. Tap the plus sign that appears in the middle of the screen (look in the bottom-right corner of the left page). The New Contact window appears along with the virtual keyboard at the bottom of the screen, as shown in Figure 23-2.

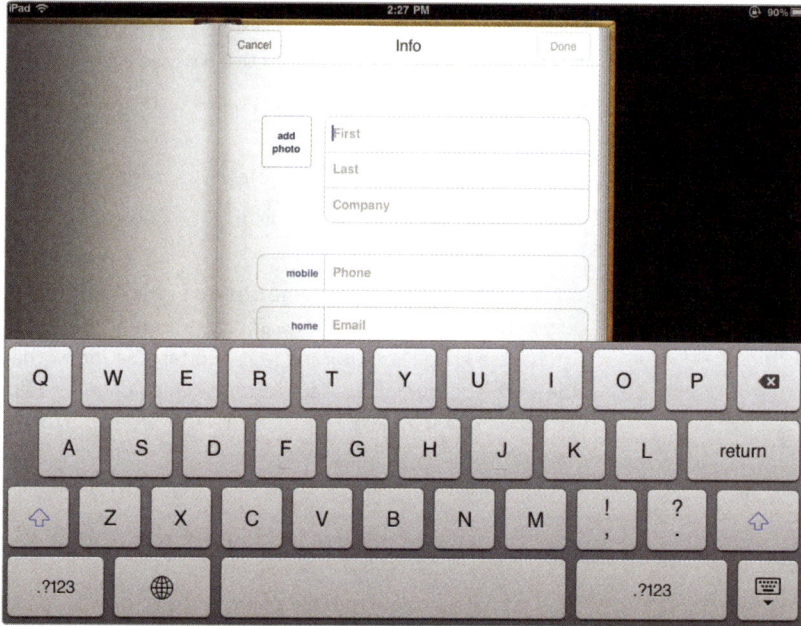

FIGURE 23-2: *The New Contact window*

3. Tap each text field where you want to add
    information (such as the First and Last text
    fields). You don't need to fill in every text
    field. For example, you might only want to
    store a person's name and email address
    but not a street address or home phone
    number.

4. (Optional) Tap the **add photo** box to
    choose a picture to represent a person.
    The Photo Albums window appears so
    you can choose a picture stored in the
    Photos app, as shown in Figure 23-3. Tap
    a picture you want to use.

5. Tap **Done** in the upper-right corner of the
    screen when you're finished typing infor-
    mation about a person.

FIGURE 23-3: *Tapping the
add photo box lets you
choose a picture stored in
one of your photo albums.*

Editing (or Deleting) a Contact

People often change phone numbers, switch email addresses, or move to different companies. To keep your contact list current, you can add, delete, or modify any information you want.

To edit contact information, follow these steps:

1. From the Home screen, tap **Contacts**. The Contacts screen appears.
2. Scroll through your list of names on the left side of the screen, and tap a name that you want to edit. The information for your chosen name appears on the right side of the screen (see Figure 23-1).
3. Tab **Edit** at the bottom middle of the screen.
4. (Optional) Tap any text field. The virtual keyboard appears to let you edit text in that text field.
5. (Optional) Tap the white dash inside a red circle that appears to the left of some fields. A red Delete button appears, as shown in Figure 23-4.

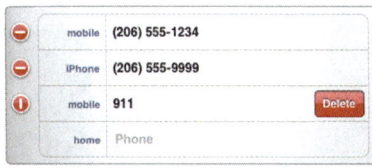

FIGURE 23-4: *Some fields display a white dash inside a red circle icon, which lets you delete that entire field.*

6. (Optional) Tap the white plus sign inside a green circle that appears to the left of a field, such as **add new address** or **add field**. Tapping the icon to the left of the add field box displays an Add Field list, as shown in Figure 23-5. Tap a field to add, such as **Nickname**, **Job Title**, or **Birthday**.
7. (Optional) If you'd like to delete a contact, tap the big red **Delete Contact** button. A dialog appears, asking if you really want to delete your contact. Tap **Delete** or **Cancel**.
8. Tap **Done** in the upper-right corner of the screen when you're done editing a contact.

* **NOTE:** When you edit contact information on your computer or iPad, you can synchronize those changes through iTunes as described in Chapter 15.

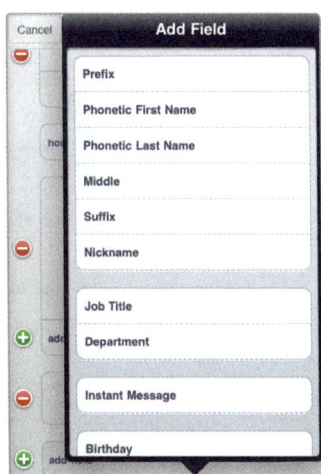

FIGURE 23-5: *You can add a new field to your contact information.*

Sending Contact Information by Email

Oftentimes you may have contact information about someone that you'd like to share with others. The simple way to do this is through email. Just pick the contact information you want to send, and your iPad attaches this contact information to an email message as a vCard (.vcf) file that practically every contact management program can import.

To email contact information, follow these steps:

1. From the Home screen, tap **Contacts**. The Contacts screen appears.
2. Find a contact that you want to send.
3. Tap **Share** at the bottom middle of the screen. An email message and the virtual keyboard appear on the screen with your contact information stored as a vCard file, as shown in Figure 23-6.

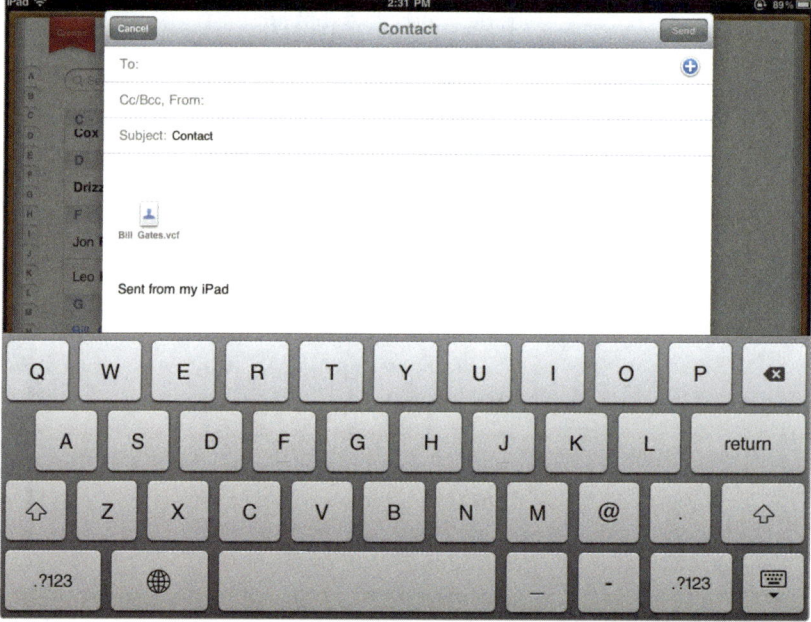

FIGURE 23-6: You can easily email contact information to others.

4. Tap the **To** text field, and type an email address. (If you tap the plus sign at the far right of the To text field, you can pick a name stored in your Contacts app.)
5. Tap the **Subject** text field, and type a subject for your message.
6. Tap the message text field where the contact information appears, and type new text or modify the existing text.
7. Tap **Send**.

Sending Email to a Contact

If you need to reach someone, you can find that person's name in the Contacts app and send an email to that person, if you've stored that person's email address.

To send email to someone from the Contacts app, follow these steps:

1. From the Home screen, tap **Contacts**. The Contacts screen appears.
2. Find a contact that you want to send an email to.
3. Tap on the person's displayed email address. An email message and the virtual keyboard appear on the screen with the recipient's email address already stored in the To field. Just type a message and subject and tap **Send**.

Getting Directions to a Contact

If you've stored someone's street address (either a home or work address) you might want to know the fastest route to that location. To get directions from your current location to a stored street address, follow these steps:

1. From the Home screen, tap **Contacts**. The Contacts screen appears.
2. Find a contact that you want to visit.
3. Tap on the person's displayed street address. The Maps screen appears and displays a red pin at the location of the street address.
4. Tap the **Directions** tab in the upper-left corner of the Maps screen. A blue direction bar appears at the bottom of the Maps screen.
5. Tap the **Car** (driving), **Bus** (mass transit), or **Man** (walking) icon and tap **Start** to see a list of directions from your current location to your destination.

* *NOTE:* You'll learn all about maps and driving directions in Chapter 25.

Additional Ideas for Using Contacts

The Contacts app is just a simple database, so feel free to store any kind of text information in it, whether it's information about your stamp collection or a list of celebrities you'd like to meet.

You can use the iPad to store emergency contact information, your software serial numbers, or just the hotel room numbers of your own room and those of your co-workers during your next business trip. Now when you need to reinstall a program or find the right room, just look in the Contacts app on your iPad.

24 Using the Calendar

By using the Calendar app on your iPad, you can organize your schedule and set appointments. To make sure you don't forget an appointment, you can set an alarm to alert you.

Since you may be tracking appointments on both your computer and your iPad, you may need to synchronize all your appointments as explained in Chapter 15. By doing this, you can make, edit, and delete appointments on either your computer or iPad and then synchronize this information with both devices.

If you're using Gmail and Google's online calendar service (or another online mail and calendar service, such as Yahoo!), you can sync your calendar when you set up your email account (see Chapter 13).

What You'll Be Using

To store and manage appointments on your iPad, you need to use the following:

 The Calendar app   The Settings screen

Understanding Calendar Views

The Calendar can display different views so you can focus on what you need to get done for a particular day or look at a long-range schedule to see what you might have coming up in the next week or month.

These are the four types of views you can see:

▶ **Day**   Displays a 24-hour timeline for all appointments for a single day

▶ **Week**   Displays a 24-hour timeline for all seven days of the week

▶ **Month**   Displays appointments (but not starting or duration times) for an entire month

▶ **List**   Lists all scheduled appointments regardless of starting date, time, or duration

To view the different ways the Calendar can display appointments, follow these steps:

1. From the Home screen, tap **Calendar**. The Calendar screen appears.
2. Tap the **Day** tab. The Day view displays a list of all your appointments for that day and a monthly calendar on the left side of the screen. On the right side of the screen, the Day view displays a timeline that shows you when each appointment is scheduled, as shown in Figure 24-1.
3. Tap any date displayed in the monthly calendar on the left side of the screen. The Day view displays your appointments for your chosen date.
4. Tap **Today** in the bottom-left corner of the screen. No matter what day you were viewing, the Today button immediately shows you your appointment list for the current day. (The Today button works in all the different views— Day, Week, Month, or List.)
5. Tap any date displayed at the bottom of the screen. In Day view, the bottom of the screen shows all the days of the month you're currently viewing, as well as buttons for the previous month and the following month.
6. Tap the **Week** tab. The Week view displays a list of all your appointments from Sunday through Saturday, as shown in Figure 24-1.
7. Tap any week displayed at the bottom of the screen. The Week view displays your appointments for your chosen week.
8. Tap the **Month** tab. The Month view displays a list of all your appointments for the entire month, as shown in Figure 24-1.
9. Tap any month displayed at the bottom of the screen. The Month view displays your appointments for your chosen month.

10. Tap the **List** tab. The List view displays all your appointments (regardless of when they're scheduled), as shown in Figure 24-1.

11. Tap any appointment on the left side of the screen. The right side of the screen displays the date for your chosen appointment.

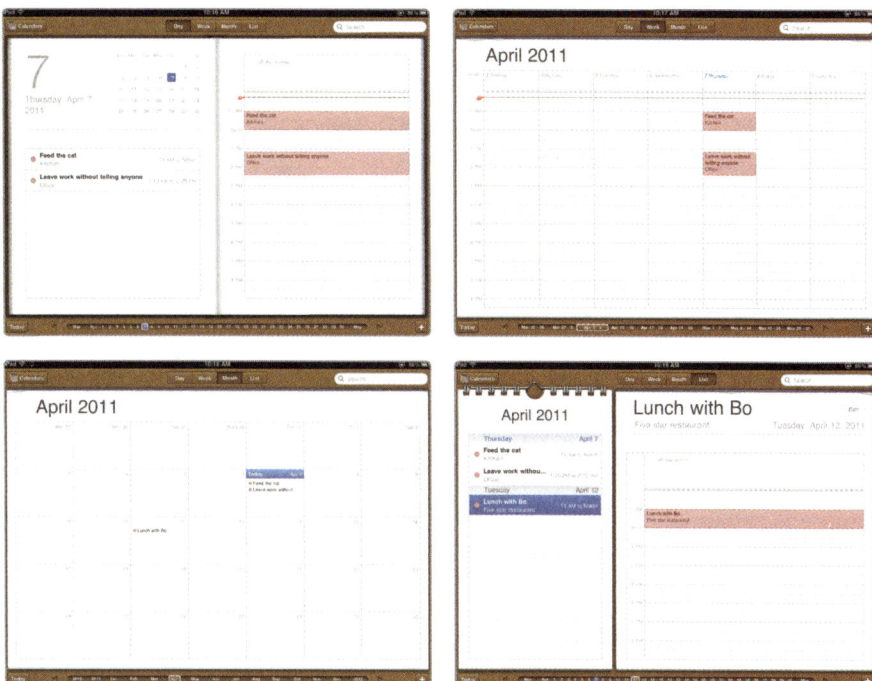

FIGURE 24-1: *The Day, Week, Month, and List views*

Setting an Appointment

When you want to set an appointment, you can define the following items:

▸ A description of the event

▸ A location

▸ Start time

▸ End time

▸ Whether to define the appointment as a repetitive event

▸ Whether to display and sound an alert before the appointment

▸ What calendar to put the appointment on (Home, On My iPad, or Work)

▸ Any additional notes about the appointment

You don't need to define all of these items. For example, you might skip defining the location of the appointment. In addition, the Calendar automatically uses default settings for every option except for the event description, location, and any additional notes you might want to add, so you can just focus on typing a description of your appointment, such as "Doctor's appointment" or "Secret meeting with Elvis Presley."

To create an appointment, follow these steps:

1. From the Home screen, tap **Calendar**. The Calendar screen appears.
2. Tap the plus sign that appears in the bottom-right corner of the screen. The Add Event window appears (see Figure 24-2) with the virtual keyboard.
3. Tap the **Title** text field, and type a description of your appointment.
4. (Optional) Tap the **Location** text field, and type a description of the location where your appointment will take place.
5. Tap the **Starts/Ends** field. The Start & End window appears, as shown in Figure 24-3.
6. Tap the **Starts** field, and then scroll through the date picker at the bottom of the Start & End window to choose a date and time.
7. Tap the **Ends** field, and then scroll through the date picker at the bottom of the Start & End window to choose a date and time.
8. (Optional) Tap the **All-day** on/off switch to read *ON* if you want to define an appointment to take an entire day.
9. Tap **Done** in the upper-right corner of the Start & End window.
10. (Optional) Tap the **Repeat** field. A Repeat Event window appears, as shown in Figure 24-4. Tap a time period, such as **Every Week** or **Every Month**, and then tap the **Done** button in the upper-right corner of the Repeat Event window.
11. (Optional) Tap the **Alert** field. The Event Alert window appears, as shown in Figure 24-5. Tap a time period, such as **5 minutes before** or **1 hour before**, and then tap **Done** in the upper-right corner of the Event Alert window.
12. (Optional) To add your event to another calendar service, tap the **Calendar** field. A Calendar window appears. Tap a calendar, such as your Google or Yahoo! calendar, and then tap **Done** in the upper-right corner of the Calendar window.

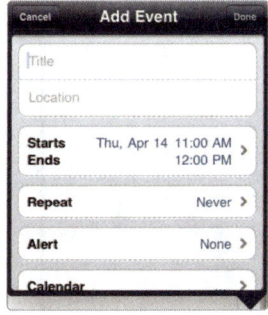

FIGURE 24-2: *The Add Event window lets you define the specifics of your appointment.*

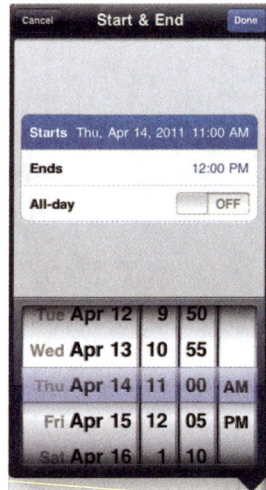

FIGURE 24-3: *The Start & End window lets you define the times of your appointment.*

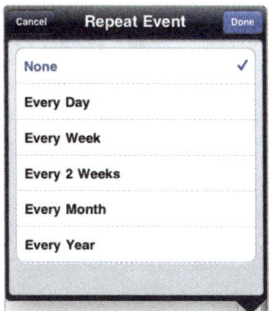

FIGURE 24-4: *The Repeat Event window lets you define a repetitive event.*

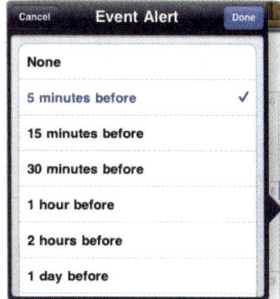

FIGURE 24-5: *The Event Alert window lets you define when an alert should sound.*

13. (Optional) Tap in the Notes text field, and type any additional description or notes you want to remember about this appointment, such as **Don't forget to bring birthday present** or **Remember, Mr. Grutchins is allergic to peanuts**.

14. Tap **Done** in the upper-right corner of the Add Event window when you're finished typing information about your appointment.

Editing (or Deleting) an Appointment

After you have defined an appointment, you can always modify it by changing the start time or date or turning an alarm off or on. You also have the option of deleting the entire appointment.

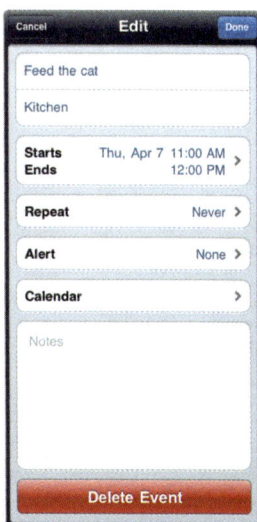

To edit an appointment, follow these steps:

1. From the Home screen, tap **Calendar**. The Calendar screen appears.

2. Tap the appointment you want to modify. A brief description of your appointment appears along with an Edit button.

3. Tap the **Edit** button. The Edit Event window appears, as shown in Figure 24-6.

4. Make any changes to your appointment.

5. (Optional) Tap **Delete Event** at the bottom of the Edit Event window if you want to delete your entire appointment. A red Delete Event button and a black Cancel button appear at the bottom of the Edit Event window. Tap **Delete Event** or **Cancel**.

6. Tap **Done** in the upper-right corner of the Edit Event window to save your changes.

FIGURE 24-6: *The Edit Event window lets you modify an existing appointment.*

Searching for an Appointment

You may have set an appointment and suddenly can't remember what date you assigned it. Rather than waste time scanning your appointments, you can search for it by typing a word or phrase that is part of your appointment, such as the location or name of the appointment.

To search for an appointment, follow these steps:

1. From the Home screen, tap **Calendar**. The Calendar screen appears.
2. Tap the **Search** field that appears in the upper-right corner of the screen. A virtual keyboard appears.
3. Type a word or phrase that appears in the appointment that you want to find. As you type, a Results window appears, listing all appointments that currently match what you typed (even if it's just one letter), as shown in Figure 24-7.
4. Tap an appointment in the Results window to view that appointment.

FIGURE 24-7: The Results window shows you which appointments match what you've typed.

Viewing and Managing Multiple Calendars

If you have many appointments, you could organize them into different calendars, such as storing your personal appointments on your Yahoo! calendar and your work-related appointments on your Google account calendar. To view the appointments you've made on a particular calendar, follow these steps:

1. From the Home screen, tap **Calendar**. The Calendar screen appears.
2. Tap the **Calendars** button that appears in the upper-left corner of the screen. The Show Calendars window appears.
3. Tap a Calendar name, such as Yahoo! or Gmail (Google), to clear or select a calendar. If you clear a checkmark from a calendar, all appointments stored on that calendar are hidden. Tap the checkmark again, and they reappear.

To define a default calendar to use for storing your appointments, follow these steps:

1. From the Home screen, tap **Settings**. The Settings screen appears.
2. Tap the **Mail, Contacts, Calendars** button that appears in the left of the screen. Scroll down the right side of the screen until you see the Default Calendar button, as shown Figure 24-8.
3. Tap the **Default Calendar** button and tap the calendar you want to make your default calendar. Now any new appointments you make will be in that calendar.

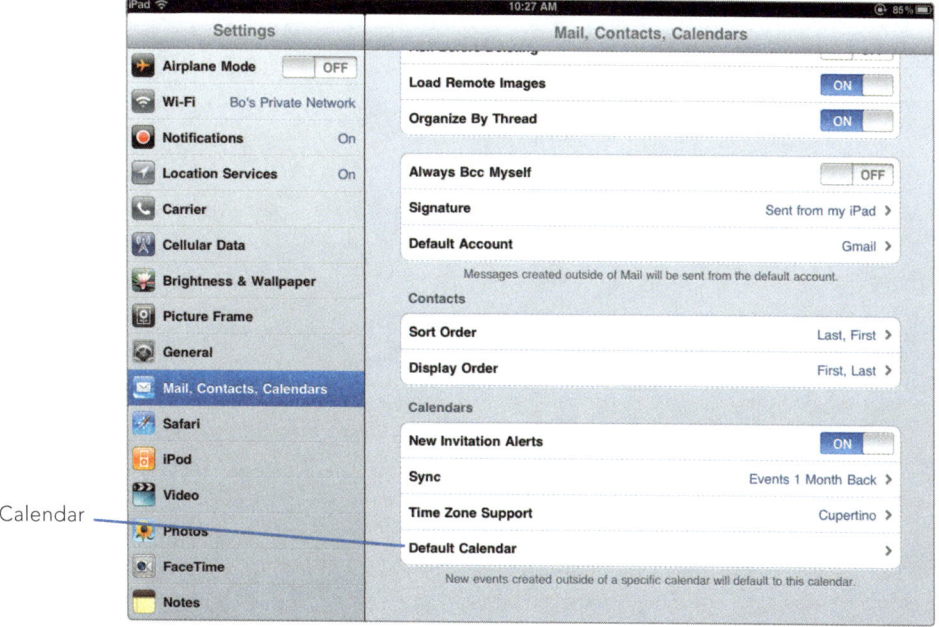

Set Default Calendar

FIGURE 24-8: *You can define the default calendar in the Settings screen.*

Additional Ideas for Using Calendars

Calendars can help keep your life organized (just as long as you take your iPad with you so you can see your calendars). If you're trying to achieve a goal, such as losing weight or giving up smoking, set a repetitive appointment with words of encouragement.

Since you can store appointments far into the future, take a moment now to set an alert for important dates, such as upcoming anniversaries, birthdays, or other events that you can't afford to forget. Now your iPad can help make you look like a genius when you remember all those birthdays of loved ones.

25 Using Maps

Maps can be fun to study just to see unusual locations. However, most people will likely use a map to help them find their way around. If you're in an unfamiliar area, just load the Maps app, find your current location, and then figure out how to get back to a freeway or which roads you need to take to head in a certain direction.

What You'll Be Using

To view maps on your iPad, you need to use the following:

▶ An Internet connection (Wi-Fi or 3G)

 The Maps app

Viewing a Map

Unlike a paper map, the Maps app can show you a dynamic map that can change, move, or expand so you can see finer details or zoom out to see a larger overview of a particular area.

Besides showing you a map, the Maps screen also displays various controls around the screen to help you use the Maps app, as shown in Figure 25-1.

Search/Directions   Current Location   Contacts   Search

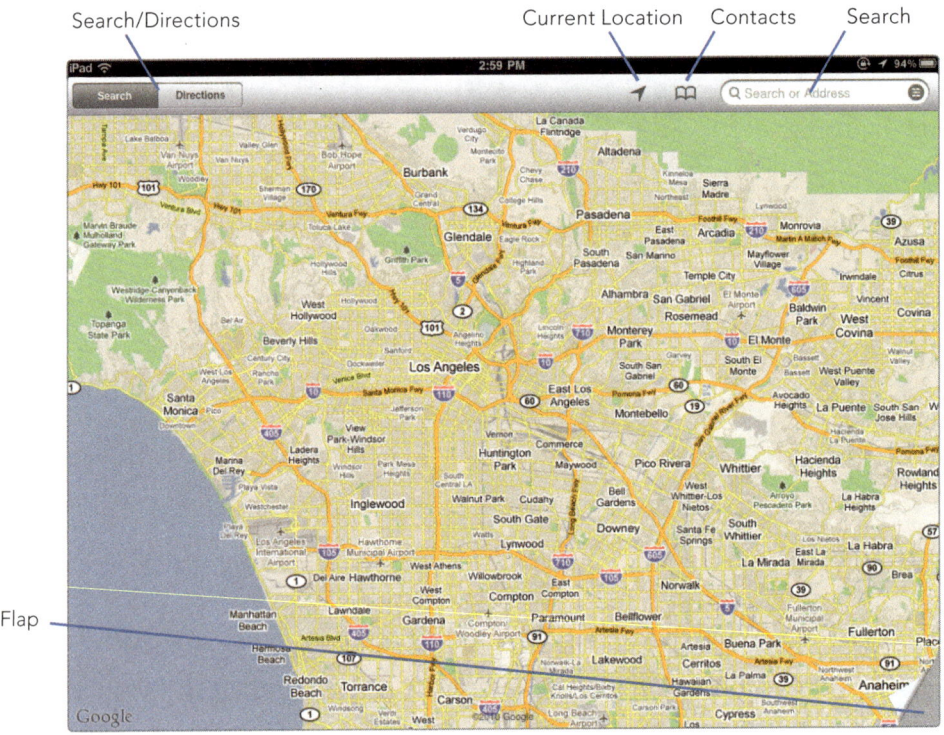

FIGURE 25-1: *The default appearance of a map, known as the Classic appearance, displays a cartoon view of an area.*

These controls are:

- **Search/Directions tab**   Lets you either search for an address or get directions between two points, such as your current location and a street address.

- **Current Location icon**   Identifies your position on a map.

- **Contacts icon**   Opens a list of names stored in the Contacts app.

- **Search field**   Lets you type in an address or type of business to find, such as **supermarket** or **gas**.

- **Flap**   Displays several options for customizing the appearance of the Maps screen.

To view and manipulate a map, follow these steps:

1. From the Home screen, tap **Maps**. The Maps screen appears (see Figure 25-1).
2. Place two fingers on the Map screen, and spread them apart and close together. The map shrinks and expands to show you a detailed or broader view of the map.
3. Press your finger on the map screen and slide it around. The map moves so you can see other parts of the map. By scrolling, you essentially have an endless map.

Changing the Appearance of a Map

Depending on how you like looking at maps, you can change a map's appearance in one of four ways:

- **Classic**   Displays the map as a graphic image

- **Satellite**   Displays an actual photograph of an area

- **Hybrid**   Displays an actual photograph with cartoon streets drawn over it

- **Terrain**   Displays a graphic map with elevation levels included

To see the four different ways to display a map, follow these steps:

1. While using Maps, tap the gray area in the bottom-right corner of the screen where the corner of the map looks like it's folded back. A list of map appearance options appears, as shown in Figure 25-2.
2. Change your map's appearance by tapping **Classic**, **Satellite**, **Hybrid**, or **Terrain**. The map now displays its new look, as shown in Figure 25-3.
3. (Optional) Tap the flap in the corner of the Maps screen again. Press the Traffic overlay on/off button to display congested roads in red and yellow.

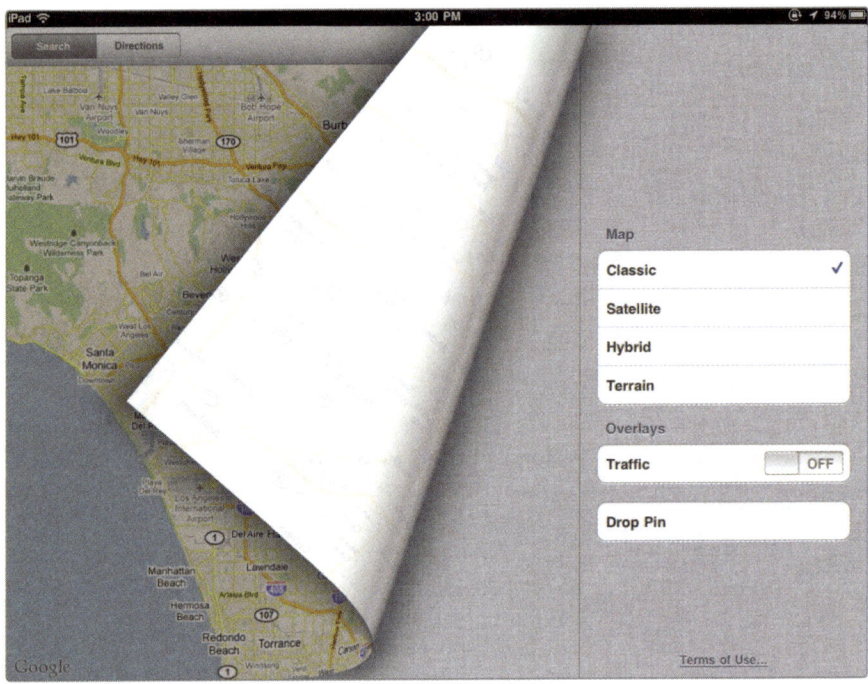

FIGURE 25-2: Options for changing the appearance of your map

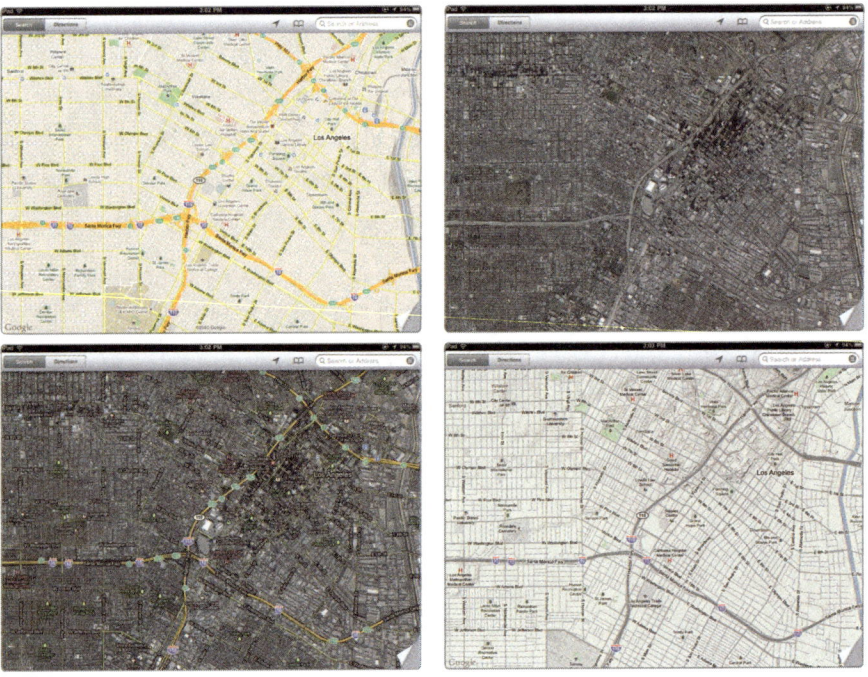

FIGURE 25-3: Different map types can be useful in different situations.

Finding Your Current Location

Every map is useless if you can't find where you are. That's why shopping center maps always have a big "You Are Here" arrow. To identify your current location, your iPad needs an Internet connection.

To find your current location on a map, follow these steps:

1. From the Home screen, tap **Maps**. The Maps screen appears.
2. Tap the **Location** icon. Your current location appears as a blue dot and a circle, as shown in Figure 25-4.

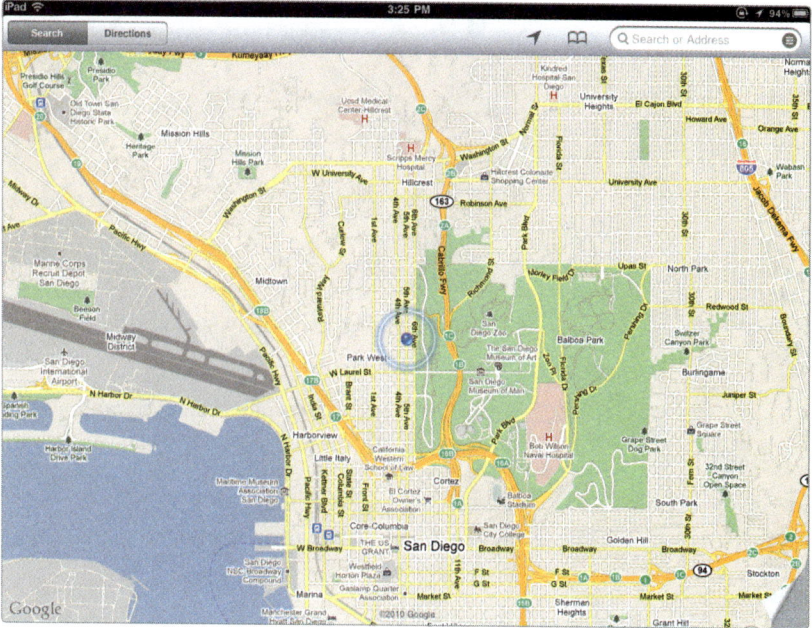

FIGURE 25-4: *A blue dot identifies your current location on the map.*

Using the Compass

A map can be handy to help you find your way around, but if you don't know which direction you're facing, you may not know whether you're heading the right way. To help you find your direction, the Maps app offers a compass.

To use the compass, follow these steps:

1. From the Home screen, tap **Maps**. The Maps screen appears.
2. Tap the **Current Location** icon twice. A compass appears in the upper-right corner, as shown in Figure 25-5. (Note how the Current Location icon changes when you turn on the compass.)

Compass

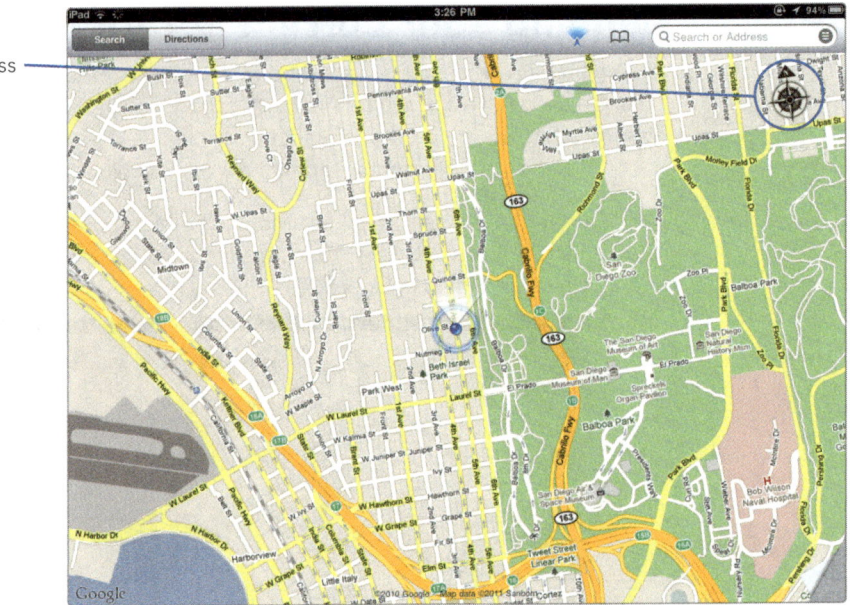

FIGURE 25-5: *The compass lets you find north on a map.*

3. Rotate the iPad. The compass shows you the direction of north, while a triangular area on the blue dot shows which direction you're currently facing. Try moving your iPad around—notice that as you change directions, the iPad's indicator moves with you.

4. Tap the **Current Location** icon once to make the compass disappear. You can also just drag the map.

Finding Places on a Map

Sometimes you know exactly where you want to go. Other times you may be searching for something you need, such as the nearest pizza restaurant, gas station, supermarket, or coffeehouse. Whether you want to find a specific address or need to find a certain kind of place, your iPad can show you the way.

Searching for an Address

If you know the exact address you want to find, you can locate it on your iPad by following these steps:

1. From the Home screen, tap **Maps**. The Maps screen appears.

2. Tap the **Search** tab in the upper-left corner of the screen. (It may already be selected.)

3. Tap the **Search** field in the upper-right corner of the screen. The virtual keyboard appears at the bottom of the screen.

4. Type an address and city. Then tap the **Search** key on the virtual keyboard. The map displays a red pin to identify the address, as shown in Figure 25-6.

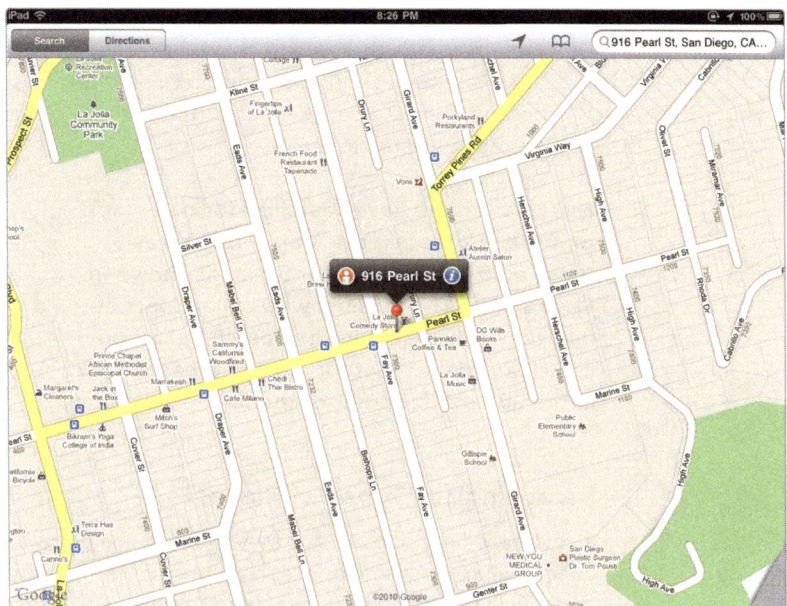

FIGURE 25-6: *The map identifies an address with a red pin.*

5.   Tap the orange circle with the white silhouette of a person in it. (Not all addresses will display this orange circle icon.) The screen shows you a photograph of the area around the address, as shown in Figure 25-7.

FIGURE 25-7: *Drag your finger across the picture for a 360-degree view of the surrounding area.*

6. Tap the screen once, and tap the **Done** button that appears in the upper-right corner of the screen. Or tap the viewing circle that appears in the bottom-right corner of the screen to return to the map.

* *NOTE:* **After you have searched for one or more addresses, the Maps app stores those addresses in a Recents list, as shown in Figure 25-8. The Recents window appears automatically when you tap the Search field. You can clear this list by tapping the Clear button in the upper-left corner of the Recents window.**

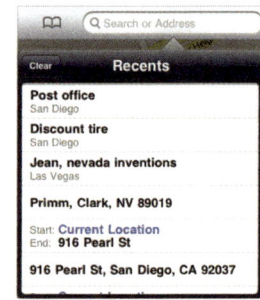

FIGURE 25-8: The Recents window stores your last searched locations.

Searching for Types of Places

If you're looking for pizza or a supermarket, the Maps app is smart enough to figure out what you want and display multiple pins identifying locations of businesses that match your search. You can also use the Search feature to find particular cities, towns, and even well-known landmarks like the Empire State Building or Golden Gate Park.

To search for places, follow these steps:

1. From the Home screen, tap **Maps**. The Maps screen appears.
2. Tap the **Search** tab in the upper-left corner of the screen.
3. Tap the **Location** icon, or simply scroll the map to an area that you want to investigate.
4. Tap the **Search** field in the upper-right corner of the screen. The virtual keyboard appears at the bottom of the screen.
5. Type a description of the place you want to find, such as **pizza** or **gas**. Red pins appear on the map to identify locations that match your search criteria.
6. Tap the **Results** icon (it looks like three white horizontal lines inside a gray circle) at the far right of the Search field. A list of names and addresses of places that match your search criteria appears, as shown in Figure 25-9.
7. Tap a name, and the map highlights the location of that business on the map.

FIGURE 25-9: The Results window lists the names and addresses of businesses that match your search criteria.

Bookmarking Favorite Locations

When you find a location on a map, you can bookmark it. That way, if you find a great restaurant, bookstore, or bar that you know you'll want to return to, you can save this location for future use or send an email message to a friend so they'll be able to find that place too.

Saving or Sharing a Location

To save a location or email it to a friend, follow these steps:

1. Search for a location using one of the instructions in "Finding Places on a Map" on page 208. Your chosen location appears on the map, marked by a red pin.
2. Tap the **Information** icon that appears (it looks like a white lowercase *i* in a blue circle). A window pops up, listing information about that location, as shown in Figure 25-10.
3. (Optional) Tap **Add to Bookmarks**. The Add Bookmark window appears. Type or edit a descriptive name, and tap **Save**.
4. (Optional) Tap **Add to Contacts**. The Create New Contact, Add to Existing Contact, and Cancel buttons appear. Tap **Create New Contact**, **Add to Existing Contact**, or **Cancel**. If you tap Create New Contact, you can edit any information before tapping the Done button. If you tap Add to Existing Contact, you'll need to pick a name in your Contacts list to store the location information.
5. (Optional) Tap **Share Location**. A new email message appears, with the contact information attached.

FIGURE 25-10: *A window listing information about the location on the map. If you tap Share Location, you can email the location to a friend.*

Placing Your Own Bookmark

Rather than look for an address or place and then create a bookmark, the Maps app also gives you the option of placing a purple pin on a map to identify any location you want. This can be handy for identifying a particular area without caring what that street address might be.

To place a bookmark on a map, follow these steps:

1. From the Home screen, tap **Maps**. The Maps screen appears.
2. Tap the gray corner in the lower-right corner of the screen. A list of options appears, as shown in Figure 25-11.
3. Tap **Drop Pin**. A purple pin appears on the map.

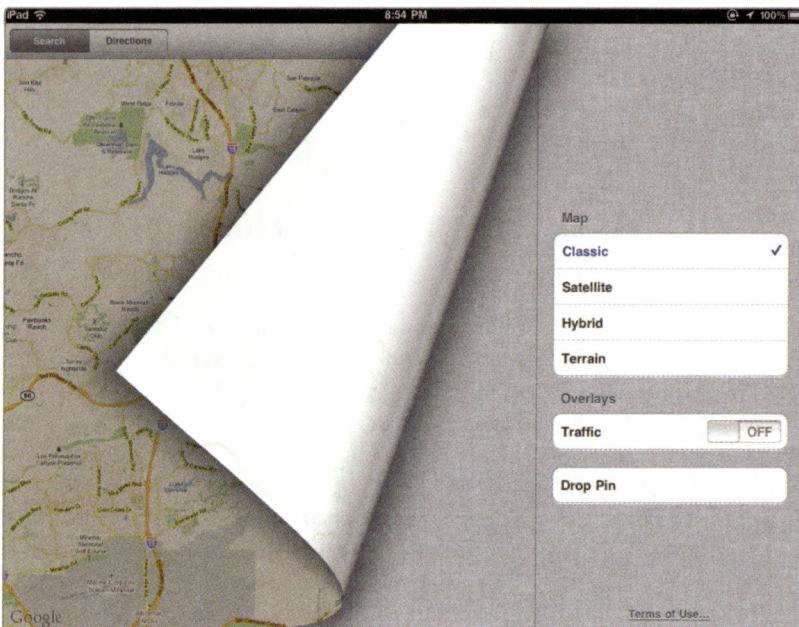

FIGURE 25-11: *Tapping the gray corner of the map displays a Drop Pin option.*

4. Tap and slide the purple pin anywhere on the map. Lift your finger when the purple pin appears where you want it.
5. Tap the **Information** icon that appears (it looks like a white lowercase *i* in a blue circle). A window pops up, listing information about that location. (You can remove the pin by tapping Remove Pin.)
6. Tap **Add to Bookmarks**. The Add Bookmark window appears.
7. Type or edit a descriptive name, and tap **Save**.

Finding an Address with Bookmarks and Contacts

If you have already stored someone's street address in the Contacts app, you don't need to retype this address into the Maps app to find its location. Instead, you can just tap that person's name, and the Maps app will find that location for you.

To see how to find an address from the Contacts app, make sure you have stored someone's street address, and then follow these steps:

1. From the Home screen, tap **Maps**. The Maps screen appears.
2. Tap the **Bookmark** icon. A window appears.
3. Tap **Contacts** at the bottom of this window. Your list of Contacts appears.
4. Tap a name. The map displays a red pin identifying the location of the address stored with that name. (If you choose a name that doesn't have a street address stored with it, you'll see a "No Street Addresses" message.)

Getting Directions

Many times you want to know where you are and the shortest route to get to your destination. Not only can your iPad show you the fastest driving directions, but it can also show you public transportation options or directions for walking. All you need to know is your current location and your destination.

Getting Directions to a Specific Address

If you know a specific address that you want to go to, you can type that address into the Maps app and get driving, mass transit, or walking directions to your destination by following these steps:

1. From the Home screen, tap **Maps**.The Maps screen appears.
2. Tap the **Directions** tab in the upper-left corner of the screen. The upper-right corner of the screen displays Start and End text fields, as shown in Figure 25-12.

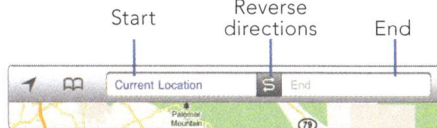

FIGURE 25-12: *The Start and End fields define the starting and ending points for directions.*

3. Tap the **End** text field. If you tap the Reverse icon (the squiggly arrow between the Start and End fields), you can reverse your starting and ending points.
4. Type an address, and tap the **Search** key on the virtual keyboard. The map displays your ending destination and shows how long it will take to drive there from your current location, as shown in Figure 25-13.

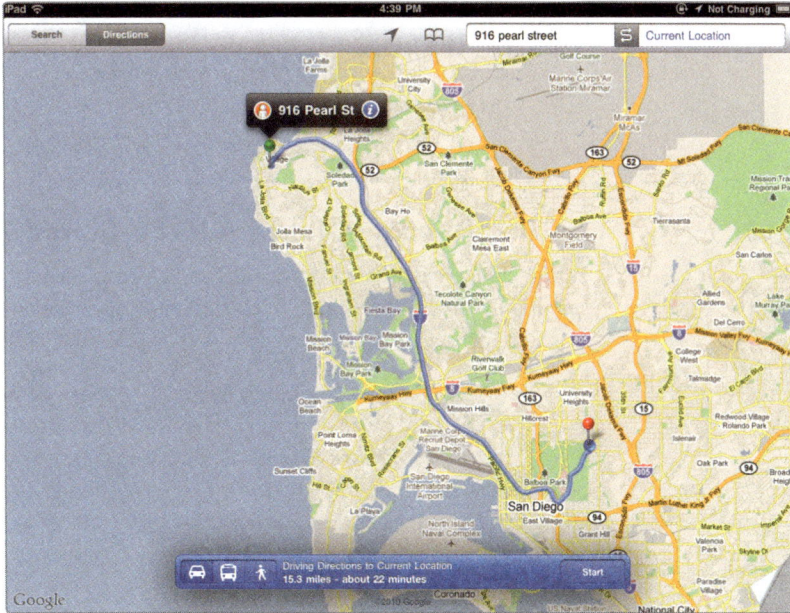

FIGURE 25-13: *Driving directions appear at the bottom of the map.*

5.   (Optional) Tap the **Bus** icon that appears at the bottom of the screen. Mass transit directions appear.

6.   (Optional) Tap the **Person** icon that appears at the bottom of the screen. Walking directions appear.

7.   Tap **Start** to get directions. To view step-by-step directions, tap the **Left** or **Right** arrow icons that appear on the blue bar, as shown in Figure 25-14. The map will zoom to each turn.

8.   To get a list of all directions, as shown in Figure 25-15, tap the **List** icon at the far left of the blue bar (shown in Figure 25-14).

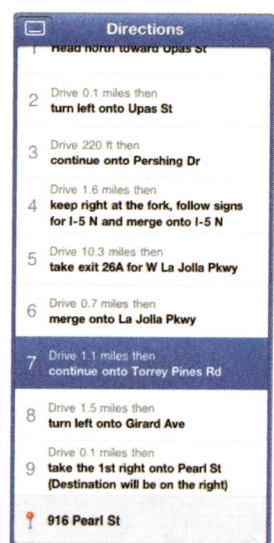

List icon   Skip ahead to   Skip back to the
             the next step   previous step

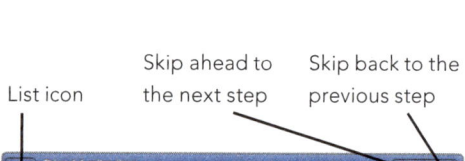

FIGURE 25-14: *Each time you tap the right arrow, another step in your direction appears.*

FIGURE 25-15: *Viewing a list of directions*

Getting Directions for an Address Stored in the Contacts App

Rather than type an address, it's often easier to take advantage of an address stored in your Contacts app. To get driving directions to an address stored in the Contacts app, follow these steps:

1.   From the Home screen, tap **Maps**. The Maps screen appears.

2.   Tap the **Directions** button in the upper-left corner of the screen.

3.   Tap the **Bookmark** icon in the upper-right corner of the screen. A window pops up.

4.   Tap **Contacts** at the bottom of this window. A list of names stored in the Contacts app appears.

5. Tap a name that has a street address stored. A window appears, displaying buttons labeled Directions To Here, Directions From Here, and Cancel, as shown in Figure 25-16.
6. Tap **Directions To Here**. A blue bar appears at the bottom of the map, letting you choose driving, mass transit, or walking directions. Tap one of these choices, and tap **Start**.

Getting Directions from the Information Icon

When the map displays a location with a red pin (such as after searching for a specific type of business like a pizza place or supermarket, as explained in "Searching for Types of Places" on page 210), you can get directions to that location by tapping the location's Information icon, which appears as a lowercase letter *i* inside a blue circle.

To get directions using the Information icon, follow these steps:

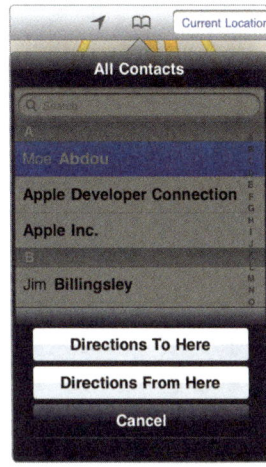

FIGURE 25-16: *Using a contact's address to get directions*

1. From the Home screen, tap **Maps**. The Maps screen appears.
2. Tap the **Bookmarks** icon, tap **Contacts** at the bottom of the window, and tap a name. Or tap the **Search** field, and type a business that you want to find, such as **supermarket** or **gas**. A red pin appears on the map, along with the name of a person or business, and the blue Information icon. Tap the **Information** icon.
3. Tap **Directions To Here**. A blue bar appears at the bottom of the map, letting you choose driving, mass transit, or walking directions. Tap one of these choices, and tap **Start**.

Additional Ideas for Finding Places and Getting Directions with Maps

Before you go to a location that you've never been to, locate it on the Maps app, and then look at its picture so you can see the surrounding area. If you're looking for something to eat, just type in the food you want in the Maps search field, such as **pizza**, **Thai food**, or **seafood**. When you see all the nearby restaurants, just tap on a name, get directions (driving, mass transit, or walking), and find a new restaurant where you can enjoy your meal.

The Maps app acts like an interactive guide to help you find your location and find nearby businesses. If you travel often, take your iPad, and you may never be lost again (unless you lose your iPad).

26

Searching Your iPad with Spotlight

If you want to find an app, a song, a video, an email message, or another item stored on your iPad, you have two choices. You could manually search your iPad, which takes time and still doesn't guarantee that you'll find what you want. A much faster and more accurate method is to search your iPad using Spotlight.

In this chapter you will learn how to use Spotlight to search for apps, songs, videos, and email messages on your iPad.

What You'll Be Using

To search for apps and other items, you need to use the following:

▸   Spotlight   The Settings screen

Searching with Spotlight

Spotlight is a special feature that acts like a search engine on your iPad. Just type all or part of a word, and Spotlight tries to find an item that matches your search criteria. By default, Spotlight will search through your Apps, Audiobooks, Calendar appointments, Contacts, Mail messages, Music, Notes, Podcasts, and Videos.

To search for any of these items, follow these steps:

1. From the Home screen, swipe your finger from left to right. The Spotlight screen appears with a Search iPad field at the top and the virtual keyboard at the bottom, as shown in Figure 26-1. (You can also get to the Spotlight search page by pressing the Home button when you're at the Home screen.)

FIGURE 26-1: *The Spotlight screen appears when you swipe the Home screen to the right.*

2.   Tap the **Search iPad** field, and type part of the word that represents what
       you want to find. For example, if you want to find a name stored in your Con-
       tacts app, type that name. If you want to find a note in the Notes app that
       contains certain information, such as your grocery list, type a word that you
       know appears on that note, such as **milk** or **eggs**. As you type each letter,
       Spotlight displays the items that match your search criteria, as shown in
       Figure 26-2.

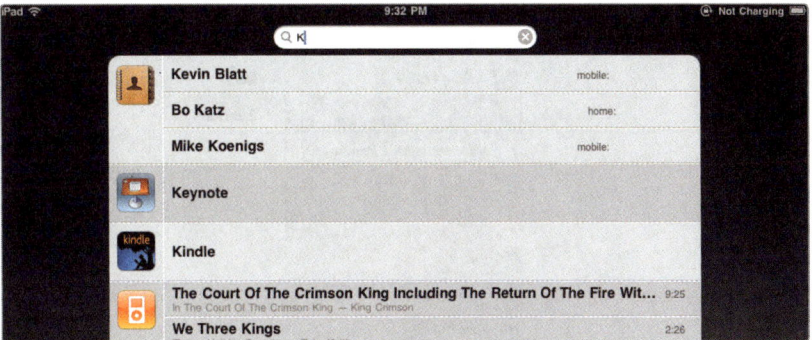

FIGURE 26-2: *As you type, Spotlight displays items that match your
search criteria.*

3.   Tap the item you want, such as a song, an app, or a note. Your iPad displays
       or plays your chosen item.

Customizing Spotlight

You can also customize the order that Spotlight searches for things. If email messages are more important to you than audiobooks, tell Spotlight to search through
your email messages first and not bother searching for audiobooks until you've
searched for everything else.

       To customize Spotlight, follow these steps:

1.   From the Home screen, tap **Settings**. The Settings screen appears.
2.   Tap **General**. The General settings screen appears.
3.   Tap **Spotlight Search**. The Spotlight Search settings screen appears, as
       shown in Figure 26-3.
4.   Tap any item, such as **Music**, **Podcasts**, or **Mail**. Spotlight will search for any
       item with a check mark next to it and ignore any items that do not have a
       check mark next to them.

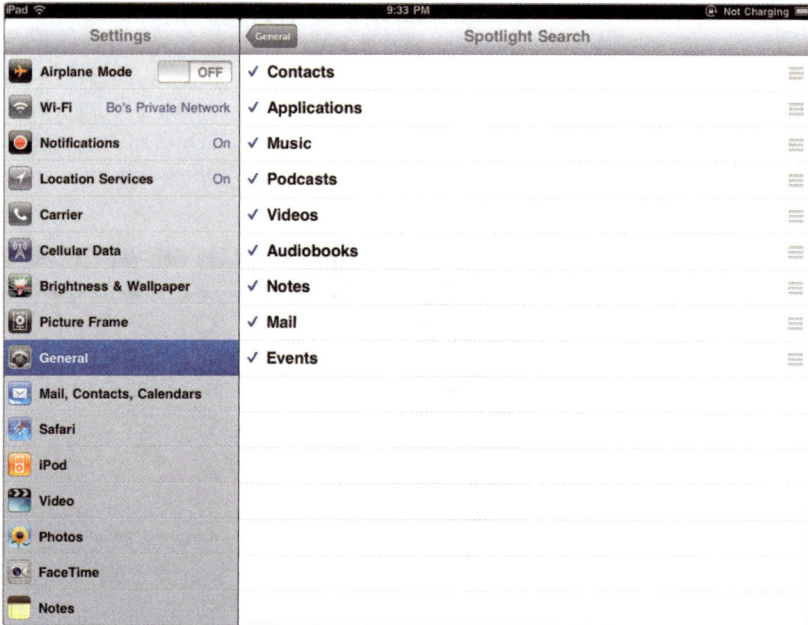

FIGURE 26-3: *The Spotlight Search settings screen lists the order of items to search.*

5.   Place your fingertip over the three horizontal lines at the far right of an item, and slide your finger up or down. This lets you rearrange the order that Spotlight searches for items, starting from the top.

6.   Press the **Home** button. The Home screen appears. Try your search again, and see the results!

Additional Ideas for Searching with Spotlight

If you collect dozens of apps, trying to find the one app you want can involve swiping through multiple panes of the Home screen. For a faster method, just swipe to reveal the Spotlight screen, and type the name of the app you want to run.

If you store notes in the Notes app, give each note a descriptive heading. Not only will this help you organize your notes within the Notes app, but it will also make it easier for Spotlight to find your note again if you can remember to search for that heading (such as "To-Do" or "Daily Goals").

With Spotlight on your iPad, you can quickly search for anything you've stored so you don't have to worry where you put it. As long as you know what you called it, you'll be able to find it again courtesy of Spotlight.

PART 6

Additional Tips

27 Making Your iPad Accessible

Using the iPad is a totally different experience from using an ordinary computer because you don't have a physical keyboard or a mouse to point to the screen. You may find the touch interface even easier to use than a traditional keyboard and mouse. Plus you can use some built-in features to make your iPad even more accessible.

The iPad can invert its color scheme so that text appears in high-contrast white on black. Also, your iPad can make it easy to zoom in on the screen to quickly enlarge images and text.

The iPad can also use a synthesized voice to read the various text, buttons, and controls on the screen. As you slide your fingers over the screen, your iPad will read whatever your finger is touching, so you'll know whether it's a button you want to press.

If you are deaf or hard of hearing, you may want to turn on closed captioning when you watch videos. You can also switch the audio to mono (rather than stereo), which can be easier to hear if your hearing is better in one ear than the other.

What You'll Be Using

To change your iPad's accessibility settings, you need to use the following:

 The Settings screen

Improving the Visual Quality of the Screen

To make the iPad's screen more readable, you can turn on "White on Black" or Zoom features. These two features are independent—you can use them together or separately.

Turning on the White on Black setting will render most text in white against a black background—as well as inverting all other colors on your iPad.

Turning on the Zoom feature lets you use three fingers to zoom the screen in and out so you can read the screen more easily. To enable the accessibility features, follow these steps:

1. From the Home screen, tap **Settings**. The Settings screen appears.
2. Tap **General**. The General settings screen appears.
3. Tap **Accessibility**. The Accessibility settings screen appears, as shown in Figure 27-1.

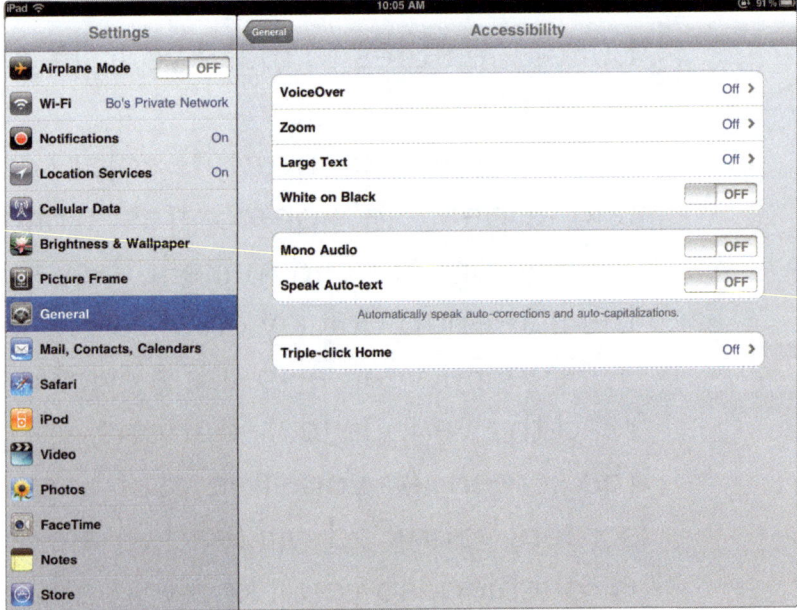

FIGURE 27-1: *The Accessibility settings screen*

4. Tap **Zoom**. The Zoom settings screen appears.
5. Tap the **Zoom** on/off switch. Note the instructions on the page.
6. Tap the **Accessibility** button to return to the Accessibility settings screen (see Figure 27-1).
7. Tap **Large Text**. A screen appears, listing different text sizes, as shown in Figure 27-2.

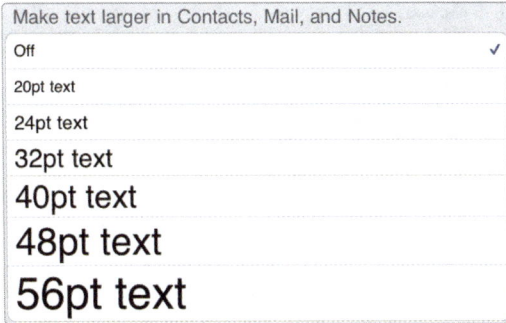

FIGURE 27-2: *Make text easier to read by choosing a larger font size.*

8. Tap a text size and then tap the **Accessibility** button to return to the Accessibility settings screen.
9. Tap the **White on Black** on/off switch. When turned on, the screen displays white text on a black background.

Turning On VoiceOver

You can also turn on the VoiceOver feature, which makes your iPad read whatever is on the screen as you touch it with your fingers. By touching the screen and hearing where your fingers are, you can control your iPad.

❋ *NOTE:* **Because Zoom and VoiceOver use the same set of shortcuts, you can enable only one or the other at a time.**

To turn on the VoiceOver feature, follow these steps:

1. From the Home screen, tap **Settings**. The Settings screen appears.
2. Tap **General**. The General settings screen appears.
3. Tap **Accessibility**. The Accessibility settings screen appears (shown earlier in Figure 27-1).
4. Tap **VoiceOver**. The VoiceOver settings screen appears, as shown in Figure 27-3.
5. Tap the **VoiceOver** on/off switch.

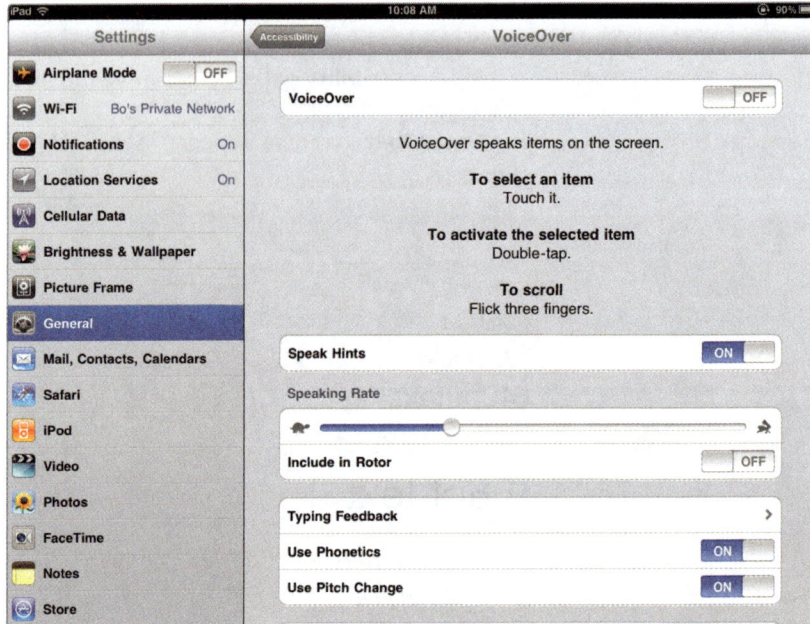

FIGURE 27-3: *The VoiceOver settings screen lets you define how your iPad can read its controls to you.*

✳ **NOTE:** Enabling this setting does more than just read the iPad's screen aloud—it actually changes iPad's behavior. Instead of single-tapping to open apps, press buttons, and toggle switches, you'll need to double-tap. You'll also need to double-tap to type. Instead of scrolling with one finger, you'll need to scroll with three fingers. This is because the usual single tap will activate VoiceOver rather than the screen element.

6. (Optional) Tap the **Speak Hints** on/off switch. Speak Hints provides a bit of context with each selection—for example, when you single-tap an app on the Home screen, your iPad will read its name aloud and say, "Double-tap to open."

7. (Optional) Slide the **Speaking Rate** slider to make the iPad's synthesized voice speak faster or slower.

8. (Optional) Tap **Typing Feedback** to display the Typing Feedback settings screen, which lets you define whether the iPad should give you audio feedback after each character, entire words, or both. Tap an option, and then tap the VoiceOver back button to view the VoiceOver screen again.

9. (Optional) Tap the **Use Phonetics** on/off switch to make your iPad pronounce words on the screen phonetically.

10. (Optional) Tap the **Use Pitch Change** on/off switch to make the iPad's synthesized voice sound more natural.
11. (Optional) Scroll down and tap **Braille** to allow your iPad to connect via Bluetooth to a Braille device.
12. (Optional) Tap the **Web Rotor**, **Language Rotor**, or **Include in Rotor** on/off switches to modify the rotor, which lets you use a two-finger rotation gesture to quickly move through text displayed on the screen.
13. Press the **Home** button. The Home screen appears again.

Turning On Closed Captioning and Mono Audio

Closed captioning lets you read what people in a video say. This can be handy if you are deaf or hard of hearing, or for watching a video in a noisy environment where you might not be able to hear the sound coming out of your iPad's speakers very well. To turn on closed captioning, follow these steps:

1. From the Home screen, tap **Settings**. The Settings screen appears.
2. Tap **Video**. The Video settings screen appears.
3. Tap the **Closed Captioning** on/off switch.
4. Press the **Home** button.

For clearer audio, you might also want to try the **Mono Audio** setting. Just tap **Settings** from the home screen, tap **General**, tap **Accessibility**, and finally tap the **Mono Audio** on/off button.

Turning Accessibility Features On and Off Rapidly

Going through the Settings screen every time you want to turn an accessibility feature on or off can be tedious, so to simplify this process, you can access these features by triple-clicking the Home button. This gives you the option of turning on (or off) VoiceOver or the White on Black feature.

If you prefer, you can also make triple-clicking the Home button display a list of options so you can turn different accessibility features on or off. To define triple-clicking the Home button, follow these steps:

1. From the Home screen, tap **Settings**. The Settings screen appears.
2. Tap **General**. The General settings screen appears.
3. Tap **Accessibility**. The Accessibility settings screen appears (shown earlier in Figure 27-1).
4. Tap **Triple-click Home**. The Home settings screen appears, as shown in Figure 27-4.

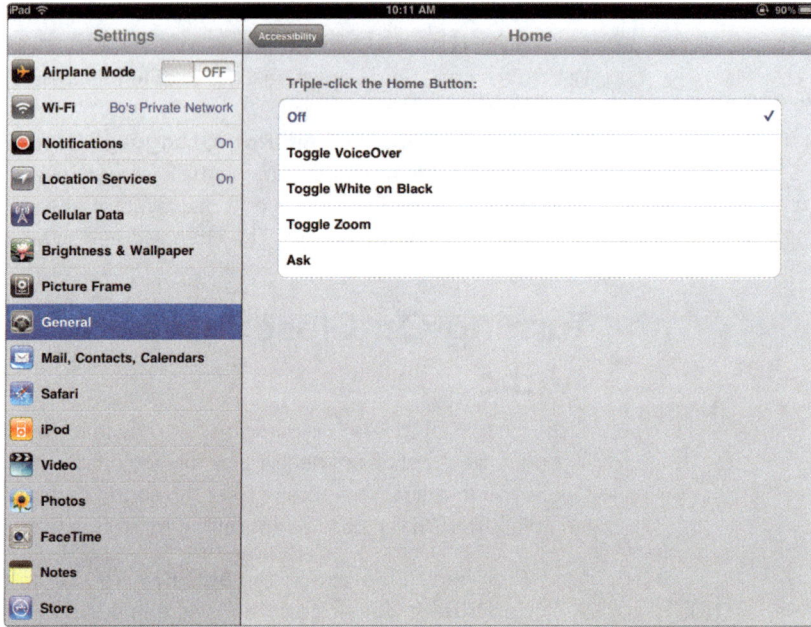

FIGURE 27-4: *The Home settings screen lets you define triple-clicking the Home button.*

5.   Tap an option, such as Toggle VoiceOver. If you choose Ask, triple-clicking the Home button displays a dialog that gives you a choice of which accessibility features to turn on or off.

6.   Press the **Home** button to return to the Home screen.

Additional Ideas for Making Your iPad Accessible

The iPad's accessibility options can be great for anyone, so give them a try. You may find that you prefer reading white-on-black text or like closed captioning on videos to make them easier to watch. You can even use the FaceTime app (see Chapter 20) to communicate in sign language, giving you yet another way to chat through your iPad. With so many different tools for controlling an iPad, you just need to think about what you want to do with it next and modify your iPad to make it easy for you to use.

28

Using Foreign Languages

Most physical keyboards are designed for a particular language, such as English, French, Russian, and so on. To type in another language with a physical keyboard, you often have to switch to a completely different keyboard or rely on odd keystroke combinations to type the characters you really want.

Fortunately, on the iPad, the virtual keyboard lets you switch between multiple languages quickly and easily. One moment you can be typing in French, the next in Russian, and the next in Chinese or Japanese. If you need to type in foreign languages on a regular basis, you'll be pleased to know that the iPad will likely accommodate the languages you need.

What You'll Be Using

To type in a foreign language, you need to use the following:

 The Settings screen

Switching the iPad's Default Language

Depending on where you bought your iPad, it will start out with an initial default language, such as English or French. If you move to another country, sell your iPad to someone in another country, or just want to practice your foreign-language skills, you can switch to a different language and make everything appear in that language.

To choose a different default language, follow these steps:

1. From the Home screen, tap **Settings**. The Settings screen appears.
2. Tap **General**. The General settings screen appears.
3. Tap **International**. The International settings screen appears.
4. Tap **Language**. A Language window appears, giving you a choice of different default languages to use, as shown in Figure 28-1.
5. Tap a language, such as Deutsch or Italiano, and tap **Done**. Your iPad now displays everything in your chosen language, as shown in Figure 28-2.

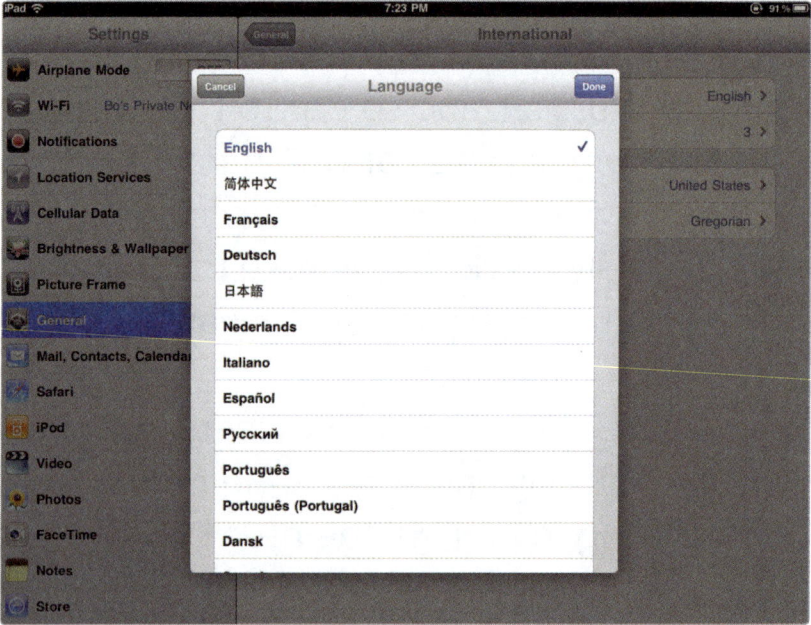

FIGURE 28-1: *The Language window lists all the default languages you can use.*

FIGURE 28-2: *Your new default language appears.*

Defining a Foreign-Language Virtual Keyboard

If you need to type in a second language, your iPad lets you switch to virtual keyboards for different languages at the tap of a key. That way, you can type in English, switch temporarily to French, Spanish, or Chinese, and then switch back again to English.

Before you can type on a foreign-language keyboard, you have to define which foreign language to use. To define a foreign-language keyboard, follow these steps:

1. From the Home screen, tap **Settings**. The Settings screen appears.
2. Tap **General**. The General settings screen appears.
3. Tap **Keyboard**. The Keyboard settings screen appears.
4. Tap **International Keyboards**. The screen displays all the available virtual keyboards on your iPad. Initially, it will display only the default language.
5. Tap **Add New Keyboard**. The Add New Keyboard screen appears, as shown in Figure 28-3.
6. Tap a foreign language. You'll return to the Keyboards page. You can follow the same steps to add another language.
7. (Optional) Tap **Edit** on the keyboard page to rearrange or delete your keyboards. Just drag the three gray bars on the right to move each keyboard around. The first keyboard on this screen will be your default keyboard.
8. Press the **Home** button. The Home screen appears.

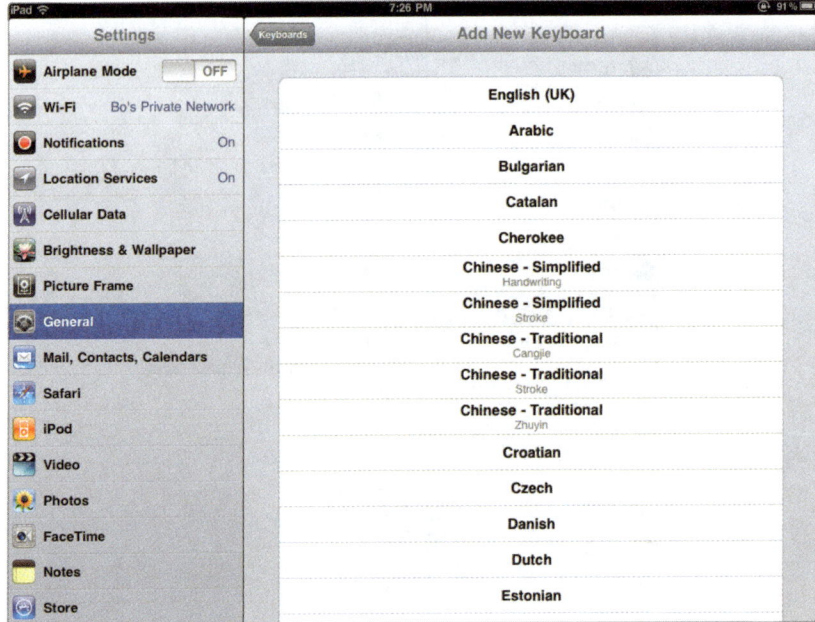

FIGURE 28-3: *The Add New Keyboard screen shows all the virtual keyboards you can add.*

Using a Foreign-Language Virtual Keyboard

After you have defined one or more foreign-language virtual keyboards, you can switch to that foreign-language keyboard any time the virtual keyboard pops up, such as when typing an email message or a note in the Notes app.

To use a foreign-language keyboard, follow these steps:

1. Run an app that displays the virtual keyboard, such as the Notes app.
2. Tap the **International** key (it looks like a globe) that appears next to the spacebar. One of your foreign-language virtual keyboards appears, as shown in Figure 28-4.
3. Type something, and when you're ready to switch to another language, tap the **International** key again until the keyboard you want appears.

✱ **NOTE:** The virtual keyboard also includes a Chinese character recognition keyboard that lets you draw a character. Then the keyboard displays a list of similar characters so you can tap the one you want to type, as shown in Figure 28-5.

International
key

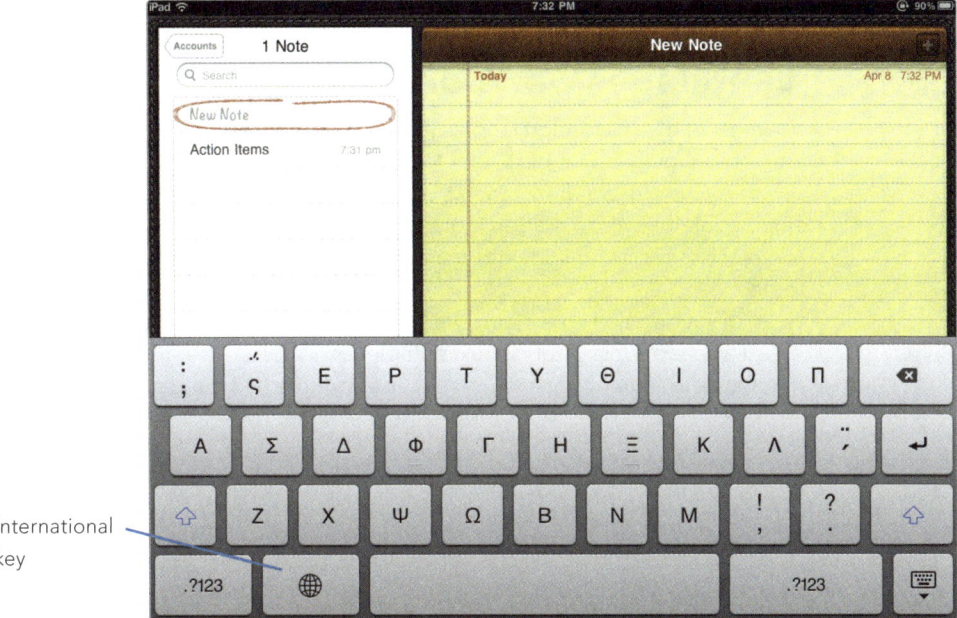

FIGURE 28-4: *Tapping the International key switches through the different language keyboards you have defined.*

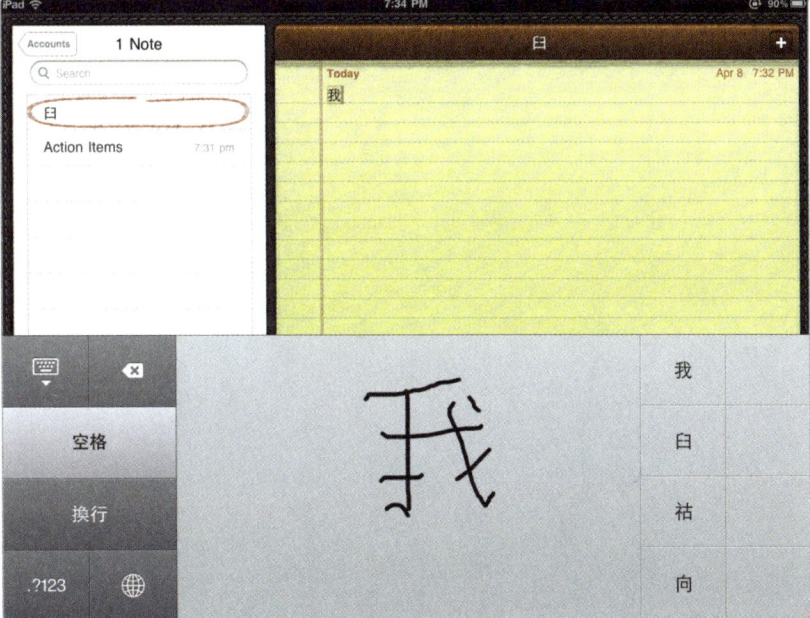

FIGURE 28-5: *The virtual keyboard can recognize Chinese characters drawn with your finger.*

Additional Ideas for Using Foreign Languages on Your iPad

Anyone learning a foreign language can switch to their foreign-language keyboard and start typing in that particular language.

If you have children, teach them the basics of typing in a foreign language. Typing foreign words is often more fun than writing them by hand, so this gives you a chance to turn your iPad into a simple foreign-language tutor for yourself or for others.

If you regularly travel to different parts of the world, or just live in a neighborhood where people often speak multiple languages, experiment with different foreign-language options so you can use your iPad no matter where you might be.

29 The Best iPad Apps

What makes the iPad so versatile isn't just its interface or touch screen but its ability to run apps to make your iPad do practically anything. Although it's possible to use your iPad without installing a single extra app, half the fun of having an iPad is downloading and using the thousands of apps available in the App Store (see Chapter 10 for more information about downloading apps from the App Store).

Surprisingly, some of the best apps are free, and others are far less expensive than comparable software for desktop or laptop computers. Whether you decide to buy apps or just download the free ones, you'll find plenty of software to expand the versatility of your iPad in ways that may surprise you.

In this chapter you will learn which types of free and commercial apps might be most useful to download and install on your iPad.

What You'll Be Using

To browse and download apps, you need to use the following:

▸ An Internet connection (Wi-Fi or 3G)

 The App Store

Office Productivity Apps

To work with word processor documents, spreadsheets, and presentations, you need an office suite for your iPad. While the iPad doesn't come with an office suite, you can buy several inexpensive apps that can turn your iPad into a replacement for a laptop.

Pages, Numbers, and Keynote

The most popular iPad office suite is Apple's own iWork, which consists of Pages, Numbers, and Keynote (shown in Figure 29-1). The three apps are sold individually, so you can pick the ones you need and skip the others.

If you use iWork on a Macintosh, you can transfer files between your Mac and iPad without converting file formats. If you use Microsoft Office files, you can open and edit them in iWork on your iPad, then transfer them back to your computer again.

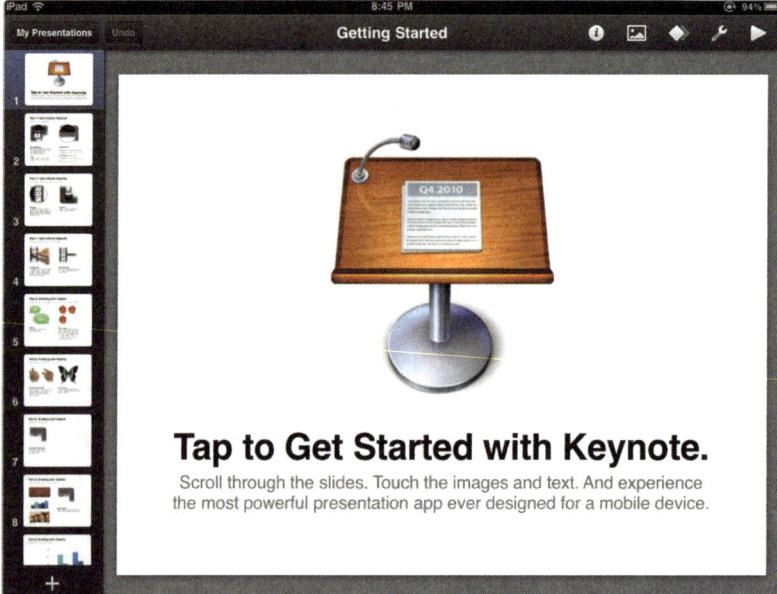

FIGURE 29-1: Keynote is just one app that's part of the iWork office suite.

Documents To Go and QuickOffice

If you don't use iWork and rely more on Microsoft Office files, you can use Documents To Go to create and edit Word, Excel, and PowerPoint files. For added convenience, Documents To Go can store and retrieve files from cloud services, such as iDisk, Dropbox, and Google Docs. This lets you access your files as long as you have an Internet connection.

Another solution for creating and editing Microsoft Office files is QuickOffice. Like Documents To Go, QuickOffice can create and edit Microsoft Word and Excel files, as shown in Figure 29-2. However, at the time of this writing, QuickOffice can only view but not edit a PowerPoint presentation, so if editing presentations is something you need on a regular basis, check the latest version to find out if it can create and edit PowerPoint presentations.

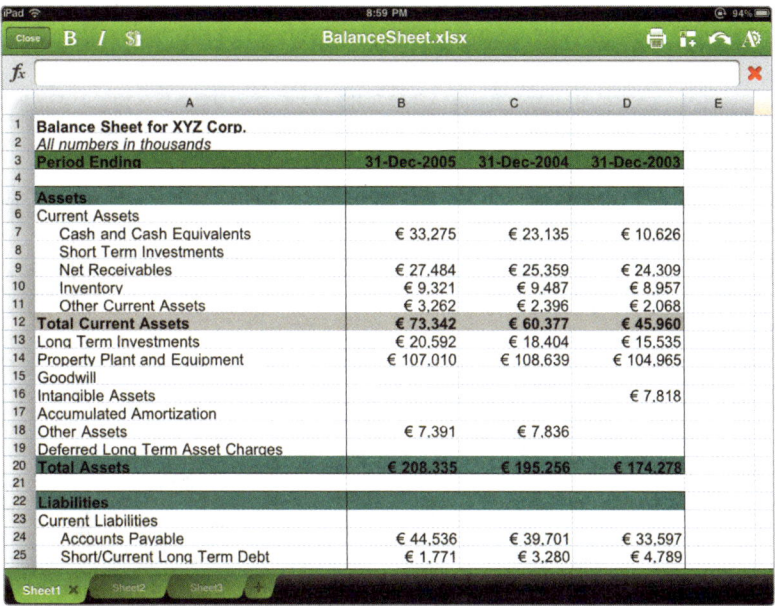

FIGURE 29-2: *QuickOffice makes it easy to edit and create Word and Excel files.*

Bento and FileMaker Go

The Contacts app that comes with the iPad is great for storing names, addresses, and phone numbers but not so flexible if you need to store other types of information. For those who need a more versatile database, grab a copy of Bento. If you have Bento on your Macintosh, you can share databases, but even if you just get Bento for the iPad, you can create custom databases for storing any type of information you might need.

For a more sophisticated database, get FileMaker Go. Not only can you develop databases directly on your iPad with FileMaker Go, but you can also use a Wi-Fi or Internet connection to remotely access FileMaker databases on your desktop computer. This gives you the ability to view and edit your database's data without storing it on your iPad.

Evernote, Simplenote, AudioNote, and PaperDesk

The Notes app that comes with the iPad can be handy for typing notes, but to synchronize your notes with your computer or an online storage site, you might want to use Evernote or Simplenote instead to make sure you never lose an idea.

If you need to store notes and record audio at the same time, then consider AudioNote. This feature can be especially useful when recording lectures so you can hear playback of exactly what was spoken while you review your typed notes.

PaperDesk lets you type notes, record audio, and draw and save pictures in your notes, as shown in Figure 29-3. One unique feature of PaperDesk is that if you tap a word that you've typed, PaperDesk will jump to the specific location in the audio recording when you typed that word so you can replay exactly what you heard when you jotted down a particular note.

FIGURE 29-3: *PaperDesk lets you sketch and type notes.*

Offline Pages

No matter which type of iPad you have (Wi-Fi only model or Wi-Fi and 3G model), you may occasionally find yourself in places without Internet access, such as on an airplane. To prepare for times without Internet access, use Offline Pages to store copies of your favorite web pages (when you do have Internet access) so you can view these pages later (when you don't have Internet access).

PCalc Lite

If you're familiar with the iPhone, you know that it comes with a free calculator app. Oddly enough, the iPad lacks this simple calculator app, so grab a free copy of PCalc Lite, which gives you a full-blown scientific calculator, as shown in Figure 29-4. Plenty of free alternative calculators are available in the App Store as well—just search for them!

FIGURE 29-4: *PCalc Lite gives your iPad a calculator app.*

Air Display

Need a little extra real estate while working on your desktop or laptop computer? The Air Display app lets you wirelessly turn your iPad into a second monitor. That way you can prop your iPad next to your computer and see more without the hassle of buying or connecting a second monitor.

News and Information

The simplest way to get the latest news is to load Safari and visit your favorite news websites. However, it's often easier to use a special app that retrieves the type of news that you want.

ABC News, AP News, BBC News, Fox News, NPR News, and Reuters News Pro

Many of the top news sites provide their own unique (and free) apps specially designed for retrieving and displaying news on an iPad. By using one of these free apps with an Internet connection through your iPad, you can read world, sports, and financial news, as shown in Figure 29-5.

The Weather Channel

If you want to know the local forecast, tap into the Weather Channel app. Not only can you see the forecast, but you can also view maps, track storms heading through your area, and watch videos of weather occurring in your area and other parts of the world, as shown in Figure 29-6.

Bloomberg for the iPad and NASDAQ QFolio

If you invest in the stock market, you may be interested in tracking your stock portfolio and keeping up with the latest financial news. (Naturally, this requires an Internet connection.) Both the Bloomberg and NASDAQ QFolio apps provide a list of the latest financial news headlines along with a list of your stocks so you can see how they're doing throughout the day.

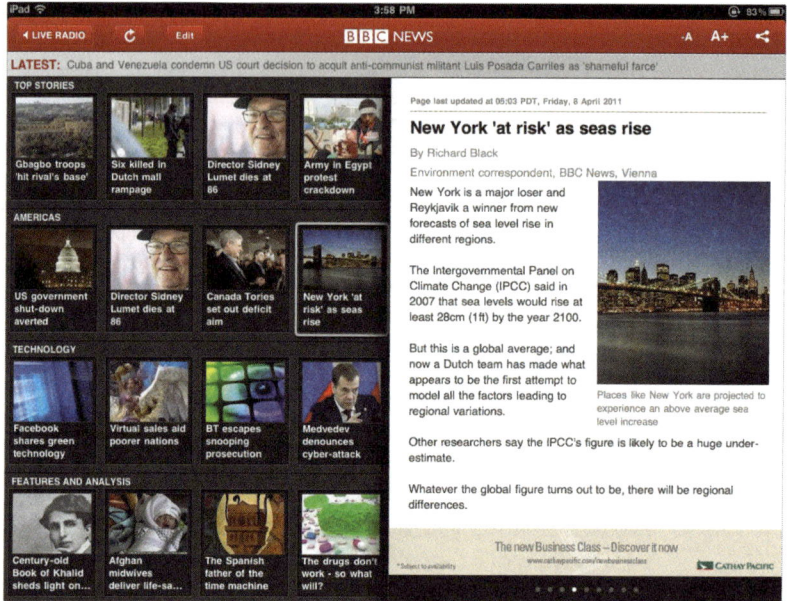

FIGURE 29-5: News apps let you choose the type of information you want to read.

FIGURE 29-6: Check your local weather conditions through the Weather Channel app.

Painting and Drawing Apps

The iPad's touch screen surface and portability make it a perfect canvas for creating anything from simple drawings to complete works of art. Get an optional stylus or just use your finger to create paintings and drawings that rival anything you could create on a computer using a dedicated graphics program, such as Photoshop or Corel Painter.

SketchBook Pro

For serious artists, grab a copy of Autodesk's SketchBook Pro. It includes Layers, Brushes, and other advanced features graphic artists will be familiar with. Based on the computer version of SketchBook Pro, this app essentially turns the surface of your iPad into a canvas for drawing or painting with your finger, as shown in Figure 29-7.

Doodle Buddy

For kids or anyone who just enjoys creating simple drawings, get a free copy of Doodle Buddy. Besides letting you draw and paint by mimicking chalk or paintbrushes, this app also includes pre-drawn images that you can paste into your creations so you can create interesting pictures even if you aren't much of an artist yourself.

FIGURE 29-7: *SketchBook Pro turns the iPad into an artistic canvas.*

Adobe Photoshop Express

While some people are capable of creating a picture from scratch, others prefer taking a real picture and modifying it. On a computer, you can use a program like Photoshop, but on an iPad, you can use a similar program from Adobe called Photoshop Express.

With Photoshop Express, you can modify digital images and turn them into art or just draw mustaches on people you don't like or scribble funny pictures on images just to keep yourself amused while waiting in line at a bank or airport (see Figure 29-8).

FIGURE 29-8: With Photoshop Express, you can use your iPad to add artistic effects to your photos.

Entertainment Apps

Most people don't get a computer to balance their budget or write business reports. Instead, most people really get a computer to play games and have fun. While you can use your iPad exclusively for business, you can easily turn your iPad into an entertainment center to watch videos, listen to Internet radio stations, or read the latest classics or best sellers.

iBooks, Kindle, and NOOK

iBooks, Apple's free reading app, gives you access to the iBookstore and lets you organize and read your ebooks. If you have a Kindle, download a free copy of the Kindle app so you can read all your Kindle ebooks on either your Kindle or your iPad.

For another alternative to Apple's iBookstore, download a free copy of the Barnes & Noble NOOK app. Just like the iBooks and Kindle apps, the NOOK app organizes your ebooks and lets you shop online for more books. With so many options for reading ebooks on your iPad, you can choose what you like best.

Netflix

If you subscribe to Netflix, download this free app, and you can watch streaming video directly on your iPad. Now you can watch movies or TV shows at your convenience without waiting for the mail to arrive.

ABC Player

Watching movies through Netflix can be nice, but if you want to watch your favorite ABC TV shows, then get the ABC Player app for free. With this app you can see what's playing or stream episodes of your favorite shows and watch them on your iPad, as shown in Figure 29-9.

FIGURE 29-9: *The ABC Player app lets you watch your favorite ABC shows on your iPad.*

JamPad and Virtuoso

One way to keep yourself amused with your iPad is to sing along while listening to the songs you've stored on your iPad. Another way to amuse yourself with music is to create your own songs. Although it's not always practical to carry around an electronic keyboard, it is possible to turn your iPad into a musical instrument with JamPad or Virtuoso, as shown in Figure 29-10.

FIGURE 29-10: *Virtuoso can teach you the notes so you can practice your keyboard skills.*

Virtuoso can help you learn the notes on a keyboard while JamPad lets you play keyboards, guitar, or drums to develop your music skills, or just play sounds to keep yourself or your kids amused on a long car ride or plane trip. If the racket gets too annoying for others to hear, bring headphones or ear buds to restrict the noise you make to your own eardrums.

Remote

While you're at home, you may prefer to play your music collection from your PC or Mac computer. The free Remote app lets you use your iPad to control iTunes on your computer from any room in the house—your iPad and computer just need to be on the same Wi-Fi network.

Pandora

No matter how large your music collection may get, chances are good you'll want to listen to something different. To help you find songs from different artists that you might enjoy, download the Pandora app.

Pandora lets you type in the name of your favorite recording artist or song, and then it plays only those songs that are similar to your chosen artist or song. By doing this, Pandora can help you discover new recording artists and songs that you might never have heard before.

iMovie and GarageBand

For aspiring movie makers and musicians, two of the best apps are iMovie and GarageBand. With iMovie, you can edit any video footage you capture through the iPad's cameras. This lets you capture a video from your iPad's camera, and then edit it to create a more polished video clip that you can share with others or upload to a video sharing site like YouTube.

GarageBand lets you turn your iPad into different musical instruments, such as drums or a keyboard, and then record your music, turning your iPad into a portable recording studio. Whether you're just learning to play an instrument or have years of experience, GarageBand can turn your iPad into an indispensable tool to further your musical aspirations.

Flipboard

The Flipboard app takes your favorite news sites, blogs, or social networking sites and turns them into an attractive digital "newspaper," as shown in Figure 29-11.

FIGURE 29-11: You can also use Flipboard to read Facebook or Twitter.

Games

The iPad has hundreds of small, cheap, and fun games perfectly suited for wasting your time. The App Store lists today's best sellers, and most games have free trials.

If you're looking to try your very first iPad game, you should try *Angry Birds*, a simple and addictive physics game with more than 100 million total downloads.

You can compare high scores with your friends and family by creating an account in the iPad's Game Center app.

Annoyed by the Game Center notification (shown in Figure 29-12) while playing games? You can turn off Game Center notifications (and any other notifications that might bother you) in the Notifications pane of the Settings screen.

FIGURE 29-12: *The Game Center notification*

Additional Ideas for Using Apps

Every day new apps arrive in the App Store, so the possibilities for your iPad continue to grow. If you still can't find an app that does what you need, you can always learn to program, create, and possibly make money distributing your own app for others to download and enjoy.

The key to the iPad's versatility is its software. No matter how old your iPad may get, it need never become obsolete as long as you can keep loading it up with apps that let you use your iPad in new and unexpected ways. Put your most crucial apps on your main Home screen, put the apps that your children play with on a different pane, and put your own entertainment apps on yet another screen.

Now with the swipe of your finger, you can convert your iPad into a business productivity tool, an entertainment center, a children's play toy, or anything else you want. All you need are the right apps.

30

Troubleshooting Your iPad

Although the iPad is trouble free 99 percent of the time, it's still a computer, and like any computer, it's prone to foul-ups and mishaps. When your iPad doesn't cooperate with your wishes, you could have a defective iPad or, more likely, your iPad just needs a swift kick in its electronic behind to make it start working again.

In this chapter you will learn several steps you can take to get an uncooperative iPad back in working condition again.

What You'll Be Using

To troubleshoot your iPad, you need to use the following:

- ▶ The Home button
- ▶ The On/Off button
- ▶ The iPad's USB cable

 The Settings screen

 iTunes on your computer

An App Is Frozen

It's rare, but sometimes the iPad seems to freeze when you're running an app, and your iPad's screen becomes unresponsive to your touch. The fix is quite simple—just press the Home button and you'll quit the app. If the app doesn't quit, try pressing and holding the Home button for five to ten seconds. If the program continues to misbehave after you restart it, you may want to check for updates to the app or even uninstall it. Updating and uninstalling apps are covered in Chapter 10.

Your iPad Runs Sluggishly or Freezes

If you're familiar with the old world of computers, you know that one of the simplest, yet mysterious, solutions to fixing a broken computer is to turn it off and turn it on again. On Windows PCs, you can accomplish this task by pressing the magical ctrl-alt-del keystroke combination, but with the iPad, you can duplicate this reset process by simply turning your iPad off, waiting a minute or two, then turning it back on.

The process of turning a computer off and back on clears its memory of any misbehaving programs that may have somehow managed to foul up your computer. Sometimes a poorly written app can mess with your iPad's memory, preventing other apps from running correctly. If an iPad app seems frozen, unresponsive, or sluggish, you may need to restart your iPad.

To restart your iPad, follow these steps:

1. Hold down the **On/Off** button and **Home** button at the same time. After a few seconds, the red slider appears at the top of the screen, and then the screen should flash off and your iPad should shut down.
2. Release both the On/Off button and Home button.
3. Wait a bit.
4. Press the **On/Off** button to turn your iPad back on.
5. (Optional) If that doesn't do the trick, try restoring your iPad (see "Restoring Your iPad" on page 250).

iTunes Won't Recognize Your iPad

To transfer files back and forth between an iPad and a computer, you must use iTunes. However, sometimes you may connect your iPad to your computer and iTunes won't recognize that it's connected, which means you can't transfer any files.

To fix this problem, you have several alternatives:

▶ Unplug your iPad's USB cable from the computer and plug it back into the computer, using the same USB port or trying a different USB port. Plug it directly into the computer's USB port and not in a USB port on a hub. Also try unplugging other devices plugged into USB ports.

▶ Keep the iPad plugged into your computer and restart your computer.

▶ Choose **iTunes ▶ Check for Updates** (Macintosh) or **Help ▶ Check for Updates** (Windows) to download and install the latest version of iTunes.

▶ Make sure you have the latest operating system version for your computer (Mac OS X or Windows).

Your iPad Cannot Access the Internet

If you're trying to get on the Internet but can't seem to connect, there could be a multitude of problems that may not be related to your iPad at all, whether you're trying to connect using Wi-Fi or a cellular telephone network. First, you could be in a "dead zone" for Wi-Fi or cellular telephone connectivity, which could be caused by buildings or poor coverage in your particular area.

If possible, try connecting through Wi-Fi using another device (such as a laptop computer) or connect to your cellular telephone network using a mobile phone. (Just make sure that mobile phone uses the same cellular telephone network as your iPad.)

If you're positive that there is adequate Wi-Fi or cellular telephone coverage in your area, then check to make sure you have turned Airplane Mode off and turned Wi-Fi on. As a last resort, you can reset the network settings. To do this, follow these steps:

1. From the Home screen, tap **Settings**.
2. Make sure the Airplane Mode on/off switch is *OFF*.
3. Tap **Wi-Fi**. The Wi-Fi Networks settings screen appears. Make sure the Wi-Fi on/off switch is *ON*. If you don't see any networks displayed under the Choose a Network category, there may not be any Wi-Fi coverage in your area.
4. (Optional) Tap **General** in the left pane. The General settings screen appears.
5. (Optional) Scroll down the General settings screen and tap **Reset**. The Reset settings screen appears.
6. (Optional) Tap **Reset Network Settings**.

✳ NOTE: **If you're connected to a Wi-Fi network and you still can't browse the Web or check your email, the Wi-Fi network you are connected to may not have Internet access. (For example, you might be in an airport or hotel where they'd like you to pay money to connect.) To stop automatically connecting to that bad Wi-Fi network, you want to forget it. See "Forgetting a Wi-Fi Network" on page 61 for instructions.**

Restoring Your iPad

Each time that you connect your iPad to your computer through its USB cable, the iTunes program on your computer makes a backup of your entire iPad. That way if your iPad malfunctions or fails completely, you can restore your backed up data to a new iPad and start working right away as if nothing had happened.

Restoring from a Backup

Restoring your iPad is an easy fix for many software troubles—give restoring a try if your iPad starts to malfunction or fails to sync properly and restarting doesn't work. Even if you lose your iPad, you can get a new one, restore your backups to this new iPad, and essentially clone your old iPad onto your new iPad.

To restore a backup from iTunes to your iPad, follow these steps:

1. Connect your iPad to your computer through its USB cable.
2. Right-click on the name of your iPad under the Devices category in the iTunes window. A pop-up menu appears, as shown in Figure 30-1.

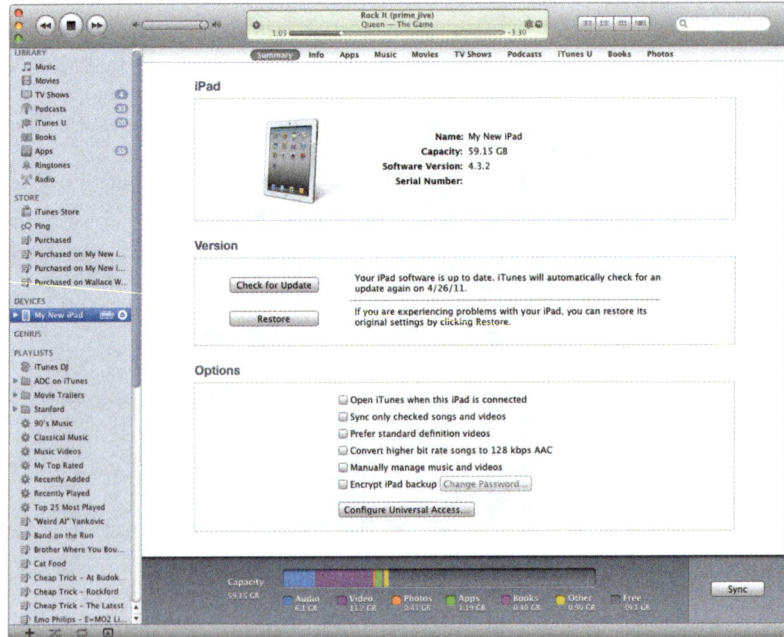

FIGURE 30-1: *Every time you connect your iPad to your computer, iTunes can back up your data.*

3. Choose **Restore from Backup**. A Restore from Backup dialog appears.
4. Choose the backup you want to use (if you have multiple choices) and click the **Restore** button.

Encrypting Your Backup

Normally iTunes on your computer just backs up your data without encrypting it. However, if you want to protect your backed up data with a password, you can turn on backup encryption by following these steps:

1. Connect your iPad to your computer through its USB cable.
2. Run the iTunes program on your computer.
3. Click the name of your iPad under the Devices category in the iTunes window.
4. Click the **Summary** tab and select (or unselect) the **Encrypt iPad backup** check box. A dialog pops up, asking you to type in a password twice as shown in Figure 30-2.
5. Type a password twice and click the **Set Password** button.

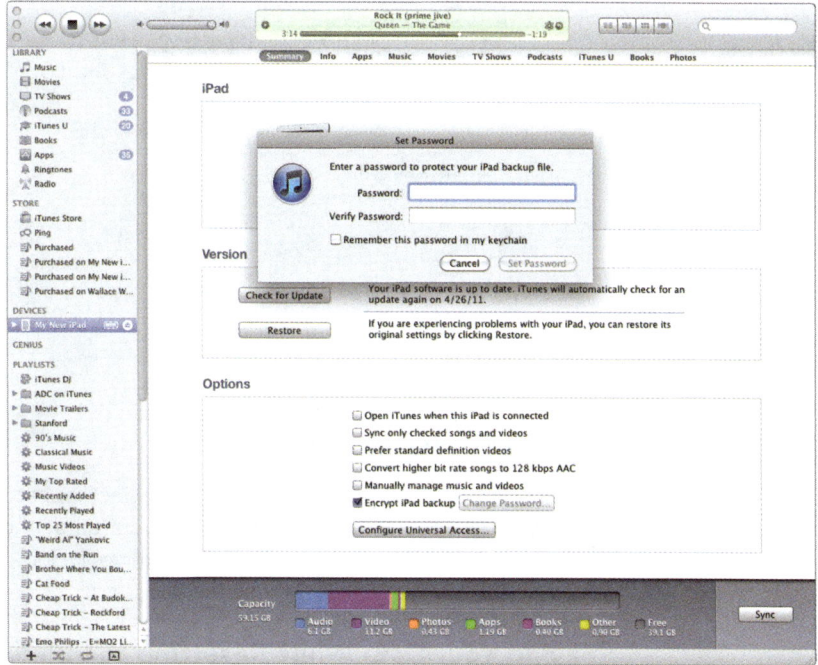

FIGURE 30-2: The Encrypt iPad backup check box lets you define a password.

* **NOTE:** You can change your password later by clicking the Change Password button on the Summary tab. Before you can restore your backup to your iPad, you'll need to type in your password, so don't forget it!

Deleting a Backup

Backing up your iPad is a good idea, which is why iTunes does this automatically. However, if you're selling or giving away your computer, you probably don't want to keep your iPad backups on that computer anymore. To remove your backups, follow these steps:

1. Run the iTunes program on your computer.
2. Choose **iTunes ▸ Preferences** (Macintosh) or **Edit ▸ Preferences** (Windows). A window appears.
3. Click the **Devices** icon or tab. A list of your backups appears, as shown in Figure 30-3.
4. Click the iPad backup you want to delete and click **OK**.

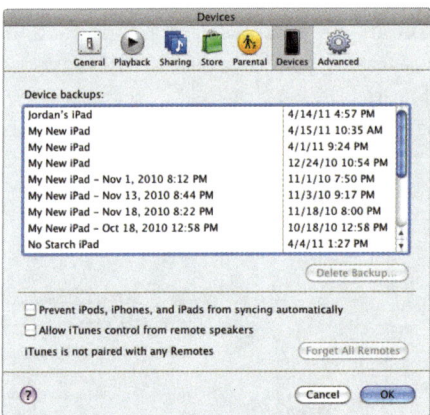

FIGURE 30-3: *You can delete your iPad backups within iTunes.*

Resetting Everything

If you want to return your iPad to its original factory settings, you have two choices. First, you can reset your iPad but leave all your data (photos, video, music, and so on) intact. Second, you can wipe out everything, including anything you have saved, such as photos or apps that you've downloaded.

Saving Your Data While Resetting the iPad

If your iPad starts acting weird and restoring doesn't do the trick, then you might need to completely reset it while preserving any data you have stored on it. To reset your iPad while preserving all your data on it, follow these steps:

1. From the Home screen, tap **Settings**. The Settings screen appears.
2. Tap **General**. The General settings screen appears.
3. Scroll down and tap **Reset**. The Reset settings screen appears, as shown in Figure 30-4.

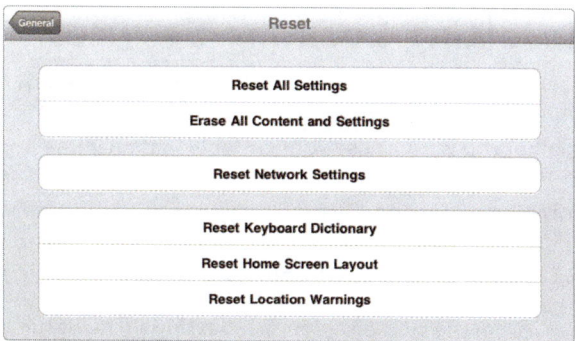

FIGURE 30-4: *The Reset settings screen*

4. Tap **Reset All Settings**. A Reset All Settings dialog appears, asking for confirmation before resetting your iPad.
5. Tap **Reset** or **Cancel**.

Resetting and Erasing Your iPad

If you plan to give away or sell your iPad, you may want to wipe out all your data and return your iPad to its original factory condition (minus any minor blemishes you may have made on the iPad's case while using it). To reset and erase your iPad completely, follow these steps:

1. From the Home screen, tap **Settings**. The Settings screen appears.
2. Tap **General**. The General settings screen appears.
3. Scroll down and tap **Reset**. The Reset settings screen appears.
4. Tap **Erase All Content and Settings**. An Erase iPad dialog appears, asking for confirmation before resetting and erasing your iPad.
5. Tap **Erase** or **Cancel**.

Resetting the Keyboard Dictionary

As you type on the virtual keyboard, it gradually learns and adapts to the words you use most often. As you type part of a word, the virtual keyboard will display the words you've used before.

Of course, after the virtual keyboard's dictionary gets trained to display certain words, you may change your writing style, so the keyboard dictionary may start suggesting words that you don't want to type. To avoid this problem, you can reset just the keyboard dictionary settings by following these steps:

1. From the Home screen, tap **Settings**. The Settings screen appears.
2. Tap **General**. The General settings screen appears.
3. Scroll down and tap **Reset**. The Reset settings screen appears.
4. Tap **Reset Keyboard Dictionary**. A Reset Dictionary dialog appears, asking for confirmation before resetting your keyboard dictionary.
5. Tap **Reset** or **Cancel**.

Resetting Location Services

If Location Services is turned on, your iPad can identify its current location. When you use certain apps, such as the Maps app, a dialog may pop up asking whether you want to use your current location in the app.

After you allow apps to use your iPad's current location, they will eventually stop asking for permission to use your current location again. However, if you prefer having a dialog alert you when your iPad is trying to identify its current location, you can reset your iPad's location warning by following these steps:

1. From the Home screen, tap **Settings**. The Settings screen appears.
2. Tap **General**. The General settings screen appears.
3. Scroll down and tap **Reset**. The Reset settings screen appears.
4. Tap **Reset Location Warnings**. A Reset Warnings dialog appears, asking whether you want to reset location warnings to the factory default settings.
5. Tap **Reset** or **Cancel**.

Finding a Stolen or Lost iPad

If someone steals your iPad or if you misplace it in a restaurant or office, you can track it down using Apple's free "Find My iPad" service.

The basic idea is that you register your iPad (and iPhone or iPod too!) using a free Apple ID. Then if you lose your iPad, you can use any computer to locate your device on a map or send a message to its screen. If you have sensitive data that you're worried might get into the wrong hands, you can send a command to "wipe" all data from your iPad! And if you've just lost your iPad among your couch cushions, you can get the iPad to play a sound for two minutes—even if it has been muted.

Turning On the Tracking Feature

Before you can track down an iPad, you must first associate it with a MobileMe account. (If you already have an Apple ID from buying music on iTunes or using the FaceTime app, you can use that email address and password for your MobileMe account.) Then turn on the tracking feature on your iPad by following these steps:

1. From the Home screen, tap **Settings**. The Settings screen appears.
2. Tap **Mail, Contacts, Calendars**. The Mail, Contacts, Calendars settings screen appears.
3. Tap **Add Account**. The Add Account screen appears.
4. Tap **MobileMe**. A MobileMe window appears. Enter your current Apple ID and password or tap Create Free Apple ID if you don't have one yet, and then follow the instructions to set up your MobileMe account.

5. Check your email and look for a message from Apple asking you to verify your MobileMe account by clicking on a verification link. After you click the link, you will be able to access your MobileMe account by visiting *http://www.me.com/*.

6. From the Home screen, tap **Settings**, tap **Mail, Contacts, Calendars**, and then tap your MobileMe account. A MobileMe account window appears, as shown in Figure 30-5.

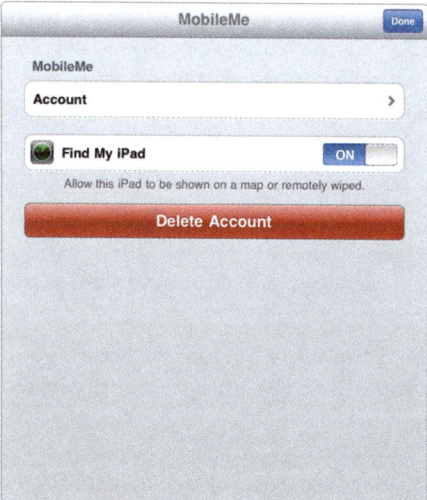

FIGURE 30-5: *The MobileMe account window displays a Find My iPad on/off switch.*

7. Tap the **Find My iPad** on/off switch to *ON*. Your iPad will now broadcast its location using its cellular or Wi-Fi Internet connection.

Locating a Lost iPad

When the Find My iPad switch is set to *ON*, you can locate your iPad on a map by following these steps:

1. Visit *http://www.me.com/* and sign in using your MobileMe account and password. MobileMe displays a list of one or more iPad, iPhone, or iPod devices you have configured to broadcast its location.

2. Tap on the name of the device that you want to locate. A blue dot displays the location of your chosen device, as shown in Figure 30-6.

FIGURE 30-6: *Locating a missing iPad through MobileMe*

3. Click the white arrow that appears in a blue circle. A window appears that displays three buttons: Display Message or Play Sound, Lock, or Wipe, as shown in Figure 30-7.

FIGURE 30-7: *The three options after you have located your iPad*

> **Display Message or Play Sound**   This lets you display a message, such as your contact number or email address, on the iPad screen so that someone finding your device can reach you. As an alternative, you can have your iPad play a sound so you can locate it in your house or office.

> **Lock**   This lets you block anyone from using your iPad if they don't know your current passcode. (If you didn't set up a passcode, go back and follow the steps in Chapter 8.)

> **Wipe**   This lets you erase all your data to prevent unauthorized access.

* **WARNING:** Clicking the Wipe button will return your iPad to its factory settings, but then you will not be able to identify its location or remotely lock it with a passcode.

4. Click the Display Message or Play Sound, Lock, or Wipe button, as shown in Figure 30-7. Depending on which option you choose, you may see additional options.

Additional Ideas for Troubleshooting Your iPad

iPad customers are eligible for free phone support from Apple for the first 90 days of ownership—US customers can call 1-800-APL-CARE (1-800-275-2273). You can also reach Apple's customer support web page at *http://www.apple.com/support/.* All new iPads come with a one-year limited warranty.

If you're fortunate enough live near an Apple Store, take your iPad in and compare its behavior to the iPads in the store. Then ask for help from one of the geniuses at the Genius Bar, and let them worry about the strange behavior of your iPad.

Despite Apple's reputation for producing quality products, there's always the possibility that you could have gotten a defective unit. If possible, back up all your data from your iPad and get a replacement. Then you can restore all your data from your computer to your new iPad.

INDEX

Updates

Visit *http://www.nostarch.com/newipad_2.htm* for updates, errata, and other information.